History of Egypt, Chaldea, Syria, Babylonia and Assyria

by Gaston Maspero and
A. H. Sayce
Volume 1

ISBN: 978-1-63923-613-8

Printed: January 2023

Published and Distributed By:
Lushena Books
607 Country Club Drive, Unit E
Bensenville, IL 60106
www.lushenabks.com

ISBN: 978-1-63923-613-8

EDITOR'S PREFACE

PROFESSOR MASPERO does not need to be introduced to us. His name is well known in England and America as that of one of the chief masters of Egyptian science as well as of ancient Oriental history and archæology. Alike as a philologist, a historian, and an archæologist, he occupies a foremost place in the annals of modern knowledge and research. He possesses that quick apprehension and fertility of resource without which the decipherment of ancient texts is impossible, and he also possesses a sympathy with the past and a power of realizing it which are indispensable if we would picture it aright. His intimate acquaintance with Egypt and its literature, and the opportunities of discovery afforded him by his position for several years as director of the Bulaq Museum, give him an unique claim to speak with authority on the history of the valley of the Nile. In the present work he has been prodigal of his abundant stores of learning and knowledge, and it may therefore be regarded as the most complete account of ancient Egypt that has ever yet been published.

In the case of Babylonia and Assyria he no longer, it is true, speaks at first hand. But he has thoroughly studied the latest and best authorities on the subject, and has weighed their statements with the judgment which comes from an exhaustive acquaintance with a similar department of knowledge.

Naturally, in progressive studies like those of Egyptology and Assyriology, a good many theories and conclusions must be tentative and provisional only. Discovery crowds so quickly on discovery, that the truth of to-day is often apt to be modified or amplified by the truth of to-morrow. A single fresh fact may throw a wholly new and unexpected light upon the results we have already gained, and cause them to assume a somewhat changed aspect. But this is what must happen in all sciences in which there is a healthy growth, and archæological science is no exception to the rule.

The spelling of ancient Egyptian proper names adopted by Professor Maspero will perhaps seem strange to many. But it must be remembered that all our attempts to represent the pronunciation of ancient Egyptian words can be approximate only; we can never ascertain with certainty how they were actually sounded. All that can be done is to determine what pronunciation was assigned to them in the Greek period, and to work backwards from this, so far as it is possible, to more remote ages. This is what Professor Maspero has done, and it must be no slight satisfaction to him to find that on the whole his system of transliteration is confirmed by the cuneiform tablets of Tel el-Amarna.

The difficulties attaching to the spelling of Assyrian names are different from those which beset our attempts to reproduce, even approximately, the names of ancient Egypt. . The cuneiform system of writing was syllabic, each character denoting a syllable, so that we know what were the vowels in a proper name as well as the consonants. Moreover, the pronunciation of the consonants resembled that of the Hebrew consonants, the transliteration of which has long since become conventional. When, therefore, an Assyrian or Babylonian name is written phonetically, its correct transliteration is not often a matter of question. But, unfortunately, the names are not always written phonetically. The cuneiform script was an inheritance from the non-Semitic predecessors of the Semites in Babylonia, and in this script the characters represented words as well as sounds. Not unfrequently the Semitic Assyrians continued to write a name in the old Sumerian way instead of spelling it phonetically, the result being that we do not know how it was pronounced in their own language. The name of the Chaldæan Noah, for instance, is written with two characters which ideographically signify "the sun" or "day of life," and of the first of which the Sumerian values were *ut, babar, khis, tam*, and *par*, while the second had the value of *zi*. Were it not that the Chaldæan historian Bêrôssos writes the name Xisuthros, we should have no clue to its Semitic pronunciation.

Professor Maspero's learning and indefatigable industry are well known to me, but I confess I was not prepared for the exhaustive acquaintance he shows with Assyriological literature. Nothing seems to have escaped his notice. Papers and books just published, and half-forgotten articles in obscure periodicals which appeared years ago, have all alike been used and quoted by him. Naturally, however, there are some points on which I should be inclined to differ from the conclusions he draws, or to which he has been led by other Assyriologists. Without being an Assyriologist himself, it was impossible for him to be acquainted with that portion of the evidence on certain disputed questions which is only to be found in still unpublished or untranslated inscriptions.

There are two points which seem to me of sufficient importance to justify my expression of dissent from his views. These are the geographical situation of the land of Magan, and the historical character of the annals of Sargon of Accad. The evidence about Magan is very clear. Magan is usually associated with the country of Melukhkha, "the salt" desert, and in *every* text in which its geographical position is indicated it is placed in the immediate vicinity of Egypt. Thus Assur-bani-pal, after stating that he had "gone to the lands of Magan and Melukhkha," goes on to say that he "directed his road to Egypt and Kush," and then describes the first of his Egyptian campaigns. Similar testimony is borne by Esarhaddon. The latter king tells us that after quitting Egypt he directed his road to the land of Melukhkha, a desert region in which there were no rivers, and which extended "to the city of Rapikh" (the modern Raphia) "at the edge of the wadi of Egypt" (the present Wadi El-Arish). After this he received camels from the king of the Arabs, and made his way to the land and city of Magan. The Tel el-Amarna tablets enable us to carry the record back to the fifteenth century B.C. In certain of the tablets now at Berlin (Winckler and Abel, 42 and 45) the Phœnician governor of the Pharaoh asks that help should be sent him from Melukhkha and Egypt: "The king should hear the words of his servant, and send ten men of the country of Melukhkha and twenty men of the country of Egypt to defend the city [of Gebal] for the king." And again, "I have sent [to] Pharaoh" (literally, "the great house") "for a garrison of men from the country of Melukhkha, and . . . the king has just despatched a garrison [from] the country of Melukhkha." At a still earlier date we have indications that Melukhkha and Magan denoted the same region of the world. In an old Babylonian geographical list which belongs to the early days of Chaldæan history, Magan is described as "the country of bronze," and Melukhkha as "the country of the *samdu*," or "malachite." It was this list which originally led Oppert, Lenormant, and myself independently to the conviction that Magan was to be looked for in the Sinaitic Peninsula. Magan included, however, the Midian of Scripture, and the city of Magan, called Makkan in Semitic Assyrian, is probably the Makna of classical geography, now represented by the ruins of Mukna.

As I have always maintained the historial character of the annals of Sargon of Accad, long before recent discoveries led Professor Hilprecht and others to adopt the same view, it is as well to state why I consider them worthy of credit. In themselves the annals contain nothing improbable; indeed, what might seem the most unlikely portion of them—that which describes the extension of Sargon's empire to the shores of the Mediterranean

—has been confirmed by the progress of research. Ammi-satana, a king of the first dynasty of Babylon (about 2200 B.C.), calls himself "king of the country of the Amorites," and the Tel el-Amarna tablets have revealed to us how deep and long-lasting Babylonian influence must have been throughout Western Asia. Moreover, the vase described by Professor Maspero in the present work proves that the expedition of Naram-Sin against Magan was an historical reality, and such an expedition was only possible if "the land of the Amorites," the Syria and Palestine of later days, had been secured in the rear. But what chiefly led me to the belief that the annals are a document contemporaneous with the events narrated in them, are two facts which do not seem to have been sufficiently considered. On the one side, while the annals of Sargon are given in full, those of his son Naram-Sin break off abruptly in the early part of his reign. I see no explanation of this, except that they were composed while Naram-Sin was still on the throne. On the other side, the campaigns of the two monarchs are coupled with the astro-logical phenomena on which the success of the campaigns was supposed to depend. We know that the Babylonians were given to the practice and study of astrology from the earliest days of their history; we know also that even in the time of the later Assyrian monarchy it was still customary for the general in the field to be accompanied by the *asipu*, or "prophet," the *ashshâph* of Dan. ii. 10, on whose interpretation of the signs of heaven the movements of the army depended; and in the infancy of Chaldæan history we should accordingly expect to find the astrological sign recorded along with the event with which it was bound up. At a subsequent period the sign and the event were separated from one another in literature, and had the annals of Sargon been a later compilation, in their case also the separation would assuredly have been made. That, on the contrary, the annals have the form which they could have assumed and ought to have assumed only at the beginning of contemporaneous Babylonian history, is to me a strong testimony in favour of their genuineness.

It may be added that Babylonian seal-cylinders have been found in Cyprus, one of which is of the age of Sargon of Accad, its style and workmanship being the same as that of the cylinder figured in vol. iii. p. 96, while the other, though of later date, belonged to a person who describes himself as "the servant of the deified Naram-Sin." Such cylinders may, of course, have been brought to the island in later times; but when we remember that a characteristic object of prehistoric Cypriote art is an imitation of the seal-cylinder of Chaldæa, their discovery cannot be wholly an accident.

Professor Maspero has brought his facts up to so recent a date that there is very little to add to what he has written. Since his manuscript was in type, however, a few additions have been made to our Assyriological knowledge. A fresh examination of the Babylonian dynastic tablet has led Professor Delitzsch to make some alterations in the published account of what Professor Maspero calls the ninth dynasty. According to Professor Delitzsch, the number of kings composing the dynasty is stated on the tablet to be twenty-one, and not thirty-one as was formerly read, and the number of lost lines exactly corresponds with this figure. The first of the kings reigned thirty-six years, and he had a predecessor belonging to the previous dynasty whose name has been lost. There would consequently have been two Elamite usurpers instead of one.

I would further draw attention to an interesting text, published by Mr. Strong in the *Babylonian and Oriental Record*, which I believe to contain the name of a king who belonged to the legendary dynasties of Chaldæa. This is Samas-natsir, who is coupled with Sargon of Accad and other early monarchs in one of the lists. The legend, if I interpret it rightly, states that "Elam shall be altogether given to Samas-natsir;" and the same prince is further described as building Nippur and Dur-ilu, as King of Babylon and as conqueror both of a certain Baldakha and of Khumba-sitir, "the king of the cedar-forest." It will be remembered that in the Epic of Gilgames, Khumbaba also is stated to have been the lord of the "cedar-forest."

But of new discoveries and facts there is a constant supply, and it is impossible for the historian to keep pace with them. Even while the sheets of his work are passing through the press, the excavator, the explorer, and the decipherer are adding to our previous stores of knowledge. In Egypt, Mr. de Morgan's unwearied energy has raised as it were out of the ground, at Kom Ombo, a vast and splendidly preserved temple, of whose existence we had hardly dreamed; has discovered twelfth-dynasty jewellery at Dahshur of the most exquisite workmanship, and at Meir and Assiut has found in tombs of the sixth dynasty painted models of the trades and professions of the day, as well as fighting battalions of soldiers, which, for freshness and lifelike reality, contrast favourably with the models which come from India to-day. In Babylonia, the American Expedition, under Mr. Haines, has at Niffer unearthed monuments of older date than those of Sargon of Accad. Nor must I forget to mention the lotiform column found by Mr. de Morgan in a tomb of the Old Empire at Abusir, or the interesting discovery made by Mr. Arthur Evans of seals and other objects from the prehistoric sites of Krete and other parts of the Ægean, inscribed with hieroglyphic characters which reveal a new system of writing that must at one time have existed by the side of the Hittite hieroglyphs, and may have had its origin in the influence exercised by Egypt on the peoples of the Mediterranean in the age of the twelfth dynasty.

In volumes IV., V., and VI. we find ourselves in the full light of an advanced culture. The nations of the ancient East are no longer each pursuing an isolated existence, and separately developing the seeds of civilization and culture on the banks of the Euphrates and the Nile. Asia and Africa have met in mortal combat. Babylonia has carried its empire to the frontiers of Egypt, and Egypt itself has been held in bondage by the Hyksôs strangers from Asia. In return, Egypt has driven back the wave of invasion to the borders of Mesopotamia, has substituted an empire of its own in Syria for that of the Babylonians, and has forced the Babylonian king to treat with its Pharaoh on equal terms. In the track of war and diplomacy have come trade and commerce; Western Asia is covered with roads, along which the merchant and the courier travel incessantly, and the whole civilised world of the Orient is knit together in a common literary culture and common commercial interests.

The age of isolation has thus been succeeded by an age of intercourse, partly military and antagonistic, partly literary and peaceful. Professor Maspero paints for us this age of intercourse, describes its rise and character, its decline and fall. For the unity of Eastern civilization was again shattered. The Hittites descended from the ranges of the Taurus upon the Egyptian province of Northern Syria, and cut off the Semites of the west from those of the east. The Israelites poured over the Jordan out of Edom and Moab, and took possession of Canaan, while Babylonia itself, for so many centuries the ruling power of the Oriental world, had to make way for its upstart rival Assyria. The old imperial powers were exhausted and played out, and it needed time before the new forces which were to take their place could acquire sufficient strength for their work.

As usual, Professor Maspero has been careful to embody in his history the very latest discoveries and information. Notice, it will be found, has been taken even of the *stela* of Meneptah, recently disinterred by Professor Petrie, on which the name of the Israelites is engraved. At Elephantinê, I found, a short time since, on a granite boulder, an inscription of Khufuânkh — whose sarcophagus of red granite is one of the most beautiful objects in the Gizeh Museum—which carries back the history of the island to the age of the pyramid-builders of the fourth dynasty. The boulder was subsequently concealed under the southern side of the city-wall, and as fragments of inscribed papyrus coeval with the sixth dynasty have been discovered in the immediate neighbourhood, on one of which mention is made of "this domain" of Pepi II., it would seem that the town of Elephantinê must have been founded between the period of the fourth dynasty and that of the sixth. Manetho is therefore justified in making the fifth and sixth dynasties of Elephantinê origin.

It is in Babylonia, however, that the most startling discoveries have been made. At Tello, M. de Sarzec has found a library of more than thirty thousand tablets, all neatly arranged, piled in order one on the other, and belonging to the age of Gudea (B.C. 2700). Many more tablets of an early date have been unearthed at Abu-Habba (Sippara) and Jokha (Isin) by Dr. Seheil, working for the Turkish government. But the most important finds have been at Niffer, the ancient Nippur, in Northern Babylonia, where the American expedition has brought to a close its long work of systematic excavation. Here Mr. Haynes has dug down to the very foundations of the great temple of El-lil, and the chief historical results of his labours have been published by Professor Hilprecht (in *The Babylonian Expedition of the University of Pennsylvania*, vol. i. pt. 2, 1896).

About midway between the summit and the bottom of the mound, Mr. Haynes laid bare a pavement constructed of huge bricks stamped with the names of Sargon of Akkad and his son Naram-Sin. He found also the ancient wall of the city, which had been built by Naram-Sin, 13·75 metres wide. The *débris* of ruined buildings which lies below the pavement of Sargon is as much as 9·25 metres in depth, while that above it, the topmost stratum of which brings us down to the Christian era, is only 11 metres in height. We may form some idea from this of the enormous age to which the history of Babylonian culture and writing reaches back. In fact, Professor Hilprecht quotes with approval Mr. Haynes's words: "We must cease to apply the adjective 'earliest' to the time of Sargon, or to any age or epoch within a thousand years of his advanced civilization." "The golden age of Babylonian history seems to include the reign of Sargon and of Ur-Gur."

Many of the inscriptions which belong to this remote age of human culture have been published by Professor Hilprecht. Among them is a long inscription, in 132 lines, engraved on multitudes of large stone vases presented to the temple of El-lil by a certain Lngal-zaggisi. Lugal-zaggisi was the son of Ukus, the *patesi* or high priest of the " Land of the Bow," as Mesopotamia, with its Bedawin inhabitants, was called. He not only conquered Babylonia, then known as Kengi, "the land of canals and reeds," but founded an empire which extended from the Persian Gulf to the Mediterranean. This was centuries before Sargon of Akkad followed in his footsteps. Erech became the capital of Lugal-zaggisi's empire, and doubtless received at this time its Sumerian title of " the city " *par excellence.*

For a long while previously there had been war between Babylonia and the " Land of the Bow," whose rulers seem to have established themselves in the city of Kis. At one time we find the Babylonian prince En-sag(sag)-ana capturing Kis and its king; at another time it is a king of Kis who makes offerings to the god of Nippur, in gratitude for his victories. To this period belongs the famous " Stela of the Vultures " found at Tello, on which is depicted the victory of E-dingir-ana-gin, the King of Lagas (Tello), over the Semitic hordes of the Land of the Bow. It may be noted that the recent discoveries have shown how correct Professor Maspero has been in assigning the kings of Lagas to a period earlier than that of Sargon of Akkad.

Professor Hilprecht would place E-dingir-ana-gin after Lugal-zaggisi, and see in the Stela of the Vultures a monument of the revenge taken by the Sumerian rulers of Lagas for the conquest of the country by the inhabitants of the north. But it is equally possible that it marks the successful reaction of Chaldæa against the power established by Lugal-zaggisi. However this may be, the dynasty of Lagas (to which Professor Hilprecht has added a new king, En-Khegal) reigned in peace for some time, and belonged to the same age as the first dynasty of Ur. This was founded by a certain Lugal-kigubnidudu, whose inscriptions have been found at Niffer. The dynasty which arose at Ur in later days (cir. B.C. 2700), under Ur-Gur and Dungi, which has hitherto been known as " the first dynasty of Ur," is thus dethroned from its position, and becomes the second. The succeeding dynasty, which also made Ur its capital, and whose kings, Ine-Sin, Pur-Sin II., and Gimil-Sin, were the immediate predecessors of the first dynasty of Babylon (to which Khammurabi belonged), must henceforth be termed the third.

Among the latest acquisitions from Tello are the seals of the *patesi*, Lugal-usumgal, which finally remove all doubt as to the identity of "Sargani, king of the city," with the famous Sargon of Akkad. The historical accuracy of Sargon's annals, moreover, have been fully vindicated. Not only have the American excavators found the contemporary monuments of him and his son Naram-Sin, but also tablets dated in the years of his campaigns against "the land of the Amorites." In short, Sargon of Akkad, so lately spoken of as "a half-mythical" personage, has now emerged into the full glare of authentic history.

That the native chronologists had sufficient material for reconstructing the past history of their country, is also now clear. The early Babylonian contract-tablets are dated by events which officially distinguished the several years of a king's reign, and tablets have been discovered compiled at the close of a reign which give year by year the events which thus characterised them. One of these tablets, for example, from the excavations at Niffer, begins with the words: (1) "The year when Pur-Sin (II.) becomes king. (2) The year when Pur-Sin the king conquers Urbillum," and ends with "the year when Gimil-Sin becomes King of Ur, and conquers the land of Zabsali" in the Lebanon.

Of special interest to the biblical student are the discoveries made by Mr. Pinches among some of the Babylonian tablets which have recently been acquired by the British Museum. Four of them relate to no less a personage than

Kudur-Laghghamar or Chedor-laomer, "King of Elam," as well as to Eri-Âku or Arioch, King of Larsa, and his son Dur-makh-ilani; to Tudghula or Tid'al, the son of Gazza[ni], and to their war against Babylon in the time of Khammu[rabi]. In one of the texts the question is asked, "Who is the son of a king's daughter who has sat on the throne of royalty? Dur-makh-ilani, the son of Eri-Âku, the son of the lady Kur . . . has sat on the throne of royalty," from which it may perhaps be inferred that Eri-Âku was the son of Kudur-Laghghamar's daughter; and in another we read, "Who is Kudur-Laghghamar, the doer of mischief? He has gathered together the Umman Manda, has devastated the land of Bel (Babylonia), and [has marched] at their side." The Umman Manda were the "Barbarian Hordes" of the Kurdish mountains, on the northern frontier of Elam, and the name corresponds with that of the Goyyim or "nations" in the fourteenth chapter of Genesis. We here see Kudur-Laghghamar acting as their suzerain lord. Unfortunately, all four tablets are in a shockingly broken condition, and it is therefore difficult to discover in them a continuous sense, or to determine their precise nature.

They have, however, been supplemented by further discoveries made by Dr. Seheil at Constantinople. Among the tablets preserved there, he has found letters from Khammurabi to his vassal Sin-idinnam of Larsa, from which we learn that Sin-idinnam had been dethroned by the Elamites Kudur-Mabug and Eri-Âku, and had fled for refuge to the court of Khammurabi at Babylon. In the war which subsequently broke out between Khammurabi and Kudur-Laghghamar, the King of Elam (who, it would seem, exercised suzerainty over Babylonia for seven years), Sin-idinnam gave material assistance to the Babylonian monarch, and Khammurabi accordingly bestowed presents upon him as a "recompense for his valour on the day of the overthrow of Kudur-Laghghamar."

I must also refer to a fine scarab—found in the rubbish-mounds of the ancient city of Kom Ombos, in Upper Egypt—which bears upon it the name of Sutkhu-Apopi. It shows us that the author of the story of the Expulsion of the Hyksôs, in calling the king Râ-Apopi, merely, like an orthodox Egyptian, substituted the name of the god of Heliopolis for that of the foreign deity. Equally interesting are the scarabs brought to light by Professor Flinders Petrie, on which a hitherto unknown Ya'aqob-hal or Jacob-el receives the titles of a Pharaoh

In volumes VII., VIII., and IX., Professor Maspero concludes his monumental work on the history of the ancient East. The overthrow of the Persian empire by the Greek soldiers of Alexander marks the beginning of a new era. Europe at last enters upon the stage of history, and becomes the heir of the culture and civilisation of the Orient. The culture which had grown up and developed on the banks of the Euphrates and Nile passes to the West, and there assumes new features and is inspired with a new spirit. The East perishes of age and decrepitude; its strength is outworn, its power to initiate is past. The long ages through which it had toiled to build up the fabric of civilisation are at an end; fresh races are needed to carry on the work which it had achieved. Greece appears upon the scene, and behind Greece looms the colossal figure of the Roman Empire.

During the past decade, excavation has gone on apace in Egypt and Babylonia, and discoveries of a startling and unexpected nature have followed in the wake of excavation. Ages that seemed prehistoric step suddenly forth into the daydawn of history; personages whom a sceptical criticism had consigned to the land of myth or fable are clothed once more with flesh and blood, and events which had been long forgotten demand to be recorded and described. In Babylonia, for example, the excavations at Niffer and Tello have shown that Sargon of Akkad, so far from being a creature of romance, was as much a historical monarch as Nebuchadrezzar himself; monuments of his reign have been discovered, and we learn from them that the empire he is said to have founded had a very real existence. Contracts have been found dated in the years when he was occupied in conquering Syria and Palestine, and a cadastral survey that was made for the purposes of taxation mentions a Canaanite who had been appointed "governor of the land of the Amorites." Even a postal service had already been established along the high-roads which knit the several parts of the empire together, and some of the clay seals which franked the letters are now in the Museum of the Louvre.

At Susa, M. de Morgan, the late director of the Service of Antiquities in Egypt, has been excavating below the remains of the Achæmenian period, among the ruins of the ancient Elamite capital. Here he has found numberless historical inscriptions, besides a text in hieroglyphics which may cast light on the origin of the cuneiform

characters. But the most interesting of his discoveries
are two Babylonian monuments that were carried off. by
Elamite conquerors from the cities of Babylonia. One of
them is a long inscription of about 1200 lines belonging to
Manistusu, one of the early Babylonian kings, whose name
has been met with at Niffer; the other is a monument of
Naram-Sin, the Son of Sargon of Akkad, which it seems
was brought as booty to Susa by Simti-silkhak, the grandfather, perhaps, of Eriaku or Arioch.

In Armenia, also, equally important inscriptions have
been found by Belck and Lehmann. More than two
hundred new ones have been added to the list of Vannic
texts. It has been discovered from them that the kingdom
of Biainas or Van was founded by Ispuinis and Menuas,
who rebuilt Van itself and the other cities which they had
previously sacked and destroyed. The older name of the
country was Kumussu, and it may be that the language
spoken in it was allied to that of the Hittites, since a tablet
in hieroglyphics of the Hittite type has been unearthed at
Toprak Kaleh. One of the newly-found inscriptions of
Sarduris III. shows that the name of the Assyrian god,
hitherto read Ramman or Rimmon, was really pronounced
Hadad. It describes a war of the Vannic king against
Assur-nirari, son of Hadad-nirari (*A-da-di-ni-ra-ri*) of
Assyria, thus revealing not only the true form of the
Assyrian name, but also the parentage of the last king
of the older Assyrian dynasty. From another inscription,
belonging to Rusas II., the son of Argistis, we learn that
campaigns were carried on against the Hittites and the
Moschi in the latter years of Sennacherib's reign, and

therefore only just before the irruption of the Kimmerians into the northern regions of Western Asia.

The two German explorers have also discovered the site and even the ruins of Muzazir, called Ardinis by the people of Van. They lie on the hill of Shkenna, near Topsanä, on the road between Kelishin and Sidek. In the immediate neighbourhood the travellers succeeded in deciphering a monument of Rusas I., partly in Vannic, partly in Assyrian, from which it appears that the Vannic king did not, after all, commit suicide when the news of the fall of Muzazir was brought to him, as is stated by Sargon, but that, on the contrary, he "marched against the mountains of Assyria" and restored the fallen city itself. Urzana, the King of Muzazir, had fled to him for shelter, and after the departure of the Assyrian army he was sent back by Rusas to his ancestral domains. The whole of the district in which Muzazir was situated was termed Lulu, and was regarded as the southern province of Ararat. In it was Mount Nizir, on whose summit the ark of the Chaldæan Noah rested, and which is therefore rightly described in the Book of Genesis as one of " the mountains of Ararat." It was probably the Rowandiz of to-day.

The discoveries made by Drs. Belok and Lehmann, however, have not been confined to Vannic texts. At the sources of the Tigris Dr. Lehmann has found two Assyrian inscriptions of the Assyrian king, Shalmaneser II., one dated in his fifteenth and the other in his thirty-first year, and relating to his campaigns against Aram of Ararat. He has further found that the two inscriptions previously known to exist at the same spot, and believed to belong

to Tiglath-Ninip and Assur-nazir-pal, are really those of
Shalmaneser II., and refer to the war of his seventh year.

But it is from Egypt that the most revolutionary revela-
tions have come. At Abydos and Kom el-Ahmar, opposite
El-Kab, monuments have been disinterred of the kings of
the first and second dynasties, if not of even earlier princes;
while at Negada, north of Thebes, M. de Morgan has found
a tomb which seems to have been that of Menes himself.
A new world of art has been opened out before us; even
the hieroglyphic system of writing is as yet immature and
strange. But the art is already advanced in many respects;
hard stone was cut into vases and bowls, and even into
statuary of considerable artistic excellence; glazed porcelain was already made, and bronze, or rather copper, was
fashioned into weapons and tools. The writing material,
as in Babylonia, was often clay, over which seal-cylinders
of a Babylonian pattern were rolled. Equally Babylonian
are the strange and composite animals engraved on some
of the objects of this early age, as well as the structure
of the tombs, which were built, not of stone, but of crude
brick, with their external walls panelled and pilastered.
Professor Hommel's theory, which brings Egyptian civilisation from Babylonia along with the ancestors of the
historical Egyptians, has thus been largely verified.

But the historical Egyptians were not the first inhabitants of the valley of the Nile. Not only have palæolithic
implements been found on the plateau of the desert; the
relics of neolithic man have turned up in extraordinary
abundance. When the historical Egyptians arrived with
their copper weapons and their system of writing, the land

was already occupied by a pastoral people, who had attained a high level of neolithic culture. Their implements of flint are the most beautiful and delicately finished that have ever been discovered; they were able to carve vases of great artistic excellence out of the hardest of stone, and their pottery was of no mean quality. Long after the country had come into the possession of the historical dynasties, and had even been united into a single monarchy, their settlements continued to exist on the outskirts of the desert, and the neolithic culture that distinguished them passed only gradually away. By degrees, however, they intermingled with their conquerors from Asia, and thus formed the Egyptian race of a later day. But they had already made Egypt what it has been throughout the historical period. Under the direction of the Asiatic immigrants and of the engineering science whose first home had been in the alluvial plain of Babylonia, they accomplished those great works of irrigation which confined the Nile to its present channel, which cleared away the jungle and the swamp that had formerly bordered the desert, and turned them into fertile fields. Theirs were the hands which carried out the plans of their more intelligent masters, and cultivated the valley when once it had been reclaimed. The Egypt of history was the creation of a twofold race: the Egyptians of the monuments supplied the controlling and directing power; the Egyptians of the neolithic graves bestowed upon it their labour and their skill.

The period treated of by Professor Maspero in these volumes is one for which there is an abundance of materials such as do not exist for the earlier portions of his history. The evidence of the monuments is supplemented by that of the Hebrew and classical writers. But on this very account it is in some respects more difficult to deal with, and the conclusions arrived at by the historian are more open to question and dispute. In some cases conflicting accounts are given of an event which seem to rest on equally good authority; in other cases, there is a sudden failure of materials just where the thread of the story becomes most complicated. Of this the decline and fall of the Assyrian empire is a prominent example; for our knowledge of it, we have still to depend chiefly on the untrustworthy legends of the Greeks. Our views must be coloured more or less by our estimate of Herodotos; those who, like myself, place little or no confidence in what he tells us about Oriental affairs will naturally form a very different idea of the death-struggle of Assyria from that formed by writers who still see in him the Father of Oriental History.

Even where the native monuments have come to our aid, they have not unfrequently introduced difficulties and doubts where none seemed to exist before, and have made the task of the critical historian harder than ever. Cyrus and his forefathers, for instance, turn out to have been kings of Anzan, and not of Persia, thus explaining why it is that the Neo-Susian language appears by the side of the Persian and the Babylonian as one of the three official languages of the Persian empire; but we still have to learn what was the relation of Anzan to Persia on the one hand, and to Susa on the other, and when it was that

Cyrus of Anzan became also King of Persia. In the Annalistic Tablet, he is called "King of Persia" for the first time in the ninth year of Nabonidos.

Similar questions arise as to the position and nationality of Astyages. He is called in the inscriptions, not a Mede, but a Manda—a name which, as I showed many years ago, meant for the Babylonian a "barbarian" of Kurdistan. I have myself little doubt that the Manda over whom Astyages ruled were the Scythians of classical tradition, who, as may be gathered from a text published by Mr. Strong, had occupied the ancient kingdom of Ellipi. It is even possible that in the Madyes of Herodotos, we have a reminiscence of the Manda of the cuneiform inscriptions. That the Greek writers should have confounded the Madâ or Medes with the Manda or Barbarians is not surprising; we find even Berossos describing one of the early dynasties of Babylonia as "Median" where Manda, and not Madâ, must plainly be meant.

These and similar problems, however, will doubtless be cleared up by the progress of excavation and research. Perhaps M. de Morgan's excavations at Susa may throw some light on them, but it is to the work of the German expedition, which has recently begun the systematic exploration of the site of Babylon, that we must chiefly look for help. The Babylon of Nabopolassar and Nebuchadrezzar rose on the ruins of Nineveh, and the story of the downfall of the Assyrian empire must still be lying buried under its mounds.

A. H. SAYCE.

TRANSLATOR'S PREFACE

In completing the translation of this great work, I have to thank Professor Maspero for kindly permitting me to appeal to him on various questions which arose while preparing the translation. His patience and courtesy have alike been unfailing in every matter submitted for his decision.

I am indebted to Miss Bradbury for kindly supplying, in the midst of much other literary work for the Egypt Exploration Fund, the translation of the chapter on the gods, and also of the earlier parts of some of the first chapters. She has, moreover, helped me in my own share of the work with many suggestions and hints, which her intimate connection with the late Miss Amelia B. Edwards fully qualified her to give.

As in the original there is a lack of uniformity in the transcription and accentuation of Arabic names, I have ventured to alter them in several cases to the form most familiar to English readers.

The spelling of the ancient Egyptian words has, at Professor Maspero's request, been retained throughout, with the exception that the French *ou* has been invariably represented by *û*, e.g. Khnoumou by Khnûmû.

By an act of international courtesy, the director of the *Imprimerie Nationale* has allowed the beautifully cut hieroglyphic and cuneiform type used in the original to be employed in the English edition, and I take advantage of this opportunity to express to him our thanks and appreciation of his graceful act.

M. L. McClure.

CONTENTS

CHAPTER I.

THE NILE AND ÆGYPT

CHAPTER II.

THE GODS OF EGYPT

CHAPTER III.

THE LEGENDARY HISTORY OF EGYPT

LIST OF ILLUSTRATIONS

THE NILE AND EGYPT

THE RIVER AND ITS INFLUENCE UPON THE FORMATION AND CHARACTER OF THE COUNTRY—THE OLDEST INHABITANTS OF THE LAND—THE FIRST POLITICAL ORGANIZATION OF THE VALLEY.

The Delta: its gradual formation, its structure, its canals—The valley of Egypt—The two arms of the river—The Eastern Nile—The appearance of its banks—The hills—The gorge of Gebel Silsileh—The cataracts: the falls of Aswân—Nubia—The rapids of Wâdy Halfah—The Takazze—The Blue Nile and the White Nile.

The sources of the Nile—The Egyptian cosmography—The four pillars and the four upholding mountains—The celestial Nile the source of the terrestrial Nile—the Southern Sea and the islands of Spirits—The tears of Isis—The rise of the Nile—The Green Nile and the Red Nile—The opening of the dykes—The fall of the Nile—The river at its lowest ebb.

The alluvial deposits and the effects of the inundation upon the soil of Egypt —Paucity of the flora: aquatic plants, the papyrus and the lotus; the sycamore and the date-palm, the acacias, the dôm-palms—The fauna: the domestic and wild animals; serpents, the uræus; the hippopotamus and the crocodile; birds; fish, the fahaka.

The Nile god: his form and its varieties— The goddess Mirit—The supposed sources of the Nile at Elephantinê—The festivals of Gebel Silsileh—Hymn to the Nile from papyri in the British Museum.

The names of the Nile and Egypt: Romitû and Qîmit—Antiquity of the Egyptian people—Their first horizon—The hypothesis of their Asiatic origin— The probability of their African origin—The language and its Semitic affinities —The race and its principal types.

The primitive civilization of Egypt—Its survival into historic times—The women of Amon—Marriage—Rights of women and children—Houses—Furniture—Dress—Jewels—Wooden and metal arms—Primitive life—Fishing and hunting—The lasso and "bolas"—The domestication of animals—Plants used for food—The lotus—Cereals—The hoe and the plough.

The conquest of the valley—Dykes—Basins—Irrigation—The princes—The nomes—The first local principalities—Late organization of the Delta—Character of its inhabitants—Gradual division of the principalities and changes of their areas—The god of the city.

CHAPTER I

THE NILE AND EGYPT

The river and its influence upon the formation of the country—The oldest inhabitants of the valley and its first political organization.

A LONG, low, level shore, scarcely rising above the sea, a chain of vaguely defined and ever-shifting lakes and marshes, then the triangular plain beyond, whose apex is thrust thirty leagues into the land—this, the Delta of Egypt, has gradually been acquired from the sea, and is as it were the gift of the Nile.[2] The Mediterranean once

[1] From a drawing by Boudier, after a photograph by the Dutch traveller Insinger, taken in 1884.

[2] The same expression has been attributed to Hecatæus of Miletus. It has often been observed that this phrase seems Egyptian on the face of it, and it certainly recalls such forms of expression as the following, taken from a formula frequently found on funerary stelæ: "All things created by heaven, given by earth, *brought by the Nile*

reached to the foot of the sandy plateau on which stand the Pyramids, and formed a wide gulf where now stretches plain beyond plain of the Delta. The last undulations of the Arabian hills, from Gebel Mokattam to Gebel Geneffeh, were its boundaries on the east, while a sinuous and shallow channel running between Africa and Asia united the Mediterranean to the Red Sea. Westward, the littoral followed closely the contour of the Libyan plateau; but a long limestone spur broke away from it at about 31° N., and terminated in Cape Abûkir. The alluvial deposits first filled up the depths of the bay, and then, under the influence of the currents which swept along its eastern coasts, accumulated behind that rampart of sand-hills whose remains are still to be seen near Benha. Thus was formed a miniature Delta, whose structure pretty accurately corresponded with that of the great Delta of to-day. Here the Nile divided into three divergent streams, roughly coinciding with the southern courses of the Rosetta and Damietta branches, and with the modern canal of Abû Meneggeh. The ceaseless accumulation of mud brought down by the river soon overpassed the first limits, and steadily encroached upon the sea until it was carried beyond the shelter furnished by Cape Abûkir. Thence it was gathered into the great littoral current flowing from Africa to Asia, and formed an incurvated coast-line ending in the headland of Casios, on the Syrian frontier. From that time Egypt made no further increase towards the

from its mysterious sources." Nevertheless, up to the present time, the hieroglyphic texts have yielded nothing altogether corresponding to the exact terms of the Greek historians—*gift* (δῶρον) *of the Nile,* or its natural *product* (ἔργον).

north, and her coast remains practically such as it was thousands of years ago:[1] the interior alone has suffered change, having been dried up, hardened, and gradually raised. Its inhabitants thought they could measure the exact length of time in which this work of creation had been accomplished. According to the Egyptians, Menes, the first of their mortal kings, had found, so they said, the valley under water. The sea came in almost as far as the Fayûm, and, excepting the province of Thebes, the whole country was a pestilential swamp. Hence, the necessary period for the physical formation of Egypt would cover some centuries after Menes. This is no longer considered a sufficient length of time, and some modern geologists declare that the Nile must have worked at the formation of its own estuary for at least seventy-four thousand years.[2] This figure is certainly exaggerated, for the alluvium would gain on the shallows of the ancient gulf far more rapidly than it gains upon the depths of the Mediterranean. But even though we reduce the period, we must still admit that the Egyptians little suspected the true age of their country. Not only did the Delta long precede the coming of Menes, but its plan was entirely completed before the first arrival of the Egyptians. The Greeks, full of the mysterious

---

[1] ÉLIE DE BEAUMONT, "The great distinction of the Nile Delta lies in the almost uniform persistence of its coast-line. . . . The present sea-coast of Egypt is little altered from that of three thousand years ago." The latest observations prove it to be sinking and shrinking near Alexandria to rise in the neighbourhood of Port Said.

[2] Others, as for example SCHWEINFURTH, are more moderate in their views, and think " that it must have taken about twenty thousand years for that alluvial deposit which now forms the arable soil of Egypt to have attained to its present depth and fertility."

virtues which they attributed to numbers, discovered that
there were seven principal branches, and seven mouths of
the Nile, and that, as compared with these, the rest were
but false mouths.   As a matter of fact, there were only
three chief outlets.   The Canopic branch flowed westward,

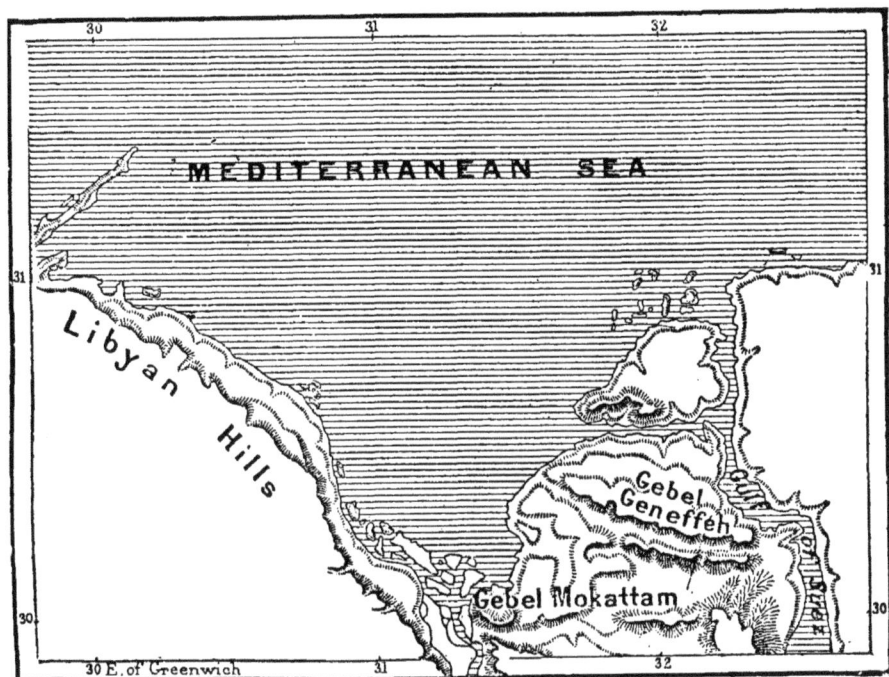

THE MOUTH OF THE NILE PREVIOUS TO THE FORMATION OF THE DELTA.

and fell into the Mediterranean near Cape Abûkir, at the
western extremity of the arc described by the coast-line.
The Pelusiac branch followed the length of the Arabian
chain, and flowed forth at the other extremity; and the
Sebennytic stream almost bisected the triangle contained
between the Canopic and Pelusiac channels.   Two
thousand years ago, these branches separated from the
main river at the city of Cerkasoros, nearly four miles

north of the site where Cairo now stands. But after the
Pelusiac branch had ceased to exist, the fork of the river
gradually wore away the land from age to age, and is now
some nine miles lower down.[1] These three great waterways are united by a network of artificial rivers and canals,
and by ditches—some natural, others dug by the hand of
man, but all ceaselessly shifting. They silt up, close, open
again, replace each other, and ramify in innumerable
branches over the surface of the soil, spreading life and
fertility on all sides. As the land rises towards the south,
this web contracts and is less confused, while black mould
and cultivation alike dwindle, and the fawn-coloured line
of the desert comes into sight. The Libyan and Arabian
hills appear above the plain, draw nearer to each other,
and gradually shut in the horizon until it seems as though
they would unite. And there the Delta ends, and Egypt
proper has begun.

It is only a strip of vegetable mould stretching north
and south between regions of drought and desolation, a
prolonged oasis on the banks of the river, made by the
Nile, and sustained by the Nile. The whole length of the
land is shut in between two ranges of hills, roughly parallel
at a mean distance of about twelve miles.[2] During the

[1] By the end of the Byzantine period, the fork of the river lay at some
distance south of Shetnûfi, the present Shatanûf, which is the spot where it
now is. The Arab geographers call the head of the Delta *Batn-el-Bagarah*,
the *Cow's Belly*. AMPÈRE, in his *Voyage en Égypte et en Nubie*, p. 120, says,
"May it not be that this name, denoting the place where the most fertile
part of Egypt begins, is a reminiscence of the Cow Goddess, of Isis, the
symbol of fecundity, and the personification of Egypt?"

[2] DE ROZIÈRE estimated the mean breadth as being only a little over
nine miles.

earlier ages, the river filled all this intermediate space, and
the sides of the hills, polished, worn, blackened to their
very summits, still bear unmistakable traces of its action.
Wasted, and shrunken within the deeps of its ancient
bed, the stream now makes a way through its own thick
deposits of mud. The bulk of its waters keeps to the
east, and constitutes the true Nile, the "Great River" of
the hieroglyphic inscriptions. A second arm flows close to
the Libyan desert, here and there formed into canals, elsewhere left to follow its own course. From the head of the
Delta to the village of Derût it is called the Bahr-Yûsuf;
beyond Derût—up to Gebel Silsileh—it is the Ibrâhimîyeh,
the Sohâgîyeh, the Raiân. But the ancient names are
unknown to us. This Western Nile dries up in winter
throughout all its upper courses: where it continues to flow,
it is by scanty accessions from the main Nile. It also
divides north of Henassieh, and by the gorge of Illahûn
sends out a branch which passes beyond the hills into the
basin of the Fayûm. The true Nile, the Eastern Nile, is
less a river than a sinuous lake encumbered with islets and
sandbanks, and its navigable channel winds capriciously
between them, flowing with a strong and steady current
below the steep, black banks cut sheer through the alluvial
earth. There are light groves of the date-palm, groups
of acacia trees and sycamores, square patches of barley
or of wheat, fields of beans or of *bersîm*,[1] and here and there
a long bank of sand which the least breeze raises into

---

[1] *Bersîm* is a kind of trefoil, the *Trifolium Alexandrinum* of LINNÆUS. It
is very common in Egypt, and the only plant of the kind generally cultivated
for fodder.

A LINE OF LADEN CAMELS EMERGES FROM A HOLLOW OF THE UNDULATING ROAD.[1]

whirling clouds. And over all there broods a great silence, scarcely broken by the cry of birds, or the song of

A DAINTY VILLAGE LOOKS FORTH SMILING FROM BENEATH ITS PALM TREES.[2]

rowers in a passing boat. Something of human life may

[1] From a drawing by Boudier, after a photograph by Insinger, taken in 1884.

[2] From a drawing by Boudier, after a photograph by Insinger, taken in 1886.

stir on the banks, but it is softened into poetry by distance. A half-veiled woman, bearing a bundle of herbs upon her head, is driving her goats before her. An irregular line of asses or of laden camels emerges from one hollow of the undulating road only to disappear within another. A group of peasants, crouched upon the shore, in the ancient posture of knees to chin, patiently awaits the return of the ferry-boat. A dainty village looks forth smiling from

GEBEL ABÛFÊDA, DREADED BY THE SAILORS.[1]

beneath its palm trees. Near at hand it is all naked filth and ugliness: a cluster of low grey huts built of mud and laths; two or three taller houses, whitewashed; an enclosed square ·shaded by sycamores; a few old men, each seated peacefully at his own door; a confusion of fowls, children, goats, and sheep; half a dozen boats made fast ashore. ·But, as we pass on, the wretchedness all fades away; meanness of detail is lost in light, and long before

[1] From a drawing by Boudier, after a photograph by Insinger, taken in 1886.

it disappears at a bend of the river, the village is again
clothed with gaiety and serene beauty. Day by day, the
landscape repeats itself. The same groups of trees
alternate with the same fields, growing green or dusty
in the sunlight according to the season of the year. With
the same measured flow, the Nile winds beneath its steep
banks and about its scattered islands. One village
succeeds another, each alike smiling and sordid under

PART OF GEBEL SHÊKH HERÎDI.[1]

its crown of foliage. The terraces of the Libyan hills,
away beyond the Western Nile, scarcely rise above the
horizon, and lie like a white edging between the green
of the plain and the blue of the sky. The Arabian hills
do not form one unbroken line, but a series of mountain
masses with their spurs, now approaching the river, and
now withdrawing to the desert at almost regular intervals.
At the entrance to the valley, rise Gebel Mokattam and

[1] From a drawing by Boudier, after a photograph by Insinger, taken
in 1882.

Gebel el-Ahmar. Gebel Hemûr-Shemûl and Gebel Shêkh Embârak next stretch in echelon from north to south, and are succeeded by Gebel et-Têr, where, according to an old legend, all the birds of the world are annually assembled.[1] Then follows Gebel Abûfêda, dreaded by the sailors for

THE HILL OF KASR ES-SAYYAD.[2]

its sudden gusts. Limestone predominates throughout, white or yellowish, broken by veins of alabaster, or of

[1] In MAKRIZI's *Description of Egypt* we read: "Every year, upon a certain day, all the herons (BOUKÎR, *Ardea bubulcus* of CUVIER) assemble at this mountain. One after another, each puts his beak into a cleft of the hill until the cleft closes upon one of them. And then forthwith all the others fly away. But the bird which has been caught struggles until he dies, and there his body remains until it has fallen into dust." The same tale is told by other Arab writers, of which a list may be seen in ÉTIENNE QUATREMÈRE, *Mémoires historiques et géographiques sur l'Égypte et quelques contrées voisines*, vol. i. pp. 31–33. It faintly recalls that ancient tradition of the Cleft at Abydos, whereby souls must pass, as human-headed birds, in order to reach the other world.

[2] From a drawing by Boudier, after a photograph by Insinger, taken in 1882.

red and grey sandstones. Its horizontal strata are so
symmetrically laid one above another as to seem more
like the walls of a town than the side of a mountain. But
time has often dismantled their summits and loosened
their foundations. Man has broken into their façades to
cut his quarries and his tombs; while the current is
secretly undermining the base, wherein it has made
many a breach. As soon as any margin of mud has
collected between cliffs and river, halfah and wild plants
take hold upon it, and date-palms grow there—whence
their seed, no one knows. Presently a hamlet rises at
the mouth of the ravine, among clusters of trees and
fields in miniature. Beyond Siût, the light becomes
more glowing, the air drier and more vibrating, and the
green of cultivation loses its brightness. The angular
outline of the dôm-palm mingles more and more with that
of the common palm and of the heavy sycamore, and
the castor-oil plant increasingly abounds. But all these
changes come about so gradually that they are effected
before we notice them. The plain continues to contract.
At Thebes it is still ten miles wide; at the gorge of
Gebelên it has almost disappeared, and at Gebel Silsileh
it has completely vanished. There, it was crossed by a
natural dyke of sandstone, through which the waters have
with difficulty scooped for themselves a passage. From
this point, Egypt is nothing but the bed of the Nile lying
between two escarpments of naked rock.

Further on the cultivable land reappears, but narrowed,
and changed almost beyond recognition. Hills, hewn out
of solid sandstone, succeed each other at distances of about

two miles, low, crushed, sombre, and formless. Presently a forest of palm trees, the last on that side, announces Aswân and Nubia. Five banks of granite, ranged in lines between latitude 24° and 18° N., cross Nubia from east to west, and from north-east to south-west, like so many ramparts thrown up between the Mediterranean and the heart of Africa. The Nile has attacked them from behind, and made its way over them one after another in rapids which have been glorified by the

ENTRANCE TO THE FIRST CATARACT.[1]

name of cataracts. Classic writers were pleased to describe the river as hurled into the gulfs of Syne with so great a roar that the people of the neighbourhood were deafened by it. Even a colony of Persians, sent thither by Cambyses, could not bear the noise of the falls, and went forth to seek a quieter situation. The first cataract is a kind of sloping and sinuous passage six and a quarter miles in length, descending from the island of Philæ to the port of Aswân, the aspect of its approach

[1] View taken from the hills opposite Elephantinê, by Insinger, in 1884.

relieved and brightened by the ever green groves of Elephantinê. Beyond Elephantinê are cliffs and sandy beaches, chains of blackened "roches moutonnées" marking out the beds of the currents, and fantastic reefs, sometimes bare and sometimes veiled by long grasses and climbing plants, in which thousands of birds have made their nests. There are islets too, occasionally large enough to have once supported something of a population, such as Amerade, Salûg, Sehêl. The granite threshold

ENTRANCE TO NUBIA[1]

of Nubia, is broken beyond Sehêl, but its *débris*, massed in disorder against the right bank, still seem to dispute the passage of the waters, dashing turbulently and roaring as they flow along through tortuous channels, where every streamlet is broken up into small cascades. The channel running by the left bank is always navigable. During the inundation, the rocks and sandbanks of the right side are completely under water, and their presence

[1] View taken from the southern point of the island of Philæ. From a photograph by Émil Brugsch-Bey.

is only betrayed by eddies. But on the river's reaching
its lowest point a fall of some six feet is established,
and there big boats, hugging the shore, are hauled up
by means of ropes, or easily drift down with the
current. All kinds of granite are found together in this
corner of Africa. There are the pink and red Syenites,
porphyritic granite, yellow granite, grey granite, both black
granite and white, and granites veined with black and
veined with white. As soon as these disappear behind us,
various sandstones begin to crop up, allied to the coarsest

LEAGUE BEYOND LEAGUE, THE HILLS STRETCH ON IN LOW IGNOBLE OUTLINE.[1]

calcaire grossier. The hill bristle with small split blocks,
with peaks half overturned, with rough and denuded
mounds. League beyond league, they stretch in low
ignoble outline. Here and there a valley opens sharply
into the desert, revealing an infinite perspective of
summits and escarpments in echelon one behind another
to the furthest plane of the horizon, like motionless

[1] From a drawing by Boudier, after a photograph by Insinger, taken
in 1881.

caravans. The now confined river rushes on with a low, deep murmur, accompanied night and day by the croaking of frogs and the rhythmic creak of the sâkieh.[1] Jetties of rough stone-work, made in unknown times by an unknown people, run out like breakwaters into midstream. From time to time waves of sand are borne over, and drown the narrow fields of durra and of barley. Scraps of close, aromatic pasturage, acacias, date-palms, and dôm-palms, together with a few shrivelled sycamores, are scattered along both banks. The ruins of a crumbling pylon mark the site of some ancient city, and, overhanging the water, is a vertical wall of rock honeycombed with tombs. Amid these relics of another age, miserable huts, scattered hamlets, a town or two surrounded with little gardens are the only evidence that there is yet life in Nubia. South of Wâdy Halfah, the second granite bank is broken through, and the second cataract spreads its rapids over a length of four leagues : the archipelago numbers more than 350 islets, of which some sixty have houses upon them and yield harvests to their inhabitants. The main characteristics of the first two cataracts are repeated with slight variations in the cases of the three which follow,—at Hannek, at Guerendid, and El-Hû-mar. It is Egypt still, but a joyless Egypt bereft of its bright-

---

[1] The *sâkieh* is made of a notch-wheel fixed vertically on a horizontal axle, and is actuated by various cog-wheels set in continuous motion by oxen or asses. A long chain of earthenware vessels brings up the water either from the river itself, or from some little branch canal, and empties it into a system of troughs and reservoirs. Thence, it flows forth to be distributed over all the neighbouring land.

ness; impoverished, disfigured, and almost desolate.
There is the same double wall of hills, now closely con-
fining the valley, and again withdrawing from each other
as though to flee into the desert. Everywhere are
moving sheets of sand, steep black banks with their

ENTRANCE TO THE SECOND CATARACT.[1]

narrow strips of cultivation, villages which are scarcely
visible on account of the lowness of their huts. The
sycamore ceases at Gebel-Barkal, date-palms become

[1] View taken from the top of the rocks of Abusîr, after a photograph by
Insinger, in 1881.

fewer and finally disappear. The Nile alone has not changed. And it was at Philæ, so it is at Berber. Here, however, on the right bank, 600 leagues from the sea, is its first affluent, the Takazze, which intermittently brings to it the waters of Northern Ethiopia. At Khartûm, the single channel in which the river flowed divides; and two other streams are opened up in a southerly direction, each of them apparently equal in volume to the main stream. Which is the true Nile? Is it the Blue Nile, which seems to come down from the distant mountains? Or is it the White Nile, which has traversed the immense plains of equatorial Africa. The old Egyptians never knew. The river kept the secret of its source from them as obstinately as it withheld it from us until a few years ago. Vainly did their victorious armies follow the Nile for months together as they pursued the tribes who dwelt upon its banks, only to find it as wide, as full, as irresistible in its progress as ever. It was a fresh-water sea, and sea—*iaûmâ, iôma*—was the name by which they called it.

The Egyptians therefore never sought its source. They imagined the whole universe to be a large box, nearly rectangular in form, whose greatest diameter was from south to north, and its least from east to west. The earth, with its alternate continents and seas, formed the bottom of the box; it was a narrow, oblong, and slightly concave floor, with Egypt in its centre. The sky stretched over it like an iron ceiling, flat according to some, vaulted according. to others. Its earthward face was capriciously sprinkled with lamps hung from strong cables, and which, extinguished or unperceived by day, were lighted, or became visible to our eyes, at night.[1] Since this ceiling could not remain in mid-air without support, four columns,

AN ATTEMPT TO REPRESENT THE EGYPTIAN UNIVERSE.[2]

or rather four forked trunks of trees, similar to those which maintained the primitive house, were supposed to uphold

[1] The variants of the sign for night—✧, ⊤— are most significant. The end of the rope to which the star is attached passes over the sky, and falls free, as though arranged for drawing a lamp up and down when lighting or extinguishing it. And furthermore, the name of the stars— khabisû—is the same word as that used to designate an ordinary lamp.

[2] Section taken at Hermopolis. To the left, is the bark of the sun on the celestial river.

it.[1] But it was doubtless feared lest some tempest[2] should overturn them, for they were superseded by four lofty peaks, rising at the four cardinal points, and connected by a continuous chain of mountains. The Egyptians knew little of the northern peak : the Mediterranean, the " Very Green," interposed between it and Egypt, and prevented their coming near enough to see it. The southern peak was named Apit-to,[3] the Horn of the Earth; that on the east was called Bâkhû, the Mountain of Birth; and the western peak was known as Manû, sometimes as Onkhit, the Region of Life. Bâkhû was not a fictitious mountain, but the highest of those distant summits seen from the Nile in looking towards the Red Sea. In the same way, Manû answered to some hill of the Libyan desert, whose

[1] Isolated, these pillars are represented under the form $\bigvee$, but they are often found together as supporting the sky $\overline{\gamma\gamma\gamma\gamma}$. BRUGSCH, who was the first to study their function, thought that all four were placed to the north, and that they denoted to the Egyptians the mountains of Armenia. He afterwards recognized that they were set up at each of the four cardinal points, but thought that this conception of their use was not older than Ptolemaic times. Like all Egyptologists, he afterwards admitted that these pillars were always placed at the four cardinal points.

[2] The words designating hurricanes, storms, or any kind of cataclysm, are followed by the sign ⊞, which represents the sky as detached and falling from its four supporting pillars. Magicians sometimes threatened to overthrow the four pillars if the gods would not obey their orders.

[3] Compare the expressions, Νότου κέρας, Ἑσπέρου κέρας, of the Greek geographers. BRUGSCH was the first to note that Apit-to is placed at the southern extremity of the world. He has hypothetically identified the Horn of the Earth with the Mountains of the Moon of the Arab geographers. I believe that the Egyptians of the great Theban period (eighteenth to twentieth dynasties) indicated by that name the mountain ranges of Abyssinia. In the course of their raids along the Blue Nile and its affluents, they saw this group of summits from afar, but they never reached it.

summit closed the horizon. When it was discovered that neither Bâkhû nor Manû were the limits of the world, the notion of upholding the celestial roof was not on that account given up. It was only necessary to withdraw the pillars from sight, and imagine fabulous peaks, invested with familiar names. These were not supposed to form the actual boundary of the universe; a great river—analogous to the Ocean-stream of the Greeks—lay between them and its utmost limits. This river circulated upon a kind of ledge projecting along the sides of the box a little below the continuous mountain chain upon which the starry heavens were sustained. On the north of the ellipse, the river was bordered by a steep and abrupt bank, which took its rise at the peak of Manû on the west, and soon rose high enough to form a screen between the river and the earth. The narrow valley which it hid from view was known as Daït from remotest times. Eternal night enfolded that valley in thick darkness, and filled it with dense air such as no living thing could breathe. Towards the east the steep bank rapidly declined, and ceased altogether a little beyond Bâkhû, while the river flowed on between low and almost level shores from east to south, and then from south to west. The sun was a disc of fire placed upon a boat. At the same equable rate, the river carried it round the ramparts of the world. From evening until morning it disappeared within the gorges of Daït; its light did not then reach us, and it was night. From morning until evening its rays, being no longer intercepted by any obstacle, were freely shed abroad from one end of the box to the other, and it was day. The Nile branched off from the celestial river at its southern bend;[1] hence the south was the chief cardinal point to the Egyptians, and by that they oriented themselves, placing sunrise to their left, and sunset to their right. Before they passed beyond the defiles of Gebel Silsileh, they thought that the spot whence the celestial waters left the sky was situate between Elephantinê and Philæ, and that they descended in an immense waterfall whose last leaps were at Syene. It may be that the tales about the first cataract told by classic writers are but a far-off echo of this tradition of a barbarous age. Conquests carried into the heart of Africa forced the Egyptians to recognize their error, but did not weaken their faith in the supernatural origin of the river. They only placed its source further south, and surrounded it with greater marvels. They told how, by going up the stream, sailors at length reached an undetermined country, a kind of borderland between this world and the next, a "Land of Shades," whose inhabitants were dwarfs, monsters, or spirits. Thence they passed into a sea sprinkled with mysterious islands, like those enchanted archipelagoes which Portuguese and Breton mariners were wont to see at times when on their voyages, and which vanished at their approach. These islands were inhabited by serpents with human voices, sometimes friendly and sometimes cruel to the shipwrecked. He who went forth from the islands could never more re-enter them: they were resolved into the

[1] The classic writers themselves knew that, according to Egyptian belief, the Nile flowed down from heaven. The legend of the Nile having its source in the ocean stream was but a Greek transposition of the Egyptian doctrine, which represented it as an arm of the celestial river whereon the sun sailed round the earth.

waters and lost within the bosom of the waves. A modern
geographer can hardly comprehend such fancies; those of
Greek and Roman times were perfectly familiar with them.
They believed that the Nile communicated with the Red
Sea near Suakin, by means of the Astaboras, and this
was certainly the route which the Egyptians of old had
imagined for their navigators. The supposed communication was gradually transferred farther and farther south ;
and we have only to glance over certain maps of the sixteenth and seventeenth centuries, to see clearly drawn
what the Egyptians had imagined—the centre of Africa as
a great lake, whence issued the Congo, the Zambesi, and
the Nile. Arab merchants of the Middle Ages believed
that a resolute man could pass from Alexandria or Cairo to
the land of the Zindjes and the Indian Ocean by rising
from river to river.[1] Many of the legends relating to this
subject are lost, while others have been collected and
embellished with fresh features by Jewish and Christian
theologians. The Nile was said to have its source in
Paradise, to traverse burning regions inaccessible to man,
and afterwards to fall into a sea whence it made its way
to Egypt. Sometimes it carried down from its celestial
sources branches and fruits unlike any to be found on
earth. The sea mentioned in all these tales is perhaps a

---

[1] JOINVILLE has given a special chapter to the description of the sources
and wonders of the Nile, in which he believed as firmly as in an article of
his creed. As late as the beginning of the seventeenth century, WENDELINUS
devoted part of his *Admiranda Nili* to proving that the river did *not* rise in
the earthly Paradise. At Gûrnah, forty years ago, RHIND picked up a legend
which stated that the Nile flows down from the sky.

less extravagant invention than we are at first inclined to
think. A lake, nearly as large as the Victoria Nyanza,
once covered the marshy plain where the Bahr el-Abiad

SOUTH AFRICA AND THE SOURCES OF THE NILE, BY ODOARDO LOPEZ.[1]

unites with the Sobat, and with the Bahr el-Ghazâl. Alluvial
deposits have filled up all but its deepest depression, which

[1] Facsimile of the map published by KIRCHER in *Œdipus Ægyptiacus*,
vol. i. (*Iconismus II*), p. 53.

is known as Birket Nû; but, in ages preceding our era,
it must still have been vast enough to suggest to Egyptian
soldiers and boatmen the idea of an actual sea, opening
into the Indian Ocean. The mountains, whose outline was
vaguely seen far to southward on the further shores, doubtless contained within them its mysterious source. There
the inundation was made ready, and there it began upon a
fixed day. The celestial Nile had its periodic rise and fall,
on which those of the earthly Nile depended. Every
year, towards the middle of June, Isis, mourning for Osiris,
let fall into it one of the tears which she shed over her
brother, and thereupon the river swelled and descended
upon earth. Isis has had no devotees for centuries, and
her very name is unknown to the descendants of her
worshippers; but the tradition of her fertilizing tears has
survived her memory. Even to this day, every one in
Egypt, Mussulman or Christian, knows that a divine drop
falls from heaven during the night between the 17th and
18th of June, and forthwith brings about the rise of the Nile.

Swollen by the rains which fall in February over the
region of the Great Lakes, the White Nile rushes northward, sweeping before it the stagnant sheets of water left
by the inundation of the previous year. On the left, the
Bahr el-Ghazâl brings it the overflow of the ill-defined
basin stretching between Darfûr and the Congo; and the
Sobat pours in on the right a tribute from the rivers which
furrow the southern slopes of the Abyssinian mountains.
The first swell passes Khartûm by the end of April, and
raises the water-level there by about a foot, then it slowly
makes its way through Nubia, and dies away in Egypt at

the beginning of June. Its waters, infected by half-putrid organic matter from the equatorial swamps, are not completely freed from it even in the course of this long journey, but keep a greenish tint as far as the Delta. They are said to be poisonous, and to give severe pains in the bladder to any who may drink them. I am bound to say that every June, for five years, I drank this green water from the Nile itself, without taking any other precaution than the usual one of filtering it through a porous jar. Neither I, nor the many people living with me, ever felt the slightest inconvenience from it. Happily, this *Green Nile* does not last long, but generally flows away in three or four days, and is only the forerunner of the real flood. The melting of the snows and the excessive spring rains having suddenly swollen the torrents which rise in the central plateau of Abyssinia, the Blue Nile, into which they flow, rolls so impetuously towards the plain that, when its waters reach Khartûm in the middle of May, they refuse to mingle with those of the White Nile, and do not lose their peculiar colour before reaching the neighbourhood of Abû Hamed, three hundred miles below. From that time the height of the Nile increases rapidly day by day. The river, constantly reinforced by floods following one upon another from the Great Lakes and from Abyssinia, rises in furious bounds, and would become a devastating torrent were its rage not checked by the Nubian cataracts. Here six basins, one above another, in which the water collects, check its course, and permit it to flow thence only as a partially filtered and moderated stream. It is signalled at Syene towards the 8th of June, at Cairo by the 17th to the 20th, and there its birth is officially celebrated during the "Night of the Drop." Two days later it reaches the Delta, just in time to save the country from drought and sterility. Egypt, burnt up by the Khamsîn, a west wind blowing continuously for fifty days, seems nothing more than an extension of the desert. The trees are covered and choked by a layer of grey dust. About the villages, meagre and laboriously watered patches of vegetables struggle for life, while some show of green still lingers along the canals and in hollows whence all moisture has not yet evaporated. The plain lies panting in the sun—naked, dusty, and ashen—scored with intersecting cracks as far as eye can see. The Nile is only half its usual width, and holds not more than a twentieth of the volume of water which is borne down in October. It has at first hard work to recover its former bed, and attains it by such subtle gradations that the rise is scarcely noted. It is, however, continually gaining ground; here a sandbank is covered, there an empty channel is filled, islets are outlined where there was a continuous beach, a new stream detaches itself and gains the old shore. The first contact is disastrous to the banks; their steep sides, disintegrated and cracked by the heat, no longer offer any resistance to the current, and fall with a crash, in lengths of a hundred yards and more. As the successive floods grow stronger and are more heavily charged with mud, the whole mass of water becomes turbid and changes colour. In eight or ten days it has turned from greyish blue to dark red, occasionally of so intense a colour as to look like newly shed blood. The "Red Nile" is not unwholesome like the

" Green Nile," and the suspended mud to which it owes its suspicious appearance deprives the water of none of its freshness and lightness. It reaches its full height towards the 15th of July; but the dykes which confine it, and the barriers constructed across the mouths of canals, still prevent it from overflowing. The Nile must be considered high enough to submerge the land adequately before it is set free. The ancient Egyptians measured its height by cubits of twenty-one and a quarter inches. At fourteen cubits, they pronounced it an excellent Nile; below thirteen, or above fifteen, it was accounted insufficient or excessive, and in either case meant famine, and perhaps pestilence at hand. To this day the natives watch its advance with the same anxious eagerness; and from the 3rd of July, public criers, walking the streets of Cairo, announce each morning what progress it has made since evening. More or less authentic traditions assert that the prelude to the opening of the canals, in the time of the Pharaohs, was the solemn casting to the waters of a young girl decked as for her bridal—the "Bride of the Nile." Even after the Arab conquest, the irruption of the river into the bosom of the land was still considered as an actual marriage; the contract was drawn up by a cadi, and witnesses confirmed its consummation with the most fantastic formalities of Oriental ceremonial. It is generally between the 1st and 16th of July that it is decided to break through the dykes. When that proceeding has been solemnly accomplished in state, the flood still takes several days to fill the canals, and afterwards spreads over the low lands, advancing little by little to the very edge of the desert. Egypt is then one sheet of turbid water spreading between two lines of rock and sand, flecked with green and black spots where there are towns or where the ground rises, and divided into irregular compartments by raised roads connecting the villages. In Nubia the river attains its greatest height towards the end of August; at Cairo and in the Delta not until three weeks or a month later. For about eight days it remains stationary, and then begins to fall imperceptibly. Sometimes there is a new freshet in October, and the river again increases in height. But the rise is unsustained; once more it falls as rapidly as it rose, and by December the river has completely retired to the limits of its bed. One after another, the streams which fed it fail or dwindle. The Tacazze is lost. among the sands before rejoining it, and the Blue Nile, well-nigh deprived of tributaries, is but scantily maintained by Abyssinian snows. The White Nile is indebted to the Great Lakes for the greater persistence of its waters, which feed the river as far as the Mediterranean, and save the valley from utter drought in winter. But, even with this resource, the level of the water falls daily, and its volume is diminished. Long-hidden sandbanks reappear, and are again linked into continuous line. Islands expand by the rise of shingly beaches, which gradually reconnect them with each other and with the shore. Smaller branches of the river cease to flow, and form a mere network of stagnant pools and muddy ponds, which fast dry up. The main channel itself is only intermittently navigable; after March boats run aground in it, and are forced to await the return of the inundation for their release. From the middle

of April to the middle of June, Egypt is only half alive, awaiting the new Nile.

Those ruddy and heavily charged waters, rising and retiring with almost mathematical regularity, bring and leave the spoils of the countries they have traversed : sand from Nubia, whitish clay from the regions of the Lakes, ferruginous mud, and the various rock-formations of Abyssinia. These materials are not uniformly disseminated in the deposits ; their precipitation being regulated both by their specific gravity and the velocity of the current. Flattened stones and rounded pebbles are left behind at the cataract between Syene and Keneh, while coarser particles of sand are suspended in the undercurrents and serve to raise the bed of the river, or are carried out to sea and form the sandbanks which are slowly rising at the Damietta and Rosetta mouths of the Nile. The mud and finer particles rise towards the surface, and are deposited upon the land after the opening of the dykes. Soil which is entirely dependent on the deposit of a river, and periodically invaded by it, necessarily maintains but a scanty flora ; and though it is well known that, as a general rule, a flora is rich in proportion to its distance from the poles and its approach to the equator, it is also admitted that Egypt offers an exception to this rule. At the most, she has not more than a thousand species, while, with equal area, England, for instance, possesses more than fifteen hundred ; and of this thousand, the greater number are not indigenous. Many of them have been brought from Central Africa by the river ; birds and winds have continued the work, and man himself has contributed his

part in making it more complete. From Asia he has at
different times brought wheat, barley, the olive, the apple,
the white or pink almond, and some twenty other species
now acclimatized on the banks of the Nile. Marsh plants
predominate in the Delta; but the papyrus, and the three
varieties of blue, white, and pink lotus which once flourished

SYCAMORES AT THE ENTRANCE OF THE MUDÎRÎYEH OF ASYÛT.[1]

there, being no longer cultivated, have now almost entirely
disappeared, and reverted to their original habitats.   The
sycamore and the date-palm, both importations from
Central Africa, have better adapted themselves to their
exile, and are now fully naturalized on Egyptian soil.   The

[1] From a drawing by Boudier, from a photograph by Insinger, taken
in 1881.

THE FOREST OF DATE-PALMS AT BEDRESHEN.

View taken from the ruins of the temple of Rameses II, after a photograph by Émil Brugsch-Bey.

sycamore grows in sand on the edge of the desert as vigorously as in the midst of a well-watered country. Its roots go deep in search of water, which infiltrates as far as the gorges of the hills, and they absorb it freely, even where drought seems to reign supreme. The heavy, squat, gnarled trunk occasionally attains to colossal dimensions, without ever growing very high. Its rounded masses of compact foliage are so wide-spreading that a single tree in the distance may give the impression of several grouped together; and its shade is dense, and impenetrable to the sun. A striking contrast to the sycamore is presented by the date-palm. Its round and slender stem rises uninterruptedly to a height of thirteen to sixteen yards; its head is crowned with a cluster of flexible leaves arranged in two or three tiers, but so scanty, so pitilessly slit, that they fail to keep off the light, and cast but a slight and unrefreshing shadow. Few trees have so elegant an appearance, yet few are so monotonously elegant. There are palm trees to be seen on every hand; isolated, clustered by twos and threes at the mouths of ravines and about the villages, planted in regular file along the banks of the river like rows of columns, symmetrically arranged in plantations, —these are the invariable background against which other trees are grouped, diversifying the landscape. The feathery tamarisk[1] and the nabk, the moringa, the carob, or locust

---

[1] The Egyptian name for the tamarisk, *asari, asri*, is identical with that given to it in Semitic languages, both ancient and modern. This would suggest the question whether the tamarisk did not originally come from Asia. In that case it must have been brought to Egypt from remote antiquity, for it figures in the Pyramid texts. Bricks of Nile mud, and Memphite and Theban tombs, have yielded us leaves, twigs, and even whole branches of the tamarisk.

tree, several varieties of acacia and mimosa—the sont, the mimosa habbas, the white acacia, the Acacia Farnesiana —and the pomegranate tree, increase in number with the distance from the Mediterranean. The dry air of the valley is marvellously suited to them, but makes the tissue of their foliage hard and fibrous, imparting an aërial aspect, and such faded tints as are unknown to their growth in

ACACIAS AT THE ENTRANCE TO A GARDEN OUTSIDE EKHMÎM.[1]

other climates. The greater number of these trees do not reproduce themselves spontaneously, and tend to disappear when neglected. The Acacia Seyal, formerly abundant by the banks of the river, is now almost entirely confined to certain valleys of the Theban desert, along with a variety

[1] From a drawing by Boudier, from a photograph by Insinger, taken in 1884.

of the kernelled dôm-palm, of which a poetical description has come down to us from the Ancient Egyptians. The common dôm-palm bifurcates at eight or ten yards from the ground; these branches are subdivided, and terminate in bunches of twenty to thirty palmate and fibrous leaves, six to eight feet long. At the beginning of this century the tree was common in Upper Egypt, but it is now becoming scarce, and we are within measurable distance of the time when its presence will be an exception north of the first cataract. Willows are decreasing in number, and the persea, one of the sacred trees of Ancient Egypt, is now only to be found in gardens. None of the remaining tree species are common enough to grow in large clusters; and Egypt, reduced to her lofty groves of date-palms, presents the singular spectacle of a country where there is no lack of trees, but an almost entire absence of shade.

If Egypt is a land of imported flora, it is also a land of imported fauna, and all its animal species have been brought from neighbouring countries. Some of these—as, for example, the horse and the camel—were only introduced at a comparatively recent period, two thousand to eighteen hundred years before our

SHE-ASS AND HER FOAL.

era; the camel still later. The animals—such as the long and short-horned oxen, together with varieties of goats and dogs—are, like the plants, generally of African origin, and the ass of Egypt preserves an original purity of form and a vigour to which the European donkey has long been a stranger. The pig and the wild boar, the long-eared hare, the hedgehog, the ichneumon, the moufflon, or maned sheep, innumerable gazelles, including the Egyptian gazelles, and antelopes with lyre-shaped horns, are as much West Asian as African, like the carnivoræ of all sizes, whose prey they are—the wild cat, the wolf, the jackal, the striped and spotted hyenas, the leopard, the panther, the hunting leopard, and the lion. On the other hand, most of the serpents, large and small, are indigenous. Some are harmless, like the colubers; others are venomous, such as the scytale, the cerastes, the haje viper, and the asp. The asp was worshipped by the Egyptians under the name of uræus. It occasionally attains to a length of six and a half feet, and when

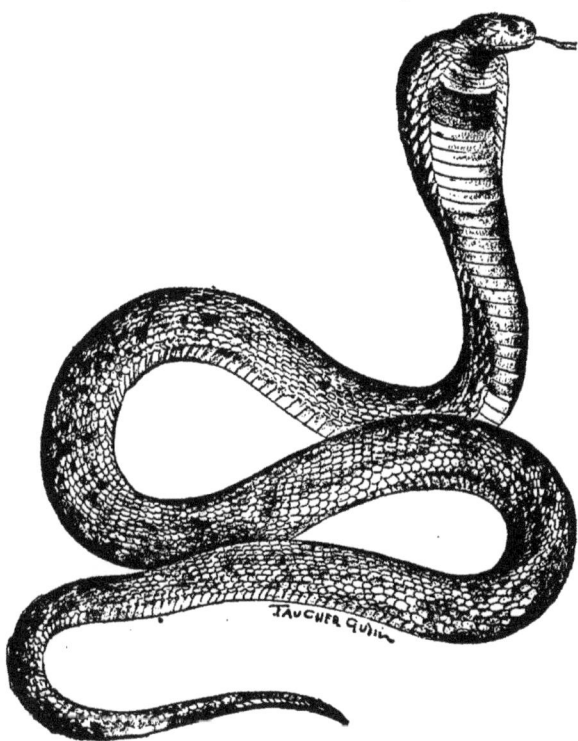

THE URÆUS OF EGYPT.[1]

[1] Drawn by Faucher-Gudin from pl. iii. of the REPTILES-SUPPLÉMENT to the *Description de l'Égypte.*

approached will erect its head and inflate its throat in readiness for darting forward. The bite is fatal, like that of the cerastes; birds are literally struck down by the strength of the poison, while the great mammals, and man himself, almost invariably succumb to it after a longer or shorter death-struggle. The uræus is rarely found except in the desert or in the fields; the scorpion crawls everywhere, in desert and city alike, and if its sting is not always followed by death, it invariably causes terrible pain. Probably there were once several kinds of gigantic serpent in Egypt, analogous to the pythons of equatorial Africa. They are still to be seen in representations of funerary scenes, but not elsewhere; for, like the elephant, the giraffe, and other animals which now only thrive far south, they had disappeared at the beginning of historic times. The hippopotamus long maintained its ground before returning to those equatorial regions whence it had been brought by the Nile. Common under the first dynasties, but afterwards withdrawing to the marshes of the Delta, it there continued to flourish up to the thirteenth century of our era. The crocodile, which came with it, has, like it also, been compelled to beat a retreat. Lord of the river throughout all ancient times, worshipped and protected in some provinces, execrated and proscribed in others, it might still be seen in the neighbourhood of Cairo towards the beginning of our century. In 1840, it no longer passed beyond the neighbourhood of Gebel et-Têr, nor beyond that of Manfalût in 1849. Thirty years later, Mariette asserted that it was steadily retreating before the guns of tourists, and the disturbance which the regular passing of steamboats produced in the deep waters. To-day, no one knows of a single crocodile existing below Aswân, but it continues to infest Nubia, and the rocks of the first cataract : one of them is occasionally carried down by the current into Egypt, where it is speedily despatched by the fellâhîn, or by some traveller in quest of adventure. The fertility of the soil, and the vastness of the lakes and marshes, attract many migratory birds; passerinæ and palmipedes flock thither from all parts of the Mediterranean. Our European swallows, our quails, our geese and wild ducks, our herons — to mention only the most familiar — come here to winter, sheltered from cold and inclement weather. Even the non-migratory birds are really, for the most part, strangers acclimatized by long sojourn. Some of them—the turtle-dove, the magpie, the kingfisher, the partridge, and the

THE IBIS OF EGYPT.[1]

sparrow—may be classed with our European species, while

[1] Drawn by Faucher-Gudin, from OISEAUX, pl. vii. 1, in the *Commission d'Égypte.*

others betray their equatorial origin in the brightness of
their colours. White and black ibises, red flamingoes,
pelicans, and cormorants enliven the waters of the river,
and animate the reedy swamps of the Delta in infinite
variety. They are to be seen ranged in long files upon
the sand-banks, fishing and basking in the sun; suddenly
the flock is seized with panic, rises heavily, and settles
away further off. In hollows of the hills, eagle and falcon,
the merlin, the bald-headed vulture, the kestrel, the golden
sparrow-hawk, find inaccessible retreats, whence they

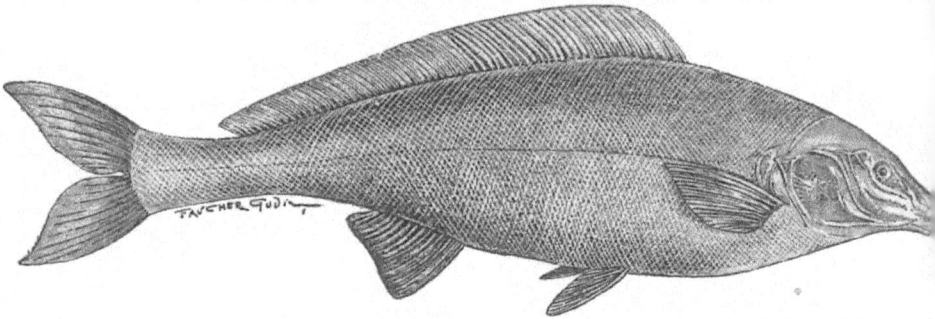

THE MORMYRUS OXYRHYNCHUS.

descend upon the plains like so many pillaging and well-
armed barons. A thousand little chattering birds come
at eventide to perch in flocks upon the frail boughs of
tamarisk and acacia. Many sea-fish make their way up-
stream to swim in fresh waters—shad, mullet, perch, and
the labrus—and carry their excursions far into the Saïd.
Those species which are not Mediterranean came originally,
and still come annually, from the heart of Ethiopia with
the rise of the Nile, including two kinds of Alestes, the
soft-shelled turtle, the Bagrus docmac, and the mormyrus.
Some attain to a gigantic size, the Bagrus bayad and the

turtle to about one yard, the latus to three and a half yards in length, while others, such as the silurus (catfish), are noted for their electric properties. Nature seems to have made the fahâka (the globe-fish) in a fit of playfulness. It is a long fish from beyond the cataracts, and it is carried by the Nile the more easily on account of the faculty it has of filling itself with air, and inflating its body at will. When swelled out immoderately, the fahâka overbalances, and drifts along upside down, its belly to the wind, covered with spikes

AHAKA.

so that it looks like a hedgehog. During the inundation, it floats with the current from one canal to another, and is cast by the retreating waters upon the muddy fields, where it becomes the prey of birds or of jackals, or serves as a plaything for children.

Everything is dependent upon the river:—the soil, the produce of the soil, the species of animals it bears, the birds which it feeds: and hence it was the Egyptians placed the river among their gods. They personified it as a man with regular features, and a vigorous and portly body, such as befits the rich of high lineage. His breasts, fully developed like those of a woman, though less firm, hang heavily upon a wide bosom where the fat lies in folds. A narrow girdle, whose ends fall free about the thighs, supports his spacious abdomen, and his attire is completed by sandals, and a close-fitting head-dress, generally surmounted with a crown of water-plants. Sometimes water springs from his breast; sometimes he presents a frog, or libation vases; or holds a bundle of the *cruces ansatæ*, as symbols of life; or bears a flat tray, full of offerings— bunches of flowers, ears of corn, heaps of fish, and geese tied together by the feet. The inscriptions call him, " Hâpi, father of the gods, lord of sustenance, who maketh food to be, and covereth the two lands of Egypt with his products; who giveth life,

TWO FISHERMEN CARRYING A LATUS WHICH THEY HAVE JUST CAUGHT.[1]

banisheth want, and filleth the granaries to overflowing." He is evolved into two personages, one being sometimes coloured red, and the other blue. The former, who wears a cluster of lotus-flowers upon his head, presides over the Egypt of the south; the latter has a bunch of papyrus for his head-dress, and watches over the Delta.[2] Two goddesses,

[1] Drawn by Faucher-Gudin, from a Medûm painting. PETRIE, *Medûm*, pl. xii.

[2] WILKINSON was the first who suggested that this god, when painted red, was the Red (that is, the High) Nile, and, when painted blue, was to be identified with the Low Nile. This opinion has since been generally

corresponding to the two Hâpis—Mirit Qimâit for Upper, and Mirit Mîhit for Lower Egypt—personified the banks of the river. They are often represented as standing with outstretched arms, as though begging for the water which should make them fertile. The Nile-god had his chapel in every province, and priests whose right it was to bury all bodies of men or beasts cast up by the river; for the god had

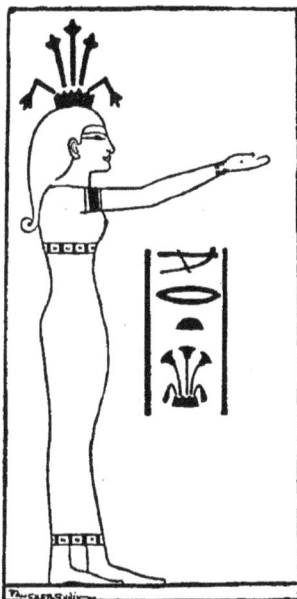

THE GODDESS MIRIT, BEARING A BUNCH
OF PAPYRUS ON HER HEAD.

THE NILE-GOD.[1]

claimed them, and to his servants they belonged. Several

adopted ; but to me it does not appear so incontrovertible as it has been considered. Here, as in other cases, the difference in colour is only a means of
making the distinction between two personages obvious to sight.

[1] Drawn by Faucher-Gudin, after a statue in the British Museum. The
dedication of this statue took place about 880 B.C. The giver was Sheshonqû,
high-priest of Amon in Thebes, afterwards King of Egypt under the name of
Sheshhonqû II., and he is represented as standing behind the leg of the god,

towns were dedicated to him : Hâthâpi, Nûit-Hâpi, Nilo-
polis. It was told in the Thebaïd how the god dwelt

within a grotto, or shrine
(*tophit*), in the island of
Biggeh, whence he issued
at the inundation. This
tradition dates from a time
when the cataract was
believed to be at the end
of the world, and to bring
down the heavenly river
upon earth. Two yawn-
ing gulfs (*qorîti*), at the
foot of the two granite
cliffs (*monîti*) between
which it ran, gave access
to this mysterious retreat.
A bas-relief from Philæ
represents blocks of stone
piled one above another,
the vulture of the south

THE SHRINE OF THE NILE AT BIGGEH.[1]

and the hawk of the north, each perched on a summit,

wearing a panther skin, with both arms upheld in adoration. The statue is
mutilated : the end of the nose, the beard, and part of the tray have
disappeared, but are restored in the illustration. The two little birds hanging alongside the geese, together with a bunch of ears of corn, are fat quails.

[1] Reproduced from a bas-relief in the small temple of Philæ, built by
Trajan and his successors. The window or door of this temple opened upon
Biggeh, and by comparing the drawing of the Egyptian artist with the view
from the end of the chamber, it is easy to recognize the original of this cliff
silhouette in the piled-up rocks of the island. By a mistake of the modern
copyist's, his drawing faces the wrong way.

and the circular chamber wherein Hâpi crouches concealed, clasping a libation vase in either hand. A single coil of a serpent outlines the contour of this chamber, and leaves a narrow passage between its overlapping head and tail through which the rising waters may overflow at the time appointed, bringing to Egypt " all things good, and sweet, and pure," whereby gods and men are fed. Towards the summer solstice, at the very moment when the sacred water from the gulfs of Syene reached Silsileh, the priests of the place, sometimes the reigning sovereign, or one of his sons, sacrificed a bull and geese, and then cast into the waters a sealed roll of papyrus. This was a written order to do all that might insure to Egypt the benefits of a normal inundation. When Pharaoh himself deigned to officiate, the memory of the event was preserved by a stela engraved upon the rocks. Even in his absence, the festivals of the Nile were among the most solemn and joyous of the land. According to a tradition transmitted from age to age, the prosperity or adversity of the year was dependent upon the splendour and fervour with which they were celebrated. Had the faithful shown the slightest lukewarmness, the Nile might have refused to obey the command and failed to spread freely over the surface of the country. Peasants from a distance, each bringing his own provisions, ate their meals together for days, and lived in a state of brutal intoxication as long as this kind of fair lasted. On the great day itself, the priests came forth in procession from the sanctuary, bearing the statue of the god along the banks, to the sound of instruments and the chanting of hymns.·

" I.—Hail to thee, Hâpi !—who appearest in the land
and comest—to give life to Egypt ;—thou who dost hide
thy coming in darkness—in this very day whereon thy
coming is sung,—wave, which spreadest over the orchards
created by Ra—to give life to all them that are athirst—
who refusest to give drink unto the desert—of the overflow of the waters of heaven ; as soon as thou descendest,
—Sibû, the earth-god, is enamoured of bread,—Napri, the
god of grain, presents his offering,—Phtah maketh every
workshop to prosper.

" II.—Lord of the fish ! as soon as he passeth the

NILE-GODS FROM THE TEMPLE OF SETI I. AT ABYDOS BRINGING FOOD TO EVERY
NOME OF EGYPT.[1]

cataract—the birds no longer descend upon the fields ;—
creator of corn, maker of barley,—he prolongeth the
existence of temples.—Do his fingers cease from their
labours, or doth he suffer ?—then are all the millions of
beings in misery ;—doth he wane in heaven ? then the
gods—themselves, and all men perish ;

[1] From a drawing by Faucher-Gudin, after a photograph by Béato.

"III.—The cattle are driven mad, and all the world— both. great and small, are in torment!—But if, on the contrary, the prayers of men are heard at his rising—and (for them) he maketh himself Khnûmû,—when he ariseth, then the earth shouts for joy,—then are all bellies joyful,— each back is shaken with laughter,—and every tooth grindeth.

"IV.—Bringing food, rich in sustenance,—creator of all good things,—lord of all seeds of life, pleasant unto his elect,—if his friendship is secured—he produceth fodder for the cattle,—and he provideth for the sacrifices of all the gods,—finer than any other is the incense which cometh from him ;—he taketh possession of the two lands—and the granaries are filled, the storehouses are prosperous,—and the goods of the poor are multiplied.

" V.—He is at the service of all prayers to answer them, —withholding nothing. To make boats to be that is his strength.—Stones are not sculptured for him—nor statues whereon the double crown is placed ;—he is unseen ;—no tribute is paid unto him and no offerings are brought unto him,—he is not charmed by words of mystery ;—the place of his dwelling is unknown, nor can his shrine be found by virtue of magic writings ;

"VI.—There is no house large enough for thee,—nor any who may penetrate within thy heart!—Nevertheless, the generations of thy children rejoice in thee—for thou dost rule as a king—whose decrees are established for the whole earth,—who is manifest in presence of the people of the South and of the North,—by whom the tears are washed from every eye,—and who is lavish of his bounties.

"VII.—Where sorrow was, there doth break forth joy —and every heart rejoiceth. Sovkû, the crocodile, the child of Nît, leaps for gladness;[1]—for the Nine gods who accompany thee have ordered all things,—the overflow giveth drink unto the fields—and maketh all men valiant; one man taketh to drink of the labour of another,—without charge being brought against him.[2]

"IX.—If thou dost enter in the midst of songs to go forth in the midst of gladness,—if they dance with joy when thou comest forth out of the unknown,—it is that thy heaviness is death and corruption.—And when thou art implored to give the water of the year,—the people of the Thebaïd and of the North are seen side by side,—each man with the tools of his trade,—none tarrieth behind his neighbour;—of all those who clothed themselves, no man clotheth himself (with festive garments)—the children of Thot, the god of riches, no longer adorn themselves with jewels,—nor the Nine gods, but they are in the night!— As soon as thou hast answered by the rising,—each one anointeth himself with perfumes.

"X.—Establisher of true riches, desire of men,—here are seductive words in order that thou mayest reply;—if thou dost answer mankind by waves of the heavenly Ocean,

---

[1] The goddess Nit, the heifer born from the midst of the primordial waters, had two crocodiles as her children, which are sometimes represented on the monuments as hanging from her bosom. Both the part played by these animals, and the reason for connecting them with the goddess, are still imperfectly understood.

[2] This is an allusion to the quarrels and lawsuits resulting from the distribution of the water in years when the Nile was poor or bad. If the inundation is abundant, disputes are at an end.

—Napri, the grain-god, presents his offering,—all the gods adore (thee),—the birds no longer descend upon the hills ; —though that which thy hand formeth were of gold—or in the shape of a brick of silver,—it is not lapis-lazuli that we eat,—but wheat is of more worth than precious stones.

"XI.—They have begun to sing unto thee upon the harp,—they sing unto thee keeping time with their hands, —and the generations of thy children rejoice in thee, and they have filled thee with salutations of praise ;—for it is the god of Riches who adorneth the earth,—who maketh barks to prosper in the sight of man—who rejoiceth the heart of women with child—who loveth the increase of the flocks.

" XII.—When thou art risen in the city of the Prince, —then is the rich man filled—the small man (the poor) disdaineth the lotus,—all is solid and of good quality,—all herbage is for his children.—Doth he forget to give food ? —prosperity forsaketh the dwellings,—and earth falleth into a wasting sickness."

The word Nile is of uncertain origin. We have it from the Greeks, and they took it from a people foreign to Egypt, either from the Phœnicians, the Khîti, the Libyans, or from people of Asia Minor. When the Egyptians themselves did not care to treat their river as the god Hâpi, they called it the sea, or the great river. They had twenty terms or more by which to designate the different phases which it assumed according to the seasons, but they would not have understood what was meant had one spoken to them of the Nile. The name Egypt also is part of the Hellenic tradition ; perhaps it was taken from the temple-name of Memphis, Hâikûphtah, which barbarian coast

tribes of the Mediterranean must long have had ringing in their ears as that of the most important and wealthiest town to be found upon the shores of their sea. The Egyptians called themselves Romitû, Rotû, and their country Qîmit, the black land. Whence came they? How far off in time are we to carry back the date of their arrival? The oldest monuments hitherto known scarcely transport us further than six thousand years, yet they are of an art so fine, so well determined in its main outlines, and reveal so ingeniously combined a system of administration, government, and religion, that we infer a long past of accumulated centuries behind them. It must always be difficult to estimate exactly the length of time needful for a race as gifted as were the Ancient Egyptians to rise from barbarism into a high degree of culture. Nevertheless, I do not think that we shall be misled in granting them forty or fifty centuries wherein to bring so complicated an achievement to a successful issue, and in placing their first appearance at eight or ten thousand years before our era. Their earliest horizon was a very limited one. Their gaze might wander westward over the ravine-furrowed plains of the Libyan desert without reaching that fabled land of Manû where the sun set every evening; but looking eastward from the valley, they could see the peak of Bâkhû, which marked the limit of regions accessible to man.

Beyond these regions lay the beginnings of To-nûtri, the land of the gods, and the breezes passing over it were laden with its perfumes, and sometimes wafted them to mortals lost in the desert.[1] Northward, the world came

---

[1] The perfumes and the odoriferous woods of the *Divine Land* were

to an end towards the lagoons of the Delta, whose inaccessible islands were believed to be the sojourning-place
of souls after death. As regards the south, precise knowledge of it scarcely went beyond the defiles of Gebel Silsileh, where the last remains of the granite threshold had
perhaps not altogether disappeared. The district beyond
Gebel Silsileh, the province of Konûsit, was still a foreign
and almost mythic country, directly connected with heaven
by means of the cataract. Long after the Egyptians had
broken through this restricted circle, the names of those
places which had as it were marked out their frontiers,
continued to be associated in their minds with the idea of
the four cardinal points. Bâkhû and Manû were still the
most frequent expressions for the extreme East and West.
Nekhabit and Bûto, the most populous towns in the neigh-
bourhoods of Gebel Silsileh and the ponds of the Delta,
were set over against each other to designate South and
North. It was within these narrow limits that Egyptian
civilization struck root and ripened, as in a closed vessel.
What were the people by whom it was developed, the
country whence they came, the races to which they belonged, is to-day unknown. The majority would place
their cradle-land in Asia,[1] but cannot agree in determining

celebrated in Egypt. A traveller or hunter, crossing the desert, "could not
but be vividly impressed by suddenly becoming aware, in the very midst
of the desert, of the penetrating scent of the *robúl* (*Pulicharia undulata*,
SCHWEINF.), which once followed us throughout a day and two nights, in
some places without our being able to distinguish whence it came ; as, for
instance, when we were crossing tracts of country without any traces of
vegetation whatever " (GOLENISCHEFF).

[1] The greater number of contemporary Egyptologists, BRUGSCH, EBERS,

the route which was followed in the emigration to Africa. Some think that the people took the shortest road across the Isthmus of Suez, others give them longer peregrinations and a more complicated itinerary. They would have them cross the Straits of Bab el-Mandeb, and then the Abyssinian mountains, and, spreading northward and keeping along the Nile, finally settle in the Egypt of to-day. A more minute examination compels us to recognize that the hypothesis of an Asiatic origin, however attractive it may seem, is somewhat difficult to maintain. The bulk of the Egyptian population presents the characteristics of those white races which have been found established from all antiquity on the Mediterranean slope of the Libyan continent; this population is of African origin, and came to Egypt from the West or South-West. In the valley, perhaps, it may have met with a black race which it drove back or destroyed; and there, perhaps, too, it afterwards received an accretion of Asiatic elements, introduced by way of the isthmus and the marshes of the Delta. But whatever may be the origin of the ancestors of the Egyptians, they were scarcely settled upon the banks of the Nile before the country conquered, and assimilated

LAUTH, LIEBLEIN, have rallied to this opinion, in the train of E. DE ROUGÉ; but the most extreme position has been taken up by HOMMEL, the Assyriologist, who is inclined to derive Egyptian civilization entirely from the Babylonian. After having summarily announced this thesis in his *Geschichte Babyloniens und Assyriens*, p. 12, et seq., he has set it forth at length in a special treatise, *Der Babylonische Ursprung der ägyptischen Kultur*, 1892, wherein he endeavours to prove that the Heliopolitan myths, and hence the whole Egyptian religion, are derived from the cults of Eridû, and would make the name of the Egyptian city Onû, or Anû, identical with that of *Nûn-ki, Nûn*, which is borne by the Chaldean.

them to itself, as it has never ceased to do in the case of strangers who have occupied it. At the time when their history begins for us, all the inhabitants had long formed but one people, with but one language.

This language seems to be connected with the Semitic tongues by many of its roots. It forms its personal pronouns, whether isolated or suffixed, in a similar way. One of the tenses of the conjugation, and that the simplest and most archaic, is formed with identical affixes. Without insisting upon resemblances which are open to doubt, it may be almost affirmed that most of the grammatical processes used in Semitic languages are to be found in a rudimentary condition in Egyptian. One would say that the language of the people of Egypt and the languages of the Semitic races, having once belonged to the same group, had separated very early, at a time when the vocabulary and the grammatical system of the group had not as yet taken definite shape. Subject to different influences, the two families would treat in diverse fashion the elements common to both. The Semitic dialects continued to develop for centuries, while the Egyptian language, although earlier cultivated, stopped short in its growth. "If it is obvious that there was an original connexion between the language of Egypt and that of Asia, this connexion is nevertheless sufficiently remote to leave to the Egyptian race a distinct physiognomy." We recognize it in sculptured and painted portraits, as well as in thousands of mummied bodies out of subterranean tombs. The highest type of Egyptian was tall and slender, with a proud and imperious air in the carriage of his head and in his whole bearing. He had wide and full shoulders, well-marked and vigorous pectoral muscles, muscular arms, a long, fine hand, slightly developed hips, and sinewy legs. The detail of the knee-joint and the muscles of the calf are strongly marked beneath the skin; the long, thin, and low-arched feet are flattened out at the extremities owing to the custom of going barefoot. The head is rather short, the face oval, the forehead somewhat retreating. The eyes are wide and fully opened, the cheek-bones not too marked, the nose fairly prominent, and either straight or aquiline. The mouth is long, the lips full, and lightly ridged along their outline; the teeth small, even, well-set, and remarkably sound; the ears are set high on the head. At birth the skin is white, but darkens in proportion to its exposure to the sun. Men are generally painted red in the pictures, though, as a matter of fact, there must already have been all the shades which we see among the present population, from a most delicate, rose-tinted complexion to that of

THE NOBLE TYPE OF EGYPTIAN.[1]

---

[1] Statue of Rânofir in the Gizeh Museum (V[th] dynasty), after a photograph by Émil Brugsch-Bey.

a smoke-coloured bronze.   Women, who were less exposed
to the sun, are generally painted yellow, the tint paler in
proportion as they rise in the social scale.   The hair was
inclined to be wavy, and even to curl into little ringlets,

HEAD OF A THEBAN MUMMY.

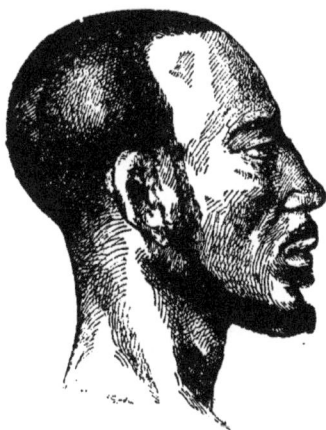

AN EGYPTIAN OF THE ORDINARY TYPE.[1]   HEAD OF A FELLAH OF UPPER EGYPT.

but without ever turning into the wool of the negro.   The
beard was scanty, thick only upon the chin.   Such was the
highest type; the commoner was squat, dumpy, and heavy.

[1] Statue of Ûsiri (VIth dynasty) in the Gizeh Museum.   From a photograph by Émil Brugsch-Bey.

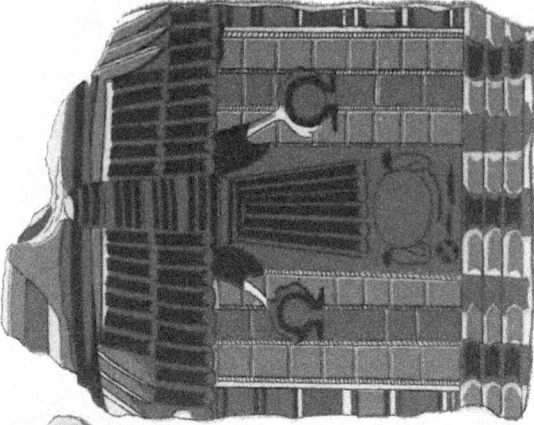

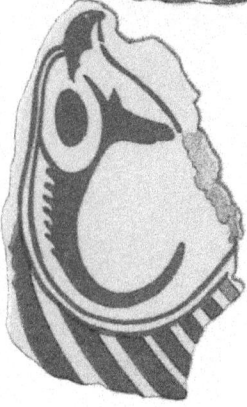

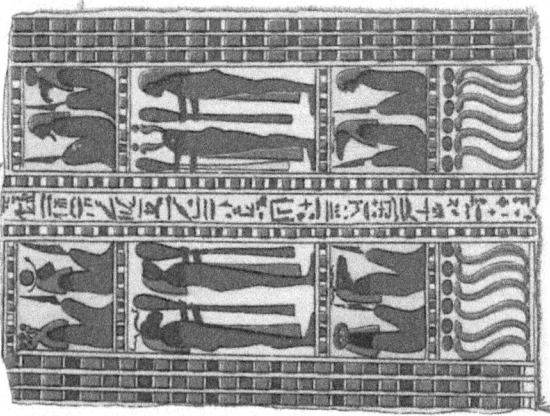

Chest and shoulders seem to be enlarged at the expense of the pelvis and the hips, to such an extent as to make the want of proportion between the upper and lower parts of the body startling and ungraceful. The skull is long, somewhat retreating, and slightly flattened on the top; the features are coarse, and as though carved in flesh by great strokes of the blocking-out chisel. Small frænated eyes, a short nose, flanked by widely distended nostrils, round cheeks, a square chin, thick, but not curling lips— this unattractive and ludicrous physiognomy, sometimes animated by an expression of cunning which recalls the shrewd face of an old French peasant, is often lighted up by gleams of gentleness and of melancholy good-nature. The external characteristics of these two principal types in the ancient monuments, in all varieties of modifications, may still be seen among the living. The profile copied from a Theban mummy taken at hazard from a necropolis of the XVIIIth dynasty, and compared with the likeness of a modern Luxor peasant, would almost pass for a family portrait. Wandering Bisharin have inherited the type of face of a great noble, the contemporary of Kheops; and any peasant woman of the Delta may bear upon her shoulders the head of a twelfth-dynasty king. A citizen of Cairo, gazing with wonder at the statues of Khafra or of Seti I. in the Gizeh Museum, is himself, feature for feature, the very image of those ancient Pharaohs, though removed from them by fifty centuries.

Until quite recently nothing, or all but nothing, had been discovered which could be attributed to the primitive races of Egypt: even the flint weapons and implements which had been found in various places could not be ascribed to them with any degree of certainty, for the Egyptians con-tinued to use stone long after metal was known to them. They made stone arrowheads, hammers, and knives, not only in the time of the Pharaohs, but under the Romans,

A FELLAH WOMAN WITH THE FEATURES OF AN ANCIENT KING.[1]

and during the whole period of the Middle Ages, and the manufacture of them has not yet entirely died out.[2]   These

[1] The face of the woman here given was taken separately, and was subse-quently attached to the figure of an Egyptian woman whom Naville had photographed sitting beside a colossal head.   The nose of the statue has been restored.

[2] An entire collection of flint tools—axes, adzes, knives, and sickles—mostly with wooden handles, were found by Prof. Petrie in the ruins of Kahun, at the entrance to the Fayûm : these go back to the time of the twelfth dynasty, more than three thousand years before our era.   Mariette had previously pointed out to the learned world the fact that a Coptic *Reis*, Salib of Abydos, in charge of the excavations, shaved his head with a flint knife, according to

objects, and the workshops where they were made, might therefore be less ancient than the greater part of the inscribed monuments. But if so far we had found no examples of any work belonging to the first ages, we met in historic times with certain customs which were out of harmony with the general civilization of the period. A comparison of these customs with analogous practices of barbarous nations threw light upon the former, completed their meaning, and showed us at the same time the successive stages through which the Egyptian people had to pass before reaching their highest civilization. We knew, for example, that even as late as the Cæsars, girls belonging to noble families at Thebes were consecrated to the service of Amon, and were thus licensed to a life of immorality, which, however, did not prevent them from making rich marriages when age obliged them to retire from office. Theban women were not the only people in the world to whom such licence was granted or imposed upon them by law; wherever in a civilized country we see a similar practice, we may recognize in it an ancient custom which in the course of centuries has degenerated into a religious observance. The institution of the women of Amon is a legacy from a time when the practice of polyandry obtained, and marriage did not yet exist. Age and maternity relieved them from this obligation, and preserved them from those incestuous connections of which we find examples in other races. A union of father and

the custom of his youth (1820-35). I knew the man, who died at over eighty years of age. in 1887; he was still faithful to his flint implement, while his sons and the whole population of El Kharbeh were using nothing but steel razors. As his scalp was scraped nearly raw by the operation, he used to cover his head with fresh leaves to cool the inflamed skin.

daughter, however, was perhaps not wholly forbidden,[1] and that of brother and sister seems to have been regarded as perfectly right and natural; the words *brother* and *sister* possessing in Egyptian love-songs the same significance as *lover* and *mistress* with us. Paternity was necessarily doubtful in a community of this kind, and hence the tie between fathers and children was slight; there being no family, in the sense in which we understand the word, except as it centred around the mother. Maternal descent was, therefore, the only one openly acknowledged, and the affiliation of the child was indicated by the name of the mother alone. When the woman ceased to belong to all, and confined herself to one husband, the man reserved to himself the privilege of taking as many wives as he wished, or as he was able to keep, beginning with his own sisters. All wives did not enjoy identical rights : those born of the same parents as the man, or those of equal rank with himself, preserved their independence. If the law pronounced him the master, *nibû*, to whom they owed obedience and·fidelity, they were mistresses of the house, *nîbît pirû*, as well as wives, *himitû*, and the two words of the title express their condition. Each of them occupied, in fact, her own house, *pirû*, which she had from her parents or her husband, and of which she was absolute mistress, *nîbît*. She lived in it and performed in it without constraint all a woman's duties; feeding the fire, grinding the corn,

---

[1] E. DE ROUGÉ held that Rameses II. married at least two of his daughters, Bint Anati and Honittui ; WIEDEMANN admits that Psammetichus I. had in the same way taken to wife Nitocris, who had been born to him by the Theban princess Shapenuapit. The Achæmenidan kings did the same : Artaxerxes married two of his own daughters.

occupying herself in cooking and weaving, making clothing and perfumes, nursing and teaching her children. When her husband visited her, he was a guest whom she received on an equal footing. It appears that at the outset these various wives were placed under the authority of an older woman, whom they looked on as their mother, and who defended their rights and interests against the master; but this custom gradually disappeared, and in historic times we read of it as existing only in the families of the gods. The female singers consecrated to Amon and other deities, owed obedience to several superiors, of whom the principal (generally the widow of a king or high priest) was called *chief-superior of the ladies of the harem of Amon.* Besides these wives, there were concubines, slaves purchased or born in the house, prisoners of war, Egyptians of inferior class, who were the chattels of the man and of whom he could dispose as he wished. All the children of one father were legitimate, whether their mother were a wife or merely a concubine, but they did not all enjoy the same advantages; those among them who were born of a brother or sister united in legitimate marriage, took precedence of those whose mother was a wife of inferior rank or a slave. In the family thus constituted, the woman, to all appearances, played the principal part. Children recognized the parental relationship in the mother alone. The husband appears to have entered the house of his wives, rather than the wives to have entered his, and this appearance of inferiority was so marked that the Greeks were deceived by it. They affirmed that the woman was supreme in Egypt; the man at the time of marriage promised obedience to her, and entered into a contract not to raise any objection to her commands.

We had, therefore, good grounds for supposing that the first Egyptians were semi-savages, like those still living in Africa and America, having an analogous organization, and similar weapons and tools. A few lived in the desert, in the oasis of Libya, or in the deep valleys of the Red Land--Doshirit, To Doshiru—between the Nile and the sea; the poverty of the country fostering their native

NEGRO PRISONERS WEARING THE PANTHER'S SKIN AS A LOIN-CLOTH.

savagery. Others, settled on the Black Land, gradually became civilized, and we have found of late considerable remains of those of their generations who, if not anterior to the times of written records, were at least contemporary with the earliest kings of the first historical dynasty. Their houses were like those of the fellahs of to-day, low huts of wattle daubed with puddled clay, or of bricks dried in the sun. They contained one room, either oblong or square, the door being the only aperture. Those of the richer class only were large enough to make it needful to support the roof by means of one or more trunks of trees, which did duty for columns. Earthen pots, turned by hand, flint knives and other implements, mats of reeds or plaited straw, two flat stones for grinding corn, a few pieces of wooden furniture, stools, and head-rests for use at night, comprised all the contents. Their ordinary pottery is heavy and almost devoid of ornament, but some of the finer kinds have been moulded and baked in wickerwork baskets, which have left a quaint trellis-like impression on the surface of the clay. In many cases the vases are bicolour, the body being of a fine smooth red, polished with a stone, while the neck and base are of an intense black, the surface of which is even more shining than that of the red part. Sometimes they are ornamented with patterns in white of flowers, palms, ostriches, gazelles, boats with undulated or broken lines, or geometrical figures of a very simple nature. More often the ground is coloured a fine yellow, and the decoration has been traced in red lines. Jars, saucers, double vases, flat plates, large cups, supports for amphoræ, trays raised on a foot—in short, every kind of form is found in use at that remote period. The men went about nearly naked, except the nobles, who wore a panther's skin, sometimes thrown over the shoulders, sometimes drawn round the waist, and covering the lower part of the body, the animal's tail touching the heels behind, as we see later in several representations of the negroes of the Upper Nile. They smeared their limbs with grease or oil, and they tattooed their faces and bodies, at least in part, but in later times this practice was retained by the lower classes only. On the other hand, the custom

of painting the face was never given up. To complete
their toilet, it was necessary to accentuate the arch of
the eyebrow with a line of kohl (antimony powder). A
similar black line surrounded and prolonged the oval of

NOTABLE WEARING THE LARGE CLOAK
OVER THE LEFT SHOULDER.[1]

PRIEST WEARING THE PANTHER'S
SKIN ACROSS THE BREAST.[2]

the eye to the middle of the temple, a layer of green
coloured the under lid, and ochre and carmine enlivened

[1] Wooden statue in the Gizeh Museum (IVth dynasty), drawn by Faucher-
Gudin, from a photograph by Béchard.

[2] Statue of the second prophet of Amon, Aa-nen, in the Turin Museum
(XVIIIth dynasty).

the tints of the cheeks and lips. The hair, plaited, curled, oiled, and plastered with grease, formed an erection which was as complicated in the case of the man as in that of the woman. Should the hair be too short, a black or blue wig, dressed with much skill, was substituted for it; ostrich feathers waved on the heads of warriors, and a large lock, flattened behind the right ear, distinguished the military or religious chiefs from their subordinates. When the art of weaving became common, a belt and loin-cloth of white linen replaced the leathern garment. Fastened round the waist, but so low as to leave the navel uncovered, the loin-cloth frequently reached to the knee; the hinder part was frequently drawn between the legs and attached in front to the belt, thus forming a kind of drawers. Tails of animals and wild beast's skin were henceforth only the insignia of authority with which priests and princes adorned themselves on great days and at religious ceremonies. The skin was sometimes carelessly thrown over the left shoulder and swayed with the movement of the body; sometimes it was carefully adjusted over one shoulder and under the other, so as to bring the curve of the chest into prominence. The head of the animal, skilfully prepared and enlivened by large eyes of enamel, rested on the shoulder or fell just below the waist of the wearer; the paws, with the claws attached, hung down over the thighs; the spots of the skin were manipulated so as to form five-pointed stars. On going out-of-doors, a large wrap was thrown over all; this covering was either smooth or hairy, similar to that in which the Nubians and Abyssinians of the present day envelop themselves. It could be draped in various ways ; transversely over the left shoulder like the fringed shawl of the Chaldeans, or hanging straight from both shoulders like a mantle.[2] In fact, it did duty as a cloak, sheltering the wearer from the sun or from the rain, from the heat or from the cold. They never sought to transform it into a luxurious garment of state, as was the case in later times with the Roman toga, whose amplitude secured a certain dignity of carriage, and whose folds, carefully adjusted beforehand, fell around the body with studied grace. The Egyptian mantle, when not required, was thrown aside and folded up. The material being fine and soft, it occupied but a small space, and was reduced to a long thin roll ; the ends being then fastened to-

A DIGNITARY WRAPPED IN HIS LARGE CLOAK.[1]

---

[1] Statue of Khiti in the Gizeh Museum (XIIth and XIIIth dynasties), drawn by Faucher-Gudin.

[2] This costume, to which Egyptologists have not given sufficient attention, is frequently represented on the monuments. Besides the two statues reproduced above, I may cite those of Uahibri and of Thoth-nofir in the Louvre, and the Lady Nofrit in the Gizeh Museum. Thothotpû in his tomb wears this mantle. Khnumhotpû and several of his workmen are represented in it at Beni-Hasan, as also one of the princes of Elephantinê in the recently discovered tombs, besides many Egyptians of all classes in the tombs of Thebes (a good example is in the tomb of Harmhabi). The

gether, it was slung over the shoulder and round the body
• like a cavalry cloak.¹ Travellers, shepherds, all those whose
occupations called them to the fields, carried it as a
bundle at the ends of their sticks; once arrived at the
scene of their work, they deposited it in a corner with
their provisions until they required it. The women were
at first contented with a loin-cloth like that of the men;
it was enlarged and lengthened till it reached the ankle
below and the bosom above, and became a tightly fitting
garment, with two bands over the shoulders, like braces, to
keep it in place. The feet were not always covered; on
certain occasions, however, sandals of coarse leather, plaited

reason why it does not figure more often is, in the first place, that the
Egyptian artists experienced actual difficulty in representing the folds of
its drapery, although these were simple compared with the complicated
arrangement of the Roman toga ; finally, the wall-paintings mostly portray
either interior scenes, or agricultural labour, or the work of various trades,
or episodes of war, or religious ceremonies, in all of which the mantle plays
no part. Every Egyptian peasant, however, possessed his own, and it was
in constant use in his daily life.

¹ Many draughtsmen, ignorant of what they had to represent, have made
incorrect copies of the manner in which this cloak was worn ; but examples
of it are numerous, although until now attention has not been called to them.
The following are a few instances taken at random of the way in which it
was used: Pepi I., fighting against the nomads of Sinai, has the cloak, but
with the two ends passed through the belt of his loin-cloth ; at Zawyet el-
Maiyitîn, Khunas, killing birds with the boomerang from his boat, wears it,
but simply thrown over the left shoulder, with the two extremities hanging
free. Khnumhotpû at Beni-Hasan, the *Khrihabi*, the overseers, or the
peasants, all have it rolled and slung round them ; the Prince of el-Bersheh
wears it like a mantle in folds over the two shoulders. If it is objected
that the material could not be reduced to such small dimensions as those
represented in these drawings of what I believe to be the Egyptian cloak, I
may cite our cavalry capes, when rolled and slung, as an instance of what
good packing will do in reducing volume.

straw, split reed, or even painted wood, adorned those shapely Egyptian feet, which, to suit our taste, should be a little shorter. Both men and women loved ornaments, and covered their necks, breasts, arms, wrists, and ankles with many rows of necklaces and bracelets. The bracelets were made of elephant ivory, mother-of-pearl, or even flint, very cleverly perforated. The necklaces were composed of strings of pierced shells,[2] interspersed with seeds and little pebbles, either sparkling or of unusual shapes.[3] Subsequently imitations in terra-cotta replaced the natural shells, and precious stones were substituted for pebbles, as were also beads of enamel,

COSTUME OF EGYPTIAN WOMAN, SPINNING.[1]

[1] Drawn by Faucher-Gudin, from one of the spinning-women at the Paris Exhibition of 1889. It was restored from the paintings in the tomb of Khnumhotpû at Beni-Hasan.

[2] The burying-places of Abydos, especially the most ancient, have furnished us with millions of shells, pierced and threaded as necklaces ; they all belong to the species of cowries used as money in Africa at the present day.

[3] Necklaces of seeds have been found in the tombs of Abydos, Thebes, and Gebelên. Of these Schweinfurth has identified, among others, the

either round, pear-shaped, or cylindrical : the necklaces were terminated and a uniform distance maintained between the rows of beads, by several slips of wood, bone, ivory, porcelain, or terra-cotta, pierced with holes, through which ran the threads. Weapons, at least among the nobility, were an indispensable part of costume. Most of

MAN WEARING WIG AND NECKLACES [1]

them were for hand-to-hand fighting : sticks, clubs, lances furnished with a sharpened bone or stone point, axes and

Cassia absus, L., "a weed of the Soudan whose seeds are sold in the drug bazaar at Cairo and Alexandria under the name of *shishm*, as a remedy, which is in great request among the natives, for ophthalmia." For the necklaces of pebbles, cf. MASPERO, *Guide du visiteur*, pp. 270, 271, No. 4129. A considerable number of these pebbles, particularly those of strange shape, or presenting a curious combination of colours, must have been regarded as amulets or fetishes by their Egyptian owners ; analogous cases, among other peoples, have been pointed out by E. B. TYLOR, *Primitive Culture*, vol. ii. p. 189.

[1] Drawn by Faucher-Gudin, from a portrait of Pharaoh Seti I. of the XIXth dynasty : the lower part of the necklace has been completed.

daggers of flint,[1] sabres and clubs of bone or wood variously shaped, pointed or rounded at the end, with blunt or sharp blades,—inoffensive enough to look at, but, wielded by a vigorous hand, sufficient to break an arm, crush in the ribs, or smash a skull with all desirable precision.[3] The plain or triple curved bow was the favourite weapon for attack at a distance,[4] but in addition to this there were the sling, the javelin, and a missile almost forgotten nowadays, the boomerang ; we have no proof, however, that the Egyptians handled the boomerang [5] with the

THE BOOMERANG AND FIGHTING BOW.[2]

[1] In several museums, notably at Leyden, we find Egyptian axes of stone, particularly of serpentine, both rough and polished.

[2] Drawn by Faucher-Gudin, from a painting in the tomb of Khnumhotpû at Beni-Hasan.

[3] In primitive times the bone of an animal served as a club. This is proved by the shape of the object held in the hand in the sign ⌣ : the hieroglyph ⨅, ⌣, which is the determinative in writing for all ideas ·of violence or brute force, comes down to us from a time when the principal weapon was the club, or a bone serving as a club.

[4] For the two principal shapes of the bow, see LEPSIUS, *Der Bogen in der Hieroglyphik* (*Zeitschrift*, 1872, pp. 79-88). From the earliest times the sign 𓌉 portrays the soldier equipped with the bow and bundle of arrows ; the quiver was of Asiatic origin, and was not adopted until much later. In the contemporary texts of the first dynasties, the idea of *weapons* is conveyed by the bow, arrow, and club or axe.

[5] The boomerang is still used by certain tribes of the Nile valley. It is

skill of the Australians, or that they knew how to throw it so as to bring it back to its point of departure.[1] Such was approximately the most ancient equipment as far as we can ascertain; but at a very early date copper and iron were known in Egypt.[2] Long before historic times, the majority of the weapons in wood were replaced by

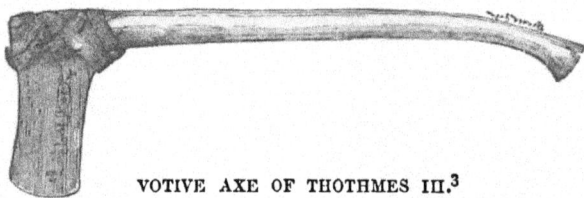

VOTIVE AXE OF THOTHMES III.[3]

those of metal,—daggers, sabres, hatchets, which preserved, however, the shape of the old wooden instruments. Those wooden weapons which were retained, were

portrayed in the most ancient tombs, and every museum possesses examples, varying in shape. Besides the ordinary boomerang, the Egyptians used one which ended in a knob, and another of semicircular shape: this latter, reproduced in miniature in cornelian or in red jasper, served as an amulet, and was placed on the mummy to furnish the deceased in the other world with a fighting or hunting weapon.

[1] The Australian boomerang is much larger than the Egyptian one ; it is about a yard in length, two inches in width, and three sixteenths of an inch in thickness. For the manner of handling it, and what can be done with it, see LUBBOCK, *Prehistoric Man*, pp. 402, 403.

[2] Metals were introduced into Egypt in very ancient times, since the class of blacksmiths is associated with the worship of Horus of Edfû, and appears in the account of the mythical wars of that God. The earliest tools we possess, in copper or bronze, date from the IVth dynasty : pieces of iron have been found from time to time in the masonry of the Great Pyramid. Mons Montélius has again and again contested the authenticity of these discoveries, and he thinks that iron was not known in Egypt till a much later period.

[3] The blade is of bronze, and is attached to the wooden handle by interlacing thongs of leather (Gizeh Museum). Drawn by Faucher-Gudin, from a photograph by Émil Brugsch-Bey.

used for hunting, or were only brought out on solemn occasions when tradition had to be respected. The war-baton became the commander's wand of authority, and at last degenerated into the walking-stick of the rich or noble. The club at length represented merely the rank of a chieftain,[1] while the crook and the wooden-handled mace, with its head of ivory, diorite, granite, or white stone, the favourite weapons of princes, continued to the last the most revered insignia of royalty.[2]

Life was passed in comparative ease and pleasure. Of the ponds left in the open country by the river at its fall, some dried up more or

KING HOLDING THE BATON, THE WHITE MACE AND THE CLUB.[3]

less quickly during the winter, leaving on the soil an immense quantity of fish, the possession of which birds and wild beasts disputed with

[1] The wooden club most commonly represented ⌡, is the usual insignia of a nobleman. Several kinds of clubs, somewhat difficult for us moderns to distinguish, yet bearing different names, formed a part of funereal furniture.

[2] The crook ⌐ is the sceptre of a prince, a Pharaoh, or a god ; the white mace ⌐ has still the value apparently of a weapon in the hands of the king who brandishes it over a group of prisoners or over an ox which he is sacrificing to a divinity. Most museums possess specimens of the stone heads of these maces, but until lately their use was not known. I had several placed in the Boulak Museum. It already possessed a model of one entirely of wood.

[3] Bas-relief in the temple of Luxor, from a photograph taken by Insinger in 1886.

man.[1] Other pools, however, remained till the returning inundation, as so many *vivaria* in which the fish were

FISHING IN THE MARSHES : TWO FISH SPEARED AT ONE STROKE OF THE HARPOON.[2]

preserved for dwellers on the banks. Fishing with the

FISHING IN THE RIVER : LIFTING A TRAP.[3]

[1] Cf. the description of these pools given by Geoffroy-Saint-Hilaire in speaking of the *fahaka*. Even at the present day the jackals come down from the mountains in the night, and regale themselves with the fish left on the ground by the gradual drying up of these ponds.

[2] Isolated figure from a great fishing scene in the tomb of Khnumhotpû at Beni-Hasan ; drawn by Faucher-Gudin after ROSELLINI.

[3] Drawn by Faucher-Gudin, from squeezes from the tomb of Ti.

harpoon, made either of stone or of metal, with the line, with a net or with traps, were all methods of fishing known and used by the Egyptians from early times. Where the ponds failed, the neighbouring Nile furnished them with inexhaustible supplies. Standing in light canoes, or rather supported by a plank on bundles of reeds bound

HUNTING IN THE MARSHES : ENCOUNTERING AND SPEARING A HIPPOPOTAMUS.[1]

together, they ventured into mid-stream, in spite of the danger arising from the ever-present hippopotamus; or they penetrated up the canals amid a thicket of aquatic plants, to bring down with the boomerang the birds which found covert there. The fowl and fish which could not be eaten

[1] Tomb of Ti. Drawn by Faucher-Gudin, from DÜMICHEN, *Resultate*, vol. ii. pl. x.

fresh, were dried, salted, or smoked, and kept for a rainy day. Like the river, the desert had its perils and its resources. Only too frequently, the lion, the leopard, the

HUNTING IN THE DESERT : BULL, LION, AND ORYX PIERCED WITH ARROWS.[1]

panther, and other large felidæ were met with there. The nobles, like the Pharaohs of later times, deemed it as

PACK FROM THE TOMB OF PTAHHOTPOU.[2]

their privilege or duty to stalk and destroy these animals, pursuing them even to their dens. The common people

[1] Drawn by Faucher-Gudin, from a painting by Beni-Hasan, LEPSIUS, *Denkm.*, ii. 136.

[2] Drawn by Faucher-Gudin, from a bas-relief of Ptahhotpû. The dogs on the upper level are of hyenoid type, those on the lower are Abyssinian greyhounds.

preferred attacking the gazelle, the oryx, the mouflon
sheep, the ibex, the wild ox, and the ostrich, but did not
disdain more humble game, such as the porcupine and
long-eared hare : nondescript packs, in which the jackal
and the hyena ran side by side with the wolf-dog and the
lithe Abyssinian greyhound, scented and retrieved for their
master the prey which he had pierced, with his arrows.
At times a hunter, returning with the dead body of the
mother, would be followed by one of her young; or a
gazelle, but slightly wounded, would be taken to the village
and healed of its hurt. Such animals,
by daily contact with man, were gradually tamed, and
formed about his
dwelling a motley
flock, kept partly
for his pleasure
and mostly for
his profit, and be-
coming in case of

CATCHING ANIMALS WITH THE BOLA.[1]

necessity a ready stock of provisions.[2] Efforts were therefore
made to enlarge this flock, and the wish to procure animals
without seriously injuring them, caused the Egyptians to
use the net for birds and the lasso and the *bola* for

---

[1] Drawn by Faucher-Gudin, from a bas-relief of Ptahhotpû. Above are
seen two porcupines, the foremost of which, emerging from his hole, has
seized a grasshopper.
[2] In the same way, before the advent of Europeans, the half-civilized
tribes of North America used to keep about their huts whole flocks of
different animals, which were tame, but not domesticated.

quadrupeds,[1]—weapons less brutal than the arrow and the javelin. The *bola* was made by them of a single rounded stone, attached to a strap about five yards in length. The stone once thrown, the cord twisted round the legs, muzzle, or neck of the animal pursued, and by the attachment thus made the pursuer, using all his strength, was enabled to bring the beast down half strangled. The lasso has no stone attached to it, but a noose prepared beforehand, and the skill of the hunter consists in throwing it round the neck of his victim while running. They caught indifferently, without distinction of size or kind, all that chance brought within their reach. The daily chase kept up these half-tamed flocks of gazelles, wild goats, water-bucks, stocks, and ostriches, and their numbers are reckoned by hundreds on the monuments of the ancient empire.[2]

[1] Hunting with the *bola* is constantly represented in the paintings both of the Memphite and Theban periods. Wilkinson has confounded it with lasso-hunting, and his mistake has been reproduced by other Egyptologists. Lasso-hunting is seen in LEPSIUS, *Denkm.*, ii. 96, in DÜMICHEN, *Resultate*, vol. i. pl. viii., and particularly in the numerous sacrificial scenes where the king is supposed to be capturing the bull of the north or south, previous to offering it to the god.

[2] As the tombs of the ancient empire show us numerous flocks of gazelles, antelopes, and storks, feeding under the care of shepherds, Fr. Lenormant concluded that the Egyptians of early times had succeeded in domesticating some species, nowadays rebels to restraint. It is my belief that the animals represented were tamed, but not domesticated, and were the result of great hunting expeditions in the desert. The facts which Lenormant brought forward to support his theory may be used against him. For instance, the fawn of the gazelle nourished by its mother does not prove that it was bred in captivity; the gazelle may have been caught before calving, or just after the birth of its young. The fashion of keeping flocks of animals taken from the desert died out between the XIIth and XVIIIth dynasties. At the time of the new empire, they had only one or two solitary

Experience alone taught the hunter to distinguish between those species from which he could draw profit, and others whose wildness made them impossible to domesticate. The subjection of the most useful kinds had not been finished when the historic period opened. The ass, the sheep, and the goat were already domesticated, but the pig was still

A SWINEHERD AND HIS PIGS.[2]

out in the marshes in a semi-wild state, under the care of special herdsmen,[1] and the religious rites preserved the remembrance of the times in which the ox was so little tamed, that in order to capture while grazing the animals needed for sacrifice or for slaughter, it was necessary to use the lasso.[3]

animals as pets for women or children, the mummies of which were sometimes buried by the side of their mistresses.

[1] The hatred of the Egyptians for the pig (HERODOTUS, ii. 47) is attributed to mythological motives. LIPPERT thinks this antipathy did not exist in Egypt in primitive times. At the outset the pig would have been the principal food of the people; then, like the dog in other regions, it must have been replaced at the table by animals of a higher order—gazelles, sheep, goats, oxen—and would have thus fallen into contempt. To the excellent reasons given by Lippert could be added others drawn from the study of the Egyptian myths, to prove that the pig has often been highly esteemed. Thus, Isis is represented, down to late times, under the form of a sow, and a sow, whether followed or not by her young is one of the amulets placed in the tomb with the deceased, to secure for him the protection of the goddess.

[2] Drawn by Faucher-Gudin, from a painting in a Theban tomb of the XVIIIth dynasty.

[3] MARIETTE, Abydos (vol. i. pl. 48 b, 53). To prevent the animal from

Europeans are astonished to meet nowadays whole peoples who make use of herbs and plants whose flavour and properties are nauseating to us : these are mostly so many legacies from a remote past; for example, castor-oil, with which the Berbers rub their limbs, and with which the fellahîn of the Saïd flavour their bread and vegetables, was preferred before all others by the Egyptians of the Pharaonic age for anointing the body and for culinary use.[1] They had begun by eating indiscriminately every kind of fruit which the country produced. Many of these, when their therapeutic virtues had been learned by experience, were gradually banished as articles of food, and their use restricted to medicine; others fell into disuse, and only reappeared at sacrifices, or at funeral feasts; several varieties continue to be eaten to the present time—the acid fruits of the nabeca and of the carob tree, the astringent figs of the sycamore, the insipid pulp of the dom-palm, besides those which are pleasant to our Western palates, such as the common fig and the date. The vine flourished, at least in Middle and Lower Egypt; from time immemorial the art of making wine from it was known, and even the most ancient monuments enumerate half a dozen famous brands, red or white.[2] Vetches, lupins, beans,

evading the lasso and escaping during the sacrifice, its right hind foot was fastened to its left horn.

[1] I have often been obliged, from politeness, when dining with the native agents appointed by the European powers at Port Saïd, to eat salads and mayonnaise sauces flavoured with castor-oil; the taste was not so disagreeable as might be at first imagined.

[2] The four kinds of canonical wine, brought respectively from the north, south, east, and west of the country, formed part of the official repast and of the wine-cellar of the deceased from remote antiquity.

chick-peas, lentils, onions, fenugreek,[1] the bamiâ,[2] the meloukhia,[3] the arum colocasia, all grew wild in the fields,

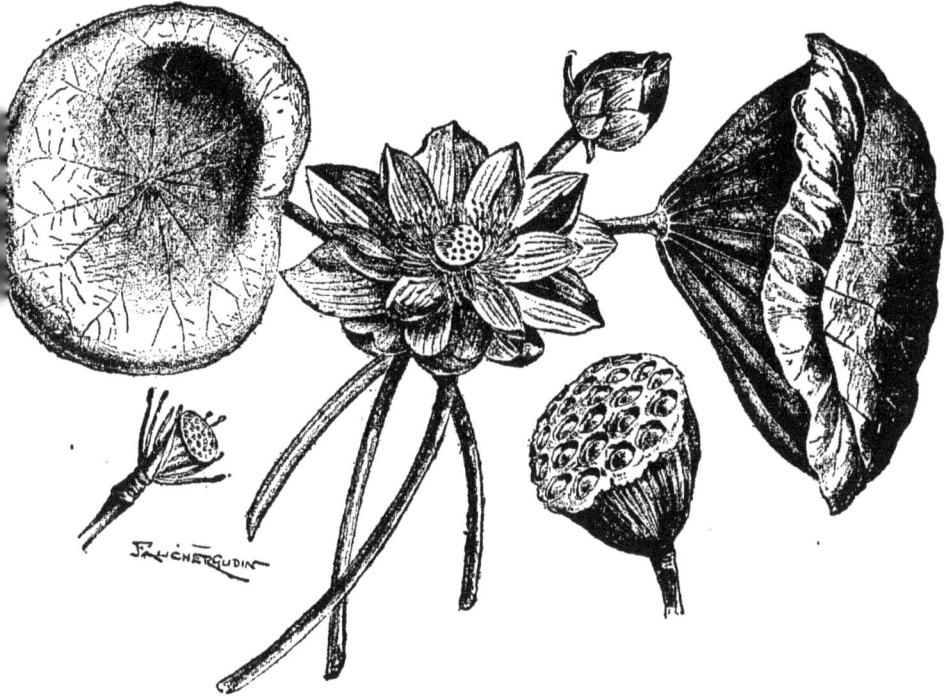

THE EGYPTIAN LOTUS.[4]

[1] All these species have been found in the tombs and identified by savants in archæological botany—Kunth, Unger, Schweinfurth (LORET, La Flore Pharaonique, pp. 17, 40, 42, 43, Nos. 33, 97, 102, 104, 105, 106).

[2] The bamiâ, Hibiscus esculentus, L., is a plant of the family of the Malvaceæ, having a fruit of five divisions, covered with prickly hairs, and containing round, white, soft seeds, slightly sweet, but astringent in taste, and very mucilaginous. It figures on the monuments of Pharaonic times.

[3] The meloukhia, Corchorus Olitorius, L., is a plant belonging to the Tilliaceæ, which is chopped up and cooked much the same as endive is with us, but which few Europeans can eat with pleasure, owing to the mucilage it contains. Theophrastus says it was celebrated for its bitterness ; it was used as food, however, in the Greek town of Alexandria.

[4] Drawn by Faucher-Gudin from the Description de l'Égypte, HISTOIRE NATURELLE, pl. 61.

and the river itself supplied its quota of nourishing plants.
Two of the species of lotus which grew in the Nile, the
white and the blue, have seed-vessels similar to those of
the poppy: the capsules contain small grains of the size
of millet-seed. The fruit of the pink lotus "grows on a
different stalk from that of the flower, and springs directly
from the root; it resembles a honeycomb in form," or, to
take a more prosaic simile, the rose of a watering-pot. The
upper part has twenty or thirty cavities, "each containing
a seed as big as an olive stone, and pleasant to eat either
fresh or dried." This is what the ancients called the bean
of Egypt. "The yearly shoots of the papyrus are also
gathered. After pulling them up in the marshes, the points
are cut off and rejected, the part remaining being about a
cubit in length. It is eaten as a delicacy and is sold in the
markets, but those who are fastidious partake of it only
after baking." Twenty different kinds of grain and fruits,
prepared by crushing between two stones, are kneaded and
baked to furnish cakes or bread; these are often mentioned
in the texts as cakes of nabeca, date cakes, and cakes of
figs. Lily loaves, made from the roots and seeds of the
lotus, were the delight of the gourmand, and appear on the
tables of the kings of the XIXth dynasty;[1] bread and cakes
made of cereals formed the habitual food of the people.
Durrah is of African origin; it is the "grain of the South"

---

[1] *Tiû*, which is the most ancient word for bread, appears in early times
to have been used for every kind of paste, whether made with fruits or
grain; the more modern word *âqû* applies specially to bread made from
cereals. The lily loaves are mentioned in the *Papyrus Anastasi*, No. 4, p.
14. l. 1.

of the inscriptions. On the other hand, it is supposed that wheat and six-rowed barley came from the region of the Euphrates. Egypt was among the first to procure and cultivate them.[1] The soil there is so kind to man, that in many places no agricultural toil is required. As soon as the water of the Nile retires, the ground is sown without previous preparation, and the grain, falling straight into the mud, grows as vigorously as in the best-ploughed furrows. Where the earth is hard it is necessary to break it up, but the extreme simplicity of the instruments with which this was done shows what a feeble resistance it offered. For a long time the hoe sufficed. It was composed either of a large stone tied to a wooden handle, or was made of two pieces of wood of unequal length, united at one of their extremities, and held together towards the middle by a slack cord : the plough, when first invented was but a slightly enlarged hoe, drawn by oxen. The cultivation of cereals, once established on the banks of the Nile, developed, from earliest times, to such a degree as to supplant all else : hunting, fishing, the rearing of cattle,

THE EGYPTIAN HOE.[2]

---

[1] The position which wheat and barley occupy in the lists of offerings, proves the antiquity of their existence in Egypt. Mariette found specimens of barley in the tombs of the Ancient Empire at Saqqarah.

[2] Bas-relief from the tomb of Ti ; drawn by Faucher-Gudin, from a photograph by Émil Brugsch-Bey.

occupied but a secondary place compared with agriculture, and Egypt became, that which she still remains, a vast granary of wheat.

The part of the valley first cultivated was from Gebel Silsileh to the apex of the Delta.[1] Between the Libyan and Arabian ranges it presents a slightly convex surface, furrowed lengthways by a depression, ·in the bottom of which the Nile is gathered and enclosed when the inunda-

PLOUGHING.[2]

tion is over. In the summer, as soon as the river had risen higher than the top of its banks, the water rushed by the force of gravity towards the lower lands, hollowing in its course long channels, some of which never completely dried

[1] This was the tradition of all the ancients. Herodotus related that, according to the Egyptians, the whole of Egypt, with the exception of the Theban nome, was a vast swamp previous to the time of Menes. Aristotle adds that the Red Sea, the Mediterranean, and the area now occupied by the Delta, formed one sea. Cf. pp. 3–5 of this volume, on the formation of the Delta.

[2] Bas-relief from the tomb of Ti ; drawn by Faucher-Gudin, from a photograph by Émil Brugsch-Bey.

up, even when the Nile reached its lowest level.[1] Cultivation was easy in the neighbourhood of these natural reservoirs, but everywhere else the movements of the river were rather injurious than advantageous to man. The inundation scarcely ever covered the higher ground in the valley, which therefore remained unproductive; it flowed rapidly over the lands of medium elevation, and moved so sluggishly in the hollows that they became weedy and stagnant pools.[2] In any year the portion not watered by the river was invaded by the sand : from the lush vegetation of a hot country, there was but one step to absolute aridity. At the present day an ingeniously established system of irrigation allows the agriculturist to direct and distribute the overflow according to his needs. From Gebel Ain to the sea, the Nile and its principal branches are bordered by long dykes, which closely follow the windings of the river and furnish sufficiently stable embankments. Numerous canals lead off to right and left, directed more or less obliquely towards the confines of the valley; they are divided at intervals by fresh dykes, starting at the one side from the river, and ending on the other either at the Bahr Yusuf or at the rising of the desert. Some of these dykes protect one district only, and consist merely of a bank of earth ; others command a large extent of territory, and a breach in them would entail the ruin of an entire province. These latter are sometimes like real ramparts, made of

[1] The whole description of the damage which can be done by the Nile in places where the inundation is not regulated, is borrowed from LINANT DE BELLEFONDS, *Mémoire sur les principaux travaux d'utilité publique*, p. 3.

[2] This physical configuration of the country explains the existence at a very early date of those gigantic serpents which I have already mentioned.

kin (Well)

crude brick carefully cemented; a few, as at Qosheish, have a core of hewn stones, which later generations have covered with masses of brickwork, and strengthened with constantly renewed buttresses of earth. They wind across the plain with many unexpected and apparently aimless turns; on closer examination, however, it may be seen that this irregularity is not to be attributed to ignorance or caprice. Experience had taught the Egyptians the art of picking out, upon the almost imperceptible relief of the soil, the easiest lines to use against the inundation : of these they have followed carefully the sinuosities, and if the course of the dykes appears singular, it is to be ascribed to the natural configuration of the ground. Subsidiary embankments thrown up between the principal ones, and parallel to the Nile, separate the higher ground bordering the river from the low lands on the confines of the valley ; they divide the larger basins into smaller divisions of varying area, in which the irrigation is regulated by means of special trenches. As long as the Nile is falling, the dwellers on its banks leave their canals in free communication with it; but they dam them up towards the end of the winter, just before the return of the inundation, and do not reopen them till early in August, when the new flood is at its height. The waters then flowing in by the trenches are arrested by the nearest transverse dyke and spread over the fields. When they have stood there long enough to saturate the ground, the dyke is pierced, and they pour into the next basin until they are stopped by a second dyke, which in its turn forces them again to spread out on either side. This operation is renewed from dyke to dyke, till the valley soon becomes a series of artificial ponds, ranged one above another, and flowing one into another from Gebel Silsileh to the apex of the Delta. In autumn, the mouth of each ditch is dammed up anew, in order to prevent the mass of water from flowing back into the stream. The transverse dykes, which have been cut in various places, are also repaired, and the basins become completely landlocked, separated by narrow causeways. In some places, the water thus imprisoned is so shallow that it is soon absorbed by the soil; in others, it is so deep, that after it has been kept in for several weeks, it is necessary to let it run off into a neighbouring depression, or straight into the river itself.

History has left us no account of the vicissitudes of the struggle in which the Egyptians were engaged with the Nile, nor of the time expended in bringing it to a successful issue. Legend attributes the idea of the system and its partial working out to the god Osiris: then Menes, the first mortal king, is said to have made the dyke of Qosheish, on which depends the prosperity of the Delta and Middle Egypt, and the fabulous Mœris is supposed to have extended the blessings of the irrigation to the Fayûm. In reality, the regulation of the inundation and the making of cultivable land are the work of unrecorded generations who peopled the valley. The kings of the historic period had only to maintain and develop certain points of what had already been done, and Upper Egypt is to this day chequered by the network of waterways with which its earliest inhabitants covered it. The work must have begun simultaneously at several points, without previous agreement, and, as it were, instinctively. A dyke protecting a village, a canal draining or watering some small province, demanded the efforts of but few individuals; then the dykes would join one another, the canals would be prolonged till they met others, and the work undertaken by chance would be improved, and would spread with the concurrence of an ever-increasing population. What happened at the end of last century, shows us that the system grew and was developed at the expense of considerable quarrels and bloodshed. The inhabitants of each district carried out the part of the work most conducive to their own interest, seizing the

BOATMEN FIGHTING ON A CANAL COMMUNICATING WITH THE NILE.[1]

supply of water, keeping it and discharging it at pleasure, without considering whether they were injuring their neighbours by depriving them of their supply or by flooding them ; hence arose perpetual strife and fighting. It became imperative that the rights of the weaker should be respected, and that the system of distribution should be co-ordinated, for the country to accept a beginning at least of social organization analogous to that which it acquired later : the

[1] Bas-relief from the tomb of Ti; drawn by Faucher-Gudin, from a photograph by É. Brugsch-Bey.

Nile thus determined the political as well as the physical constitution of Egypt.

The country was divided among communities, whose members were supposed to be descended from the same

A GREAT EGYPTIAN LORD, TI, AND HIS WIFE.[1]

seed (*pâît*) and to belong to the same family (*pâîtû*): the chiefs of them were called *ropâîtû*, the guardians, or pastors

[1] Drawn by Faucher-Gudin, from a photograph by DUMICHEN, *Resultate*, vol. ii. pl. vii.

THE PRINCES OF THE NOMES

of the family, and in later times their name became a title
applicable to the nobility in general. Families combined
and formed groups of various importance under the
authority of a head chief—*ropâtû-hâ*. They were, in fact,
hereditary lords, dispensing justice, levying taxes in kind
on their subordinates, reserving to themselves the re-
distribution of land, leading their men to battle, and
sacrificing to the gods.[1] The territories over which they
exercised authority formed small states, whose boundaries
even now, in some places, can be pointed out with
certainty. The principality of the Terebinth[2] occupied
the very heart of Egypt, where the valley is widest, and
the course of the Nile most advantageously disposed by
nature—a country well suited to be the cradle of an infant
civilization. Siaût (Siût), the capital, is built almost at
the foot of the Libyan range, on a strip of land barely
a mile in width, which separates the river from the hills.
A canal surrounds it on three sides, and makes, as it
were, a natural ditch about its walls; during the inundation it is connected with the mainland only by narrow
causeways—shaded with mimosas—and looking like a raft
of verdure aground in the current.[3] The site is as happy

---

[1] These prerogatives were still exercised by the princes of the nomes
under the Middle and New Empires ; they only enjoyed them then by the
good will of the reigning sovereign.

[2] The Egyptian word for the tree which gives its name to this principality
is *atf, iatf, iôtf*: it is only by a process of elimination that I have come to
identify it with the *Pistacia Terebinthus*, L., which furnished the Egyptians
with the scented resin *snûtir*.

[3] Boudier's drawing, reproduced on p. 31, and taken from a photograph
by Beato, gives most faithfully the aspect presented by the plain and the
modern town of Siout during the inundation.

as it is picturesque; not only does the town command

NOMES
of
MIDDLE ÉGYPT

Scale

L. Thuillier, del.ᵗ

the two arms of the river, opening or closing the water-way at will, but from time immemorial the most frequented of the routes into Central Africa has terminated at its gates, bringing to it the commerce of the Soudan. It held sway, at the outset, over both banks, from range to range, northward as far as Deyrût, where the true Bahr Yusuf leaves the Nile, and southward to the neighbourhood of Gebel Sheikh Haridi. The extent and original number of the other principalities is not so easily deter-

mined. The most important, to the north of Siût, were those

of the Hare and the Oleander. The principality of the Hare
never reached the dimensions of that of its neighbour the
Terebinth, but its chief town was Khmûnû, whose antiquity
was so remote, that a universally accepted tradition made
it the scene of the most important acts of creation.[1] That
of the Oleander, on the contrary, was even larger than
that of the Terebinth, and from Hininsû, its chief governor
ruled alike over the marshes of the Fayûm and the plains
of Beni-Suef.[2] To the south, Apû on the right bank
governed a district so closely shut in between a bend of
the Nile and two spurs of the range, that its limits have
never varied much since ancient times. Its inhabitants
were divided in their employment between weaving and
the culture of cereals. From early times they possessed
the privilege of furnishing clothing to a large part of
Egypt, and their looms, at the present day, still make
those checked or striped "melayahs" which the fellah
women wear over their long blue tunics.[3] Beyond Apû,
Thinis, the Girgeh of the Arabs, situate on both banks
of the river, rivalled Khmûnû in antiquity and Siût in
wealth: its plains still produce the richest harvests and

---

[1] Khmûnû, the present Ashmûneîn, is the Hermopolis of the Greeks,
the town of the god Thot.

[2] Hininsû is the *Heracleopolis Magna* of the Greeks, the present Henassieh,
called also Ahnas-el-Medineh. The Egyptian word for the tree which gives
its name to this principality, is Nârît. Loret has shown that this tree,
Nârît, is the oleander.

[3] Apû was the Panopolis or Chemmis of the Greeks, the town of the
god Mîn or ithyphallic Khimû. Its manufactures of linen are mentioned by
Strabo; the majority of the beautiful Coptic woven fabrics and embroideries
which have been brought to Europe lately, come from the necropolis of the
Arab period at Apû.

feed the most numerous herds of sheep and oxen in the
Saïd. As we approach the cataract, information becomes
scarcer· Qûbti and Aûnû of the South, the Coptos and

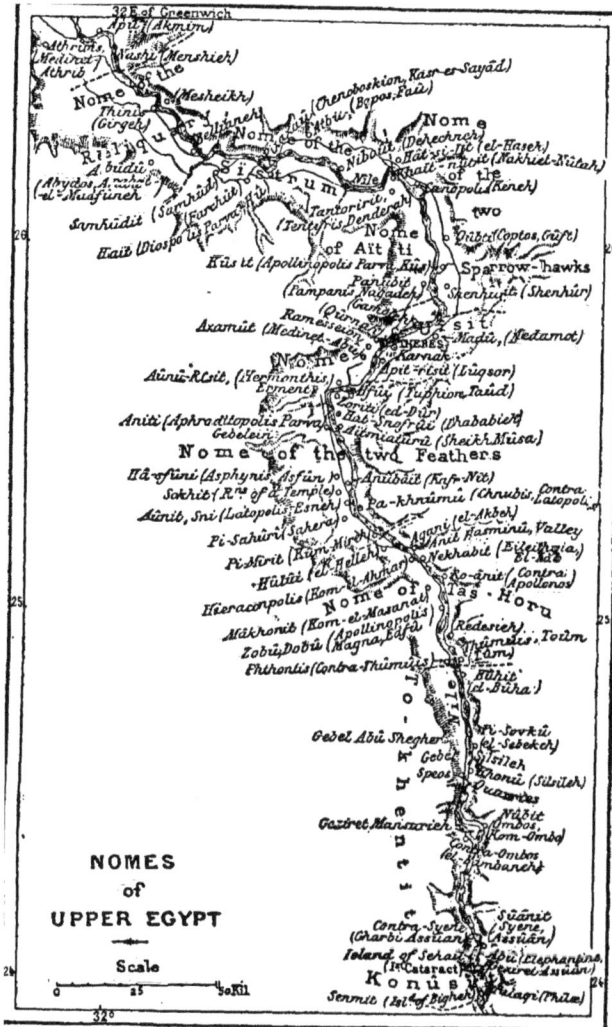

L. Thuillier, del.ᵗ

Hermonthis of the Greeks, shared peaceably the plain
occupied later on by Thebes and its temples, and Nekhabît
and Zobû watched over the safety of Egypt. Nekhabît
soon lost its position as a frontier town, and that portion

of Nubia lying between Gebel Silsileh and the rapids of Syene formed a kind of border province, of which Nubît-Ombos was the principal sanctuary and Abû-Elephantine the fortress: beyond this were the barbarians, and those inaccessible regions whence the Nile descended upon our earth.

The organization of the Delta, it would appear, was more slowly brought about. It must have greatly resembled that of the lowlands of Equatorial Africa, towards the confluence of the Bahr el Abiad and the Bahr el Ghazâl. Great tracts of mud, difficult to describe as either solid or liquid, marshes dotted here and there with sandy islets, bristling with papyrus reeds, water-lilies, and enormous plants through which the arms of the Nile sluggishly pushed their ever-shifting course, low-lying wastes intersected with streams and pools, unfit for cultivation and scarcely available for pasturing cattle. The population of such districts, engaged in a ceaseless struggle with nature, always preserved relatively ruder manners, and a more rugged and savage character, impatient of all authority. The conquest of this region began from the outer edge only. A few principalities were established at the apex of the Delta in localities where the soil had earliest been won from the river. It appears that one of these divisions embraced the country south of and between the bifurcation of the Nile: Aûnû of the North, the Heliopolis of the Greeks, was its capital. In very early times the principality was divided, and formed three new states, independent of each other. Those of Aûnû and the Haunch were opposite to each other, the

first on the Arabian, the latter on the Libyan bank of the
Nile. The district of the White Wall marched with that
of the Haunch on the north, and on the south touched
the territory of the Oleander. Further down the river,
between the more important branches, the governors of
Saïs and of Bubastis, of Athribis and of Busiris, shared
among themselves the primitive Delta. Two frontier
provinces of unequal size, the Arabian on the east in the
Wady Tumilat, and the Libyan on the west to the south
of Lake Mareotis, defended the approaches of the country
from the attacks of Asiatic Bedâwins and of African
nomads. The marshes of the interior and the dunes of
the littoral, were not conducive to the development of any
great industry or civilization. They only comprised tracts
of thinly populated country, like the principalities of the
Harpoon and of the Cow, and others whose limits varied
from century to century with the changing course of the
river. The work of rendering the marshes salubrious and
of digging canals, which had been so successful in the
Nile Valley, was less efficacious in the Delta, and proceeded
more slowly. Here the embankments were not supported
by a mountain chain: they were continued at random
across the marshes, cut at every turn to admit the waters
of a canal or of an arm of the river. The waters left
their usual bed at the least disturbing influence, and made
a fresh course for themselves across country. If the inundation were delayed, the soft and badly drained soil again
became a slough: should it last but a few weeks longer
than usual, the work of several generations was for a long
time undone. The Delta of one epoch rarely presented

the same aspect as that of previous periods, and Northern
Egypt never became as fully mistress of her soil as the
Egypt of the south.

These first principalities, however small they appear to

us, were yet too large to remain undivided. In those
times of slow communication, the strong attraction which a
capital exercised over the provinces under its authority did
not extend over a wide radius. That part of the population

of the Terebinth, living sufficiently near to Siût to come into the town for a few hours in the morning, returning in the evening to the villages when business was done, would not feel any desire to withdraw from the rule of the prince who governed there. On the other hand, those who lived outside that restricted circle were forced to seek elsewhere some places of assembly to attend the administration of justice, to sacrifice in common to the national gods, and to exchange the produce of the fields and of local manufactures. Those towns which had the good fortune to become such rallying-points naturally played the part of rivals to the capital, and their chiefs, with the district whose population, so to speak, gravitated around them, tended to become independent of the prince. When they succeeded in doing this, they often preserved for the new state thus created, the old name, slightly modified by the addition of an epithet. The primitive territory of Siût was in this way divided into three distinct communities; two, which remained faithful to the old emblem of the tree—the Upper Terebinth, with Siût itself in the centre, and the Lower Terebinth, with Kûsit to the north; the third, in the south and east, took as their totem the immortal serpent which dwelt in their mountains, and called themselves the Serpent Mountain, whoso chief town was that of the Sparrow Hawk. The territory of the Oleander produced by its dismemberment the principality of the Upper Oleander, that of the Lower Oleander, and that of the Knife. The territory of the Harpoon in the Delta divided itself into the Western and Eastern Harpoon. The fission in most cases could not have been accomplished without struggles;

but it did take place, and all the principalities having a domain of any considerable extent had to submit to it, however they may have striven to avoid it. This parcelling out was continued as circumstances afforded opportunity, until the whole of Egypt, except the half desert districts about the cataract, became but an agglomeration of petty states nearly equal in power and population.[1]

The Greeks called them nomes, and we have borrowed the word from them; the natives named them in several ways, the most ancient term being " nûît," which may be translated *domain*, and the most common appellation in recent times being " hospû," which signifies *district*. The number of the nomes varied considerably in the course of centuries: the hieroglyphic monuments and classical authors fixed them sometimes at thirty-six, sometimes at forty, sometimes at forty-four, or even fifty. The little that we know of their history, up to the present time, explains the reason of this variation. Ceaselessly quarrelled over by the princely families who possessed them, the nomes were alternately humbled and exalted by civil wars, marriages, and conquest, which caused them continually to pass into fresh hands, either entire or divided. The Egyptians, whom we are accustomed to consider as a people respecting the established order of things, and conservative of ancient tradition, showed

[1] Examples of the subdivision of ancient nomes and the creation of fresh nomes are met with long after primitive times. We find, for example, the nome of the Western Harpoon divided under the Greeks and Romans into two districts—that of the Harpoon proper, of which the chief town was Sonti-nofir ; and that of Ranûfir, with the Onûphis of classical geographers for its capital.

themselves as restless and as prone to modify or destroy the work of the past, as the most inconstant of our modern nations. The distance of time which separates them from us, and the almost complete absence of documents, gives them an appearance of immobility, by which we are liable to be unconsciously deceived; when the monuments still existing shall have been unearthed, their history will present the same complexity of incidents, the same agitations, the same instability, which we suspect or know to have been characteristic of most other Oriental nations. One thing alone remained stable among them in the midst of so many revolutions, and which prevented them from losing their individuality and from coalescing in a common unity. This was the belief in and the worship of one particular deity. If the little capitals of the petty states whose origin is lost in a remote past—Edfû and Denderah, Nekhabît and Bûto, Siût, Thinis, Khmûnû, Saîs, Bubastis, Athribis—had only possessed that importance which resulted from the presence of an ambitious petty prince, or from the wealth of their inhabitants, they would never have passed safe and sound through the long centuries of existence which they enjoyed from the opening to the close of Egyptian history. Fortune raised their chiefs, some even to the rank of rulers of the world, and in turn abased them : side by side with the earthly ruler, whose glory was but too often eclipsed, there was enthroned in each nome a divine ruler, a deity, a god of the domain, " nûtir nûiti," whose greatness never perished. The princely families might be exiled or become extinct, the extent of the territory might diminish or increase, the town might be doubled in size and population or fall in ruins : the god lived on through all these vicissitudes, and his presence alone preserved intact the rights of the state over which he reigned as sovereign. If any disaster befell his worshippers, his temple was the spot where the survivors of the catastrophe rallied around him, their religion preventing them from mixing with the inhabitants of neighbouring towns and from becoming lost among them. The survivors multiplied with that extraordinary rapidity which is the characteristic of the Egyptian fellah, and a few years of peace sufficed to repair losses which apparently were irreparable. Local religion was the tie which bound together those divers elements of which each principality was composed, and as long as it remained, the nomes remained; when it vanished, they disappeared with it.

THE GODS OF EGYPT

THEIR NUMBER AND NATURE—THE FEUDAL GODS, LIVING AND DEAD—TRIADS—
THE TEMPLES AND PRIESTHOOD—THE COSMOGONIES OF THE DELTA—THE
ENNEADS OF HELIOPOLIS AND HERMOPOLIS.

*Multiplicity of the Egyptian gods: the commonalty of the gods, its varieties,
human, animal, and intermediate between man and beast; gods of foreign
origin, indigenous gods, and the contradictory forms with which they were
invested in accordance with various conceptions of their nature.*

*The Star-gods—The Sun-god as the Eye of the Sky; as a bird, as a calf,
and as a man; its barks, voyages round the world, and encounters with the
serpent Apopi—The Moon-god and its enemies—The Star-gods: the Haunch of
the Ox, the Hippopotamus, the Lion, the five Horus-planets; Sothis Sirius, and
Sahú Orion.*

*The feudal gods and their classes: the Nile-gods, the earth-gods, the sky-
gods and the sun-god, the Horus-gods—The equality of feudal gods and*

goddesses ; their persons, alliances, and marriages: their children—The triads and their various developments.

The nature of the gods: the double, the soul, the body, death of men and gods, and their fate after death—The necessity for preserving the body, mummification—Dead gods the gods of the dead—The living gods, their temples and images—The gods of the people, trees, serpents, family fetiches—The theory of prayer and sacrifice: the servants of the temples, the property of the gods, the sacerdotal colleges.

The cosmogonies of the Delta: Sîbû and Nûît, Osiris and Isis, Sît and Nephthys—Heliopolis and its theological schools: Râ, his identification with Horus, his dual nature, and the conception of Atûmû—The Heliopolitan Enneads: formation of the Great Ennead—Thot and the Hermopolitan Ennead: creation by articulate words and by voice alone—Diffusion of the Enneads: their connection with the local triads, the god One and the god Eight—The one and only gods.

SOLEMN SACRIFICIAL PROCESSION OF THE FATTED BULL[1]

CHAPTER II

THE GODS OF EGYPT

Their number and their nature—The feudal gods, living and dead—The Triads—Temples and priests—The cosmogonies of the Delta—The Enneads of Heliopolis and of Hermopolis.

KING SETI I. KNEELING.[2]

THE incredible number of religious scenes to be found among the representations on the ancient monuments of Egypt is at first glance very striking. Nearly every illustration in the works of Egyptologists brings before us the figure

[1] Bas-relief in the temple of Luxor. Drawn by Boudier, from a photograph by Beato, taken in 1890. The two personages marching in front, carrying great bouquets, and each with an uplifted hand, are the last in a long procession of the sons of Rameses II.

[2] Drawn by Boudier, from a bas-relief of the temple of Abydos.

of some deity receiving with an impassive countenance ⸍ the prayers and offerings of a worshipper   One would think that the country had been inhabited for the most part by gods, and contained just sufficient men and animals to satisfy the requirements of their worship

On penetrating into this mysterious world, we are confronted by an actual rabble of gods, each one of whom has always possessed but a limited and almost unconscious existence   They sever ally represented a function, a moment in the life of man or of the universe thus Naprît was identified with the ripe ear, or the grain of wheat · [2] Maskhonît appeared by the child s cradle at the very moment of its birth ; [3] and Raninît presided over

THE GODDESS NAPRÎT, NAPÎT.[1]

[1] The goddess Naprît, Napît ; bas-relief from the first chamber of Osiris, on the east side of the great temple of Denderah.   Drawn by Faucher-Gudin.

[2] The word *naprît* means *grain*, the grain of wheat.   The grain-god is represented in the tomb of Seti I. as a man wearing two full ears of wheat or barley upon his head.   He is mentioned in the *Hymn to the Nile* about the same date, and in two or three other texts of different periods.   The goddess *Naprît*, . or *Napît*, to whom reference is here made, was his duplicate ; her head-dress is a sheaf of corn, as in the illustration.

[3] This goddess, whose name expresses and whose form personifies the brick or stone couch, the child-bed or -chair, upon which women in labour bowed themselves, is sometimes subdivided into two or four secondary divinities.   She is mentioned along with Shait, *destiny*, and Raninît, *suckling*.

the naming and the nurture of the newly born.[1] Neither
Raninît, the fairy godmother, nor Maskhonît exercised over
nature as a whole that sovereign authority which we are
accustomed to consider the primary attribute of deity.
Every day of every year was passed by the one in easing
the pangs of women in travail; by the other, in choosing
for each baby a name of an auspicious sound, and one
which would afterwards serve to exorcise the influences
of evil fortune. No sooner were their tasks accomplished
in one place than they hastened to another, where
approaching birth demanded their presence and their
care. From child-bed to child-bed they passed, and if
they fulfilled the single offices in which they were
accounted adepts, the pious asked nothing more of them.
Bands of mysterious cynocephali haunting the Eastern
and the Western mountains concentrated the whole of
their activity on one passing moment of the day. They
danced and chattered in the East for half an hour, to
salute the sun at his rising, even as others in the West
hailed him on his entrance into night.[2] It was the duty

Her part of fairy godmother at the cradle of the new-born child is indicated
in the passage of the *Westcar Papyrus* giving a detailed account of the births
of three kings of the fifth dynasty. She is represented in human form, and
often wears upon her head two long palm-shoots, curling over at their ends.

[1] *Raninît* presides over the child's suckling, but she also gives him his
name, and hence, his fortune. She is on the whole the nursing goddess.
Sometimes she is represented as a human-headed woman, or as lioness-
headed, most frequently with the head of a serpent ; she is also the uræus,
clothed, and wearing two long plumes on her head, and a simple uræus, as
represented in the illustration on p. 169.

[2] This is the subject of a vignette in the *Book of the Dead*, ch. xvi.,
where the cynocephali are placed in echelon upon the slopes of the hill on

of certain genii to open gates in Hades, or to keep the paths daily traversed by the sun.[1] These genii were always at their posts, never free to leave them, and possessed no other faculty than that of punctually fulfilling their appointed offices. Their existence, generally unperceived, was suddenly revealed at the very moment when the specific acts of their lives were on the point of accomplishment. These being completed, the divinities fell back into their state of inertia, and were, so to speak, reabsorbed by

SOME FABULOUS BEASTS OF THE EGYPTIAN DESERT.[2]

their functions until the next occasion.[3] Scarcely visible even by glimpses, they were not easily depicted; their

the horizon, right and left of the radiant solar disk, to which they offer worship by gesticulations.

[1] MASPERO, Études de Mythologie et d'Archéologie Égyptiennes, vol. ii. pp. 34, 35.

[2] Drawn by Faucher-Gudin from Champollion's copies, made from the tombs of Beni-Hassan. To the right is the *sha*, one of the animals of Sît, and an exact image of the god with his stiff and arrow-like tail. Next comes the *safir*, the griffin ; and, lastly, we have the serpent-headed *saza*.

[3] The Egyptians employed a still more forcible expression than our word "absorption" to express this idea. It was said of objects wherein these genii concealed themselves, and whence they issued in order to re-enter them immediately, that these forms *ate* them, or that they *ate* their own forms.

real forms being often unknown, these were approximately conjectured from their occupations. The character and costume of an archer, or of a spear-man, were ascribed to such as roamed through Hades, to pierce the dead with arrows or with javelins. Those who prowled around souls to cut their throats and hack them to pieces were represented as women armed with knives, carvers—*donît*—or else as lacerators—*nokît*. Some appeared in human form; others as animals—bulls or lions, rams or monkeys, serpents, fish, ibises, hawks; others dwelt in inanimate things, such as trees,[1] sistrums, stakes stuck in the ground;[2] and lastly, many betrayed a mixed origin in their combinations of human and animal forms. These latter would be regarded by us as monsters; to the Egyptians, they were beings, rarer perhaps than the rest, but not the less real, and their like might be encountered in the neighbourhood of Egypt.[3]

[1] Thus, the sycamores planted on the edge of the desert were supposed to be inhabited by Hâthor, Nûît, Selkît, Nît, or some other goddess. In vignettes representing the deceased as stopping before one of these trees and receiving water and loaves of bread, the bust of the goddess generally appears from amid her sheltering foliage. But occasionally, as on the sarcophagus of Petosiris, the transformation is complete, and the trunk from which the branches spread is the actual body of the god or goddess. Finally, the whole body is often hidden, and only the arm of the goddess to be seen emerging from the midst of the tree, with an overflowing libation vase in her hand.

[2] The trunk of a tree, disbranched, and then set up in the ground, seems to me the origin of the Osirian emblem called *tat* or *didû*. The symbol was afterwards so conventionalized as to represent four columns seen in perspective, one capital overtopping another; it thus became the image of the four pillars which uphold the world.

[3] The belief in the real existence of fantastic animals was first noted by Maspero, *Études de Mythologie et d'Archéologie Égyptiennes*, vol. i. pp. 117, 118, 132, and vol. ii. p. 213. Until then, scholars only recognized the

How could men who believed themselves surrounded by sphinxes and griffins of flesh and blood doubt that there were bull-headed and hawk-headed divinities with human busts? The existence of such paradoxical creatures was proved by much authentic testimony; more than one hunter had distinctly seen them as they ran along the furthest planes of the horizon, beyond the herds of gazelles of which he was in chase ; and shepherds dreaded them for their flocks as truly as they dreaded the lions, or the great felidæ of the desert.[1]

This nation of gods, like nations of men, contained foreign elements, the origin of which was known to the Egyptians themselves. They knew that Hâthor, the milch cow, had taken up her abode in their land from very ancient times, and they called her the Lady of Pûanît, after the name of her native country. Bîsû had followed her in course of time, and claimed his share of honours and worship along with her. He first appeared as a leopard; then he became a man clothed in a leopard's skin, but of strange countenance and alarming character, a big-headed dwarf with high cheek-bones, and a wide and open mouth, whence hung an enormous tongue ; he

sphinx, and other Egyptian monsters, as allegorical combinations by which the priesthood claimed to give visible expression in one and the same being to physical or moral qualities belonging to several different beings. The later theory has now been adopted by WIEDEMANN, and by most contemporary Egyptologists.

[1] At Beni-Hassan and in Thebes many of the fantastic animals mentioned in the text, griffins, hierosphinxes, serpent-headed lions, are placed along with animals which might be encountered by local princes hunting in the desert.

was at once jovial and martial, the friend of the dance and of battle.[1] In historic times all nations subjugated by the Pharaohs transferred some of their principal divinities to their conquerors, and the Libyan Shehadidi was enthroned in the valley of the Nile, in the same way as the Semitic Baâlû and his retinue of Astartes, Anitis, Reshephs, and Kadshûs. These divine colonists fared like all foreigners who have sought to settle on the banks of the Nile : they were promptly assimilated, wrought, moulded, and made into Egyptian deities scarcely distinguishable from those of the old race. This mixed pantheon

SOME FABULOUS BEASTS OF THE EGYPTIAN DESERT.[2]

had its grades of nobles, princes, kings, and each of its members was representative of one of the elements constituting the world, or of one of the forces which regulated its government. The sky, the earth, the stars, the sun, the Nile, were so many breathing and thinking beings whose lives were daily manifest in the life of the universe.

[1] Bisû, pp. 111–184. The tail-piece to the summary of this chapter is a figure of Bisû, drawn by Faucher-Gudin from an amulet in blue enamelled pottery.

[2] The hawk-headed monster with flower-tipped tail was called the *saga.*

They were worshipped from one end of the valley to the other, and the whole nation agreed in proclaiming their sovereign power. But when the people began to name them, to define their powers and attributes, to particularize their forms, or the relationships that subsisted among them, this unanimity was at an end. Each principality, each nome, each city, almost every village, conceived and represented them differently. Some said that the sky was the Great Horus, Haroêris, the sparrow-hawk of mottled plumage which hovers in highest air, and whose gaze embraces the whole field of creation. Owing to a punning assonance between his name and the word *horû*, which designates the human countenance, the two senses were combined, and to the idea of the sparrow-hawk there was added that of a divine face, whose two eyes opened in turn, the right eye being the sun, to give light by day, and the left eye the moon, to illumine the night. The face shone also with a light of its own, the zodiacal light, which appeared unexpectedly, morning or evening, a little before sunrise, and a little after sunset. These luminous beams, radiating from a common centre, hidden in the heights of the firmament, spread into a wide pyramidal sheet of liquid blue, whose base rested upon the earth, but whose apex was slightly inclined towards the zenith. The divine face was symmetrically framed, and attached to earth by four thick locks of hair; these were the pillars which upbore the firmament and prevented its falling into ruin. A no less ancient tradition disregarded as fabulous all tales told of the sparrow-hawk, or of the face, and taught that heaven and earth are wedded gods, Sibû, and Nûit, from

whose marriage came forth all that has been, all that is
and all that shall be Most people invested them with
human form and represented
the earth god Sibû as extended
beneath Nûit the Starry One;
the goddess stretched out her
arms stretched out her slender
legs stretched out her body
above the clouds, and her dis-
hevelled head drooped west
ward But there were also
many who believed that Sibû
was concealed under the form
of a colossal gander whose mate
once laid the Sun Egg, and
perhaps still laid it daily. From
the piercing cries wherewith
he congratulated her, and announced the good news to all
who cared to hear it—after the
manner of his kind—he had
received the flattering epithet
of *Ngagu oîrû*, the Great Cack-
ler. Other versions repudiated
the goose in favour of a vigorous
bull, the father of gods and
men, whose companion was a
cow, a large eyed Hâthor of

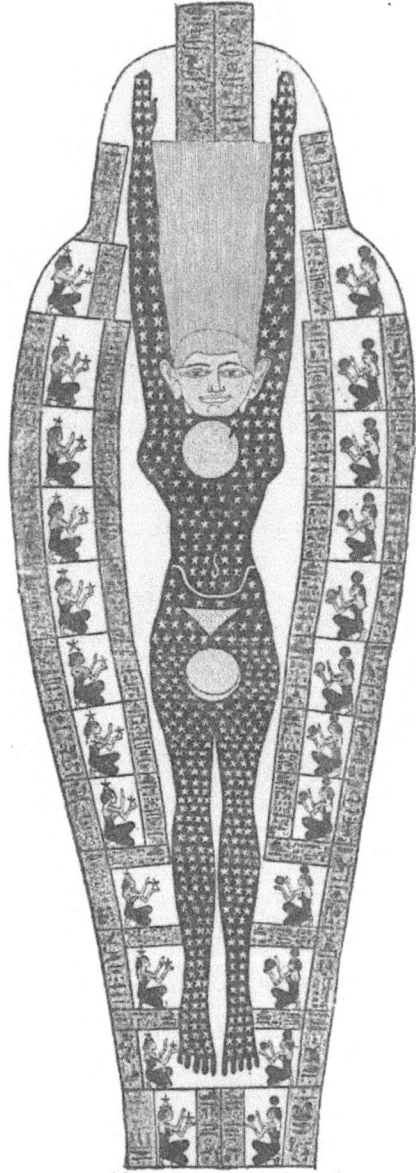

NÛÎT THE STARRY ONE [1]

[1] Drawn by Faucher-Gudin, from a painted coffin of the XXIst dynasty
in Leyden.

beautiful countenance. The head of the good beast rises into the heavens, the mysterious waters which cover the world flow along her spine; the star-covered underside of her body, which we call the firmament, is visible to the inhabitants of earth, and her four legs are the four pillars standing at the four cardinal points of the world.

THE GOOSE-GOD FACING THE CAT-GODDESS, THE LADY OF HEAVEN.[1]

The planets, and especially the sun, varied in form and nature according to the prevailing conception of the heavens. The fiery disk *Atonû*, by which the sun revealed himself to men, was a living god, called Râ, as was also

---

[1] Drawn by Faucher-Gudin, from a stella in the museum of Gizeh. This is not the goose of Sibû, but the goose of Amon, which was nurtured in the temple of Karnak, and was called Smonû. Facing it is the cat of Maût, the wife of Amon. Amon, originally an earth-god, was, as we see, confounded with Sibû, and thus naturally appropriated that deity's form of a goose.

the planet itself.[1]   Where the sky was regarded as Horus, Râ formed the right eye of the divine face : when Horus opened his eyelids in the morning, he made the dawn and day; when he closed them in the evening, the dusk and night were at hand. Where the sky was looked upon as the incarnation of a goddess, Râ was considered as her son,[2] his

[1] The name of Râ has been variously explained. The commonest etymology is that deriving the name from a verb RÂ, *to give, to make* to be a person or a thing, so that Râ would thus be the great organizer, the author of all things. LAUTH goes so far as to say that "notwithstanding its brevity, Râ is a composite word (R-A, *maker—to be*)." As a matter of fact, the word is simply the name of the planet applied to the god. It means the *sun*, and nothing more.

THE COW HÂTHOR, THE LADY OF HEAVEN.[3]

[2] Several passages from the Pyramid texts prove that the *two eyes* were very anciently considered as belonging to the face of Nûit, and this conception persisted to the last days of Egyptian paganism.   Hence, we must not be surprised if the inscriptions generally represent the god Râ as coming forth from Nûit under the form of a disc, or a scarabæus, and born of her even as human children are born.

[3] Drawn by Boudier, from a XXXth dynasty statue of green basalt in the Gizeh Museum (MASPERO, *Guide du Visiteur*, p. 345, No. 5243).   The statue was also published by MARIETTE, *Monuments divers*, pl. 96 A–B, and in the *Album photographique du Musée de Boulaq*, pl. x.

father being the earth-god, and he was born again with
every new dawn, wearing a sidelock, and with his finger to
his lips as human children were conventionally represented. He was also that luminous egg, laid and hatched in

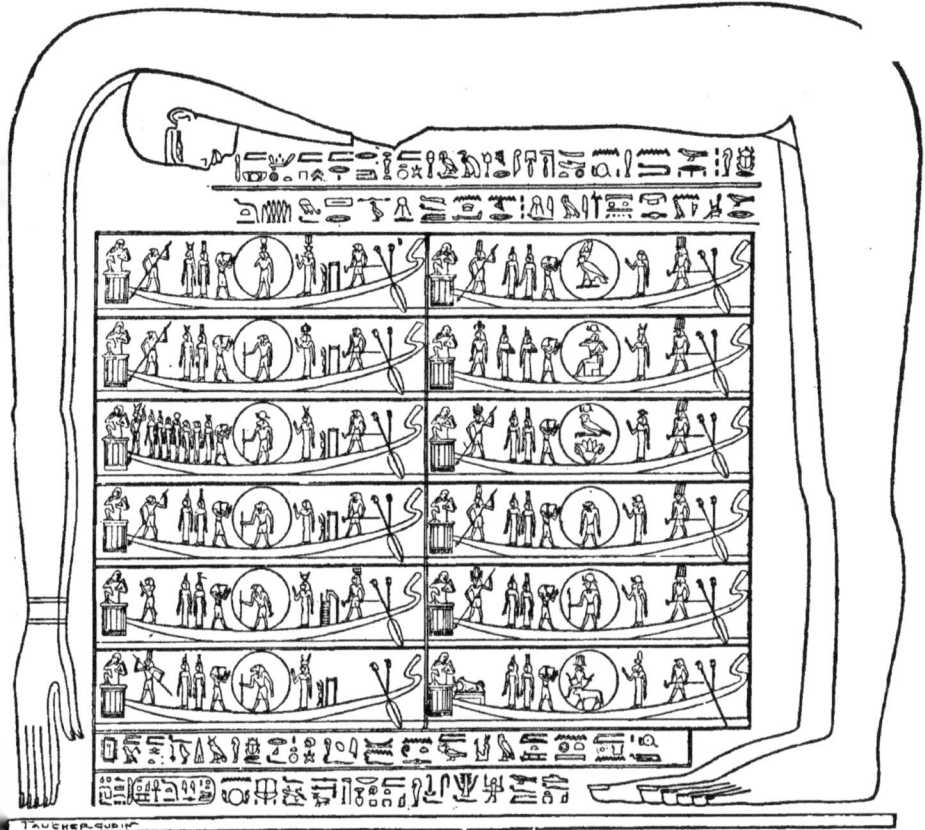

THE TWELVE STAGES IN THE LIFE OF THE SUN AND ITS TWELVE FORMS
THROUGHOUT THE DAY.[1]

the East by the celestial goose, from which the sun breaks
forth to fill the world with its rays.[2] Nevertheless, by an

[1] The twelve forms of the sun during the twelve hours of the day, from
the ceiling of the Hall of the New Year at Edfû. Drawing by Faucher-
Gudin.

[2] These are the very expressions used in the seventeenth chapter of the

anomaly not uncommon in religions, the egg did not always contain the same kind of bird ; a lapwing, or a heron, might come out of it,[1] or perhaps, in memory of Horus, one of the beautiful golden sparrow-hawks of Southern Egypt. A Sun-Hawk, hovering in high heaven on outspread wings, at least presented a bold and poetic image ; but what can be said for a Sun-Calf? Yet it is under the innocent aspect of a spotted calf, a " sucking calf of pure mouth,"[2] that the Egyptians were pleased to describe the Sun-God when Sibû, the father, was a bull, and Hâthor a heifer. But the prevalent conception was that in which the life of the sun was likened to the life of man. The two deities presiding over the East received the orb upon their hands at its birth, just as midwives receive a new-born child, and cared for it during the first hour of the day and of its life. It soon left them, and proceeded "under the belly of Nûit," growing and strengthening from minute to minute, until at noon it had become a triumphant hero whose splendour is shed abroad over all. But as night comes on his strength forsakes him and his glory is obscured; he is bent and broken down, and heavily drags himself along like an old man leaning upon his stick. At length he

Book of the Dead (NAVILLE's edition, vol. i. pl. xxv. lines 58–61; LEPSIUS, *Todtenbuch*, pl. ix. ll. 50, 51).

[1] The lapwing or the heron, the Egyptian *bonú*, is generally the Osirian bird. The persistence with which it is associated with Heliopolis and the gods of that city shows that in this also we have a secondary form of Râ.

[2] The calf is represented in ch. cix. of the *Book of the Dead* (NAVILLE's edition, pl..cxx.), where the text says (lines 10, 11), "I know that this calf is Harmakhis the Sun, and that it is no other than the Morning Star, daily saluting Râ." The expression "*sucking calf of pure mouth*" is taken word for word from a formula preserved in the Pyramid texts (*Ûnas*, l. 20).

passes away beyond the horizon, plunging westward into the mouth of Nûît, and traversing her body by night to be born anew the next morning, again to follow the paths along which he had travelled on the preceding day.

A first bark, the *saktît*, awaited him at his birth, and carried him from the Eastern to the Southern extremity of the world. *Mâzît*, the second bark, received him at noon, and bore him into the land of Manû, which is at the entrance into Hades; other barks, with which we are less familiar, conveyed him by night, from his setting until his rising at morn.[1] Sometimes he was supposed to enter the barks alone, and then they were magic and self-directed, having neither oars, nor sails, nor helm.[2] Sometimes they were equipped with a full crew, like that of an Egyptian boat—a pilot at the prow to take soundings in the channel and forecast the wind, a pilot astern to steer, a quarter-master in the midst to transmit the orders of the pilot at the prow to the pilot at the stern, and half a dozen sailors to handle poles or oars. Peacefully the bark glided along the celestial river amid the acclamations of the gods who dwelt upon its shores. But, occasionally, Apôpi, a gigantic serpent, like that which hides within the earthly Nile and devours its banks, came forth from the depth of the waters

---

[1] In the formulæ of the *Book of Knowing that which is in Hades*, the dead sun remains in the bark Saktît during part of the night, and it is only to traverse the fourth and fifth hours that he changes into another.

[2] Such is the bark of the sun in the other world. Although carrying a complete crew of gods, yet for the most part it progresses at its own will, and without their help. The bark containing the sun alone is represented in many vignettes of the *Book of the Dead*, and at the head of many stelæ.

and arose in the path of the god.[1] As soon as they caught sight of it in the distance, the crew flew to arms, and entered upon the struggle against him with prayers and spear-thrusts. Men in their cities saw the sun faint and fail, and sought to succour him in his distress; they cried aloud, they were beside themselves with excitement, beating their breasts, sounding their instruments of music, and striking with all their strength upon every metal vase or utensil in their possession, that their clamour might rise to heaven and terrify the monster. After a time of anguish, Râ emerged from the darkness and again went on his way, while Apôpi sank back into the abyss,[2] paralysed by the magic of the gods, and pierced with many a wound. Apart from these temporary eclipses, which no one could foretell, the Sun-King steadily followed his course round the world,

[1] In Upper Egypt there is a widespread belief in the existence of a monstrous serpent, who dwells at the bottom of the river, and is the genius of the Nile. It is he who brings about those falls of earth (*batabît*) at the decline of the inundation which often destroy the banks and *eat* whole fields. At such times, offerings of durrah, fowls, and dates are made to him, that his hunger may be appeased, and it is not only the natives who give themselves up to these superstitious practices. Part of the grounds belonging to the Karnak hotel at Luxor having been carried away during the autumn of 1884, the manager, a Greek, made the customary offerings to the serpent of the Nile.

[2] The character of Apôpi and of his struggle with the sun was, from the first, excellently defined by CHAMPOLLION as representing the conflict of darkness with light. Occasionally, but very rarely, Apôpi seems to win, and his triumph over Râ furnishes one explanation of a solar eclipse. A similar explanation is common to many races. In one very ancient form of the Egyptian legend, the sun is represented by a wild ass running round the world along the sides of the mountains that uphold the sky, and the serpent which attacks it is called *Haiû*.

according to laws which even his will could not change. Day after day he made his oblique ascent from east to south, thence to descend obliquely towards the west. During the summer months the obliquity of his course diminished, and he came closer to Egypt; during the winter it increased, and he went farther away. This double movement recurred with such regularity from equinox to solstice, and from solstice to equinox, that the day of the god's departure and the day of his return could be confidently predicted. The Egyptians explained this phenomenon according to their conceptions of the nature of the world. The solar bark always kept close to that bank of the celestial river which was nearest to men; and when the river overflowed at the annual inundation, the sun was carried along with it outside the regular bed of the stream, and brought yet closer to Egypt. As the inundation abated, the bark descended and receded, its greatest distance from earth corresponding with the lowest level of the waters. It was again brought back to us by the rising strength of the next flood; and, as this phenomenon was yearly repeated, the periodicity of the sun's oblique movements was regarded as the necessary consequence of the periodic movements of the celestial Nile.

The same stream also carried a whole crowd of gods, whose existence was revealed at night only to the inhabitants of earth. At an interval of twelve hours, and in its own bark, the pale disk of the moon— *Yâûhû Aûhû*—followed the disk of the sun along the ramparts of the world. The moon, also, appeared in many various forms—here, as a man born of Nûît;[1] there, as a cynocephalus or an ibis;[2] elsewhere, it was the left eye of Horus,[3] guarded by the ibis or cynocephalus. Like Râ, it had its enemies incessantly upon the watch for it: the crocodile, the hippopotamus,

EGYPTIAN CONCEPTION OF THE PRINCIPAL CONSTELLATIONS OF THE NORTHERN SKY.[4]

and the sow. But it was when at the full, about the 15th of each month, that the lunar eye was in greatest peril.

[1] He may be seen as a child, or man, bearing the lunar disk upon his head, and pressing the lunar eye to his breast. Passages from the Pyramid text of Ûnas indicate the relationship subsisting between Thot, Sibû, and Nûit, making Thot the brother of Isis, Sît, and Nephthys. In later times he was considered a son of Râ.

[2] Even as late as the Græco-Roman period, the temple of Thot at Khmûnû contained a sacred ibis, which was the incarnation of the god, and said to be immortal by the local priesthood. The temple sacristans showed it to Apion the grammarian, who reports the fact, but is very sceptical in the matter.

[3] The texts quoted by Chabas and Lepsius to show that the sun is the right eye of Horus also prove that his left eye is the moon.

[4] Drawn by Faucher-Gudin, from the ceiling of the Ramesseum. On the right, the *female hippopotamus* bearing the *crocodile*, and leaning on the *Monâît;* in the middle, the *Haunch,* here represented by the whole bull; to the left, *Selkit* and the *Sparrow-hawk*, with the *Lion*, and the *Giant fighting the Crocodile.*

The sow fell upon it, tore it out of the face of heaven, and cast it, streaming with blood and tears, into the celestial Nile, where it was gradually extinguished, and lost for days; but its twin, the sun, or its guardian, the cynocephalus, immediately set forth to find it and to restore it to Horus. No sooner was it replaced, than it slowly recovered,

THE LUNAR BARK, SELF-PROPELLED, UNDER THE PROTECTION OF THE TWO EYES.

and renewed its radiance; when it was well—*ûzaît*—the sow again attacked and mutilated it, and the gods rescued and again revived it. Each month there was a fortnight of youth and of growing splendour, followed by a fortnight's agony and ever-increasing pallor. It was born to die, and died to be born again twelve times in the year, and each of these cycles measured a month for the inhabitants of the

world.   One invariable accident from time to time disturbed the routine of its existence.   Profiting by some
distraction of the guardians, the sow greedily swallowed
it, and then its light went out suddenly, instead of fading
gradually.   These eclipses, which alarmed mankind at least
as much as did those of the sun, were scarcely more than
momentary, the gods compelling the monster to cast up
the eye before it had been destroyed.   Every evening the
lunar bark issued out of Hades by the door which Râ had

THE HAUNCH, AND THE FEMALE HIPPOPOTAMUS.[1]

passed through in the morning, and as it rose on the horizon, the star-lamps scattered over the firmament appeared
one by one, giving light here and there like the camp-fires
of a distant army.   However many of them there might
be, there were as many Indestructibles—*Akhîmû Sokû*—or
Unchanging Ones—*Akhîmû Ûrdû*—whose charge it was to
attend upon them and watch over their maintenance.[2]

[1] Drawn by Faucher-Gudin, from the rectangular zodiac carved upon the
ceiling of the great temple of Denderah (Dümichen, *Resultate*, vol. ii. pl.
xxxix.).

[2] The *Akhîmû-Sokû* and the *Akhîmû-Ûrdû* have been very variously
defined by different Egyptologists who have studied them.   Chabas considered them to be gods or genii of the constellations of the ecliptic, which

They were not scattered at random by the hand which
had suspended them, but their distribution had been
ordered in accordance with a certain plan, and they were
arranged in fixed groups like so many star republics, each
being independent of its neighbours. They represented the
outlines of bodies of men and animals dimly traced out
upon the depths of night, but shining with greater bril-
liancy in certain important places. The seven stars which
we liken to a chariot (Charles's Wain) suggested to the
Egyptians the haunch of an ox placed on the northern edge
of the horizon.[1] Two lesser stars connected the haunch
—*Maskhaît*—with thirteen others, which recalled the silhouette of a female hippopotamus—*Rirît*—erect upon her

mark the apparent course of the sun through the sky. Following the indications given by Dévéria, he also thought them to be the sailors of the solar
bark, and perhaps the gods of the twelve hours, divided into two classes :
the *Akhîmû-Sokû* being those who are rowing, and the *Akhîmû-Ûrdû* those
who are resting. But texts found and cited by BRUGSCH show that the
Akhîmû-Sokû are the planets accompanying Râ in the northern sky, while
the *Akhîmû-Ûrdû* are his escort in the south. The nomenclature of the stars
included in these two classes is furnished by monuments of widely different
epochs. The two names should be translated according to the meaning of
their component words : *Akhîmû Sokû*, those who know not destruction, the
Indestructibles ; and *Akhîmû Ûrdû* (*Ûrzû*), those who know not the immobility
of death, the *Imperishables.*

[1] The forms of the constellations, and the number of stars composing
them in the astronomy of different periods, are known from the astronomical
scenes of tombs and temples. The identity of the *Haunch* with the *Chariot*,
or *Great Bear* of modern astronomy, was discovered by LEPSIUS and confirmed by BIOT. MARIETTE pointed out that the Pyramid Arabs applied the
name of the *Haunch* (*er-Rigl*) to the same group of stars as that thus
designated by the ancient Egyptians. CHAMPOLLION had noted the position
of the *Haunch* in the northern sky, but had not suggested any identification.
The *Haunch* appertained to Sît-Typhon.

hind legs,[1] and jauntily carrying upon her shoulders a monstrous crocodile whose jaws opened threateningly above her head. Eighteen luminaries of varying size and splendour, forming a group hard by the hippopotamus, indicated

ORION, SOTHIS, AND TWO HORUS-PLANETS STANDING IN THEIR BARKS.[2]

the outline of a gigantic lion couchant, with stiffened tail, its head turned to the right, and facing the Haunch.[3] Most

[1] The connection of *Rirît*, the female hippopotamus, with the Haunch is made quite clear in scenes from Philæ and Edfû, representing Isis holding back Typhon by a chain, that he might do no hurt to Sâbû-Osiris. JOLLOIS and DEVILLIERS thought that the hippopotamus was the *Great Bear*. BIOT contested their conclusions, and while holding that the hippopotamus might at least in part present our constellation of the Dragon, thought that it was probably included in the scene only as an ornament, or as an emblem. The present tendency is to identify the hippopotamus with the Dragon and with certain stars not included in the constellations surrounding it.

[2] From the astronomic ceiling in the tomb of Seti I. (LEFÉBURE, 4th part, pl. xxxvi.).

[3] The Lion, with its eighteen stars, is represented on the tomb of Seti I.; on the ceiling of the Ramesseum; and on the sarcophagus of Htari.

of the constellations never left the sky : night after night they were to be found almost in the same places, and always shining with the same even light. Others borne by a slow movement passed annually beyond the limits of sight for months at a time. Five at least of our planets were known from all antiquity, and their characteristic colours and appearances carefully noted. Sometimes each was thought to be a hawk-headed Horus. Ûapshetatûi, our Jupiter, Kahiri-(Saturn), Sobkû-(Mercury), steered their barks straight ahead like Iâûhû and Râ; but Mars-Doshiri, the red, sailed backwards. As a star Bonû, the bird (Venus) had a dual personality; in the evening it was Ûati, the lonely star which is the first to rise, often before nightfall; in the morning it became Tiûnûtiri, the god who hails the sun before his rising and proclaims the dawn of day.

Sahû and Sopdît, Orion and Sirius, were the rulers of this mysterious world. Sahû consisted of fifteen stars, seven large and eight

SAHÛ-ORION.[1]

The Lion is sometimes shown as having a crocodile's tail. According to BIOT the Egyptian Lion has nothing in common with the Greek constellation of that name, nor yet with our own, but was composed of smaller stars, belonging to the Greek constellation of the Cup or to the continuation of the Hydra, so that its head, its body, and its tail would follow the a of the Hydra, between the ψ' and ξ of that constellation, or the γ of the Virgin.

[1] Drawn by Faucher-Gudin, from a small bronze in the Gizeh Museum, published by MARIETTE, in the *Album photographique du Musée de Boulaq*, pl. 9. The legs are a modern restoration.

small, so arranged as to represent a runner darting through space, while the fairest of them shone above his head, and marked him out from afar to the admiration of mortals. With his right hand he flourished the *crux ansata*, and turning his head towards Sothis as he beckoned her on with his left, seemed as though inviting her to follow

ORION AND THE COW SOTHIS SEPARATED BY THE SPARROW-HAWK.[1]

him. The goddess, standing sceptre in hand, and crowned with a diadem of tall feathers surmounted by her most radiant star, answered the call of Sahû with a gesture, and quietly embarked in pursuit as though in no anxiety to overtake him. Sometimes she is represented as a cow lying down in her bark, with tree stars along her back, and Sirius flaming from between her

[1] Scene from the rectangular zodiac of Denderah, drawn by Faucher-Gudin, from a photograph taken with magnesium light by DÜMICHEN.

horns.[1] Not content to shine by night only, her bluish rays, suddenly darted forth in full daylight and without any warning, often described upon the sky the mystic lines of the triangle which stood for her name. It was then that she produced those curious phenomena of the zodiacal light which other legends attributed to Horus himself. One, and perhaps the most ancient of the innumerable accounts of this god and goddess, represented Sahû as a wild hunter. A world as vast as ours rested upon the other side of the iron firmament; like ours, it was distributed into seas, and continents divided by rivers and canals, but peopled by races unknown to men. Sahû traversed it during the day, surrounded by genii who presided over the lamps forming his constellation. At his appearing " the stars prepared themselves for battle, the heavenly archers rushed forward, the bones of the gods upon the horizon trembled at the sight of him," for it was no common game that he hunted, but the very gods themselves. One attendant secured the prey with a lasso, as bulls are caught in the pastures, while another examined each capture to decide if it were pure and good for food. This being determined, others bound the divine victim, cut its throat, disembowelled it, cut up its carcass, cast the joints into a pot, and superintended their cooking. Sahû did not devour indifferently all that the fortune of the chase might bring him, but classified his game in

[1] The identity of the cow with Sothis was discovered by JOLLOIS and DEVILLIERS. It is under this animal form that Sothis is represented in most of the Græco-Roman temples, at Denderah, Edfû, Esneh, Dêr el-Medineh.

accordance with his wants. He ate the great gods at his breakfast in the morning, the lesser gods at his dinner towards noon, and the small ones at his supper; the old were rendered more tender by roasting. As each god was assimilated by him, its most precious virtues were transfused into himself; by the wisdom of the old was his wisdom

AMON-RÂ, AS MÎNÛ OF COPTOS, AND INVESTED WITH HIS EMBLEMS.[1]

strengthened, the youth of the young repaired the daily waste of his own youth, and all their fires, as they penetrated his being, served to maintain the perpetual splendour of his light.

[1] Scene on the north wall of the Hypostyle Hall at Karnak ; drawn by Boudier, from a photograph by Insinger, taken in 1882. The king, Seti I., is presenting bouquets of leaves to Amon-Minû. Behind the god stands Isis (of Coptos), septre and *crux ansata* in hand.

The nome gods who presided over the destinies of Egyptian cities, and formed a true feudal system of divinities, belonged to one or other of these natural categories. In vain do they present themselves under the most shifting aspects and the most deceptive attributes; in vain disguise themselves with the utmost care; a closer examination generally discloses the principal features of their original physiognomies. Osiris of the Delta, Khnûmû of the Cataract, Harshâfîtû of Heracleopolis, were each of them incarnations of the fertilizing and life-sustaining Nile. Wherever there is some important change in the river, there they are more especially installed and worshipped: Khnûmû at the place of its entering into Egypt, and again at the town of Hâûrit, near the point where a great arm branches off from the Eastern stream to flow towards the Libyan hills and form the Bahr-Yûsuf: Harshâfîtû at the gorges of the Fayûm, where the Bahr-Yûsuf leaves the valley; and, finally, Osiris at Mendes and at Busiris, towards the mouth of the middle branch, which was held to be the true Nile by the people of the land. Isis of Bûto denoted the black vegetable mould of the valley, the distinctive soil of Egypt annually covered and fertilized by the inundation.[1] But the earth in general, as distinguished from the sky—the earth with its continents, its seas, its alternation of barren deserts and fertile lands —was represented as a man: Phtah at Memphis, Amon

---

[1] In the case of Isis, as in that of Osiris, we must mark the original character; and note her characteristics as goddess of the Delta before she had become a multiple and contradictory personality through being confounded with other divinities.

at Thebes, Mînû at Coptos and at Panopolis. Amon seems rather to have symbolized the productive soil, while Mînû reigned over the desert. But these were fine distinctions, not invariably insisted upon, and his worshippers often invested Amon with the most significant attributes of Mînû. The Sky-gods, like the Earth-gods, were separated into two groups, the one consisting of women : Hâthor of Denderah, or Nît of Saïs; the other composed of men identical with Horus, or derived from him : Anhûri-Shû of Sebennytos and Thinis; Harmerati, Horus of the two eyes, at Pharbæthos ; Har-Sapdi, Horus the source of the zodiacal light, in the Wâdy Tumilât; and finally Harhûdîti at Edfû. Râ, the solar disk, was enthroned at Heliopolis, and sun-gods were numerous among the nome deities, but they were sun-gods closely connected with gods representing the sky, and resembled Horus quite as much as Râ. Whether under the name of Horus or of Anhûri, the sky was early identified with its most brilliant luminary, its solar eye, and its divinity was as it were fused into that of the Sun. Horus the Sun, and Râ, the Sun-God of Heliopolis, had

ANHÔRI.[1]

so permeated each other that none could say where the one began and the other ended. One by one all the

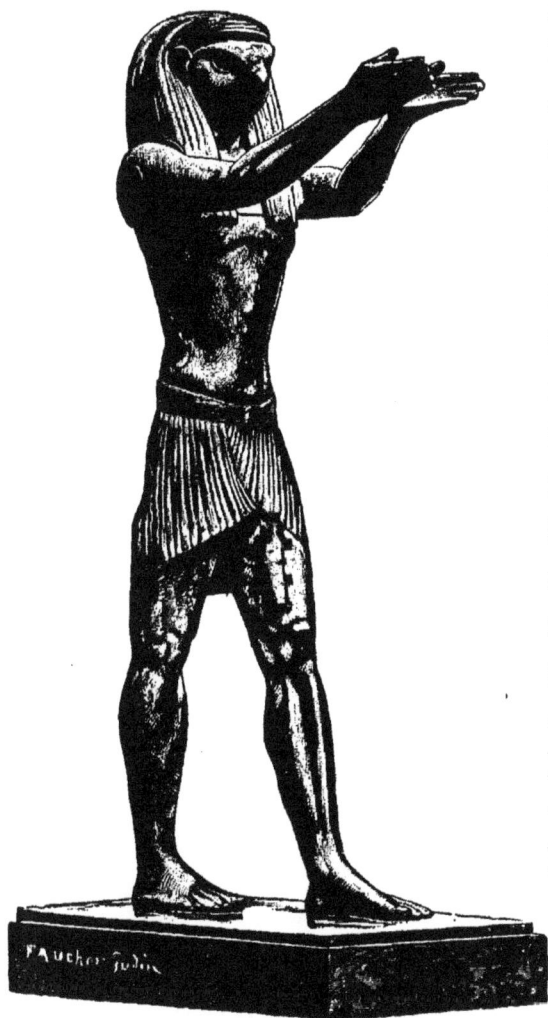

functions of Râ had been usurped by Horus, and all the designations of Horus had been appropriated by Râ. The sun was styled Harmakhûîti, the Horus of the two mountains — that is, the Horus who comes forth from the mountain of the east in the morning, and retires at evening into the mountain of the west;[1] or Hartimâ, Horus the Pikeman, that Horus whose lance spears the hippopotamus or the serpent of the celestial river; or Harnûbi, the Golden Horus, the great golden

THE HAWK-HEADED HORUS [2]

[1] From the time of Champollion, Harmakhûîti has been identified with the Harmachis of the Greeks, the great Sphinx.

[2] A bronze of the Saïte period, from the Posno collection, and now in the Louvre; drawn by Faucher-Gudin. The god is represented as upholding a libation vase with both hands, and pouring the life-giving water upon the king, standing, or prostrate, before him. In performing this ceremony, he

sparrow-hawk with mottled plumage, who puts all other birds to flight; and these titles were indifferently applied to each of the feudal gods who represented the sun. The latter were numerous. Sometimes, as in the case of Harkhobi, Horus of Khobiû,¹ a geographical qualification was appended to the generic term of Horus, while specific names, almost invariably derived from the parts which they were supposed to play, were borne by others. The sky-god worshipped at Thinis in Upper Egypt, at Zarit and at Sebennytos in Lower Egypt, was called Anhûri. When he assumed the attributes of Râ, and took upon himself the solar nature, his name was interpreted as denoting the conqueror of the sky. He was essentially combative. Crowned with a group of upright plumes, his spear raised and ever ready to strike the foe, he advanced along the firmament and triumphantly traversed it day by day.² The sun-god who at Medamôt Taûd and Erment had preceded Amon as ruler of the Theban plain, was also a warrior, and his name of Montû had reference to his method of fighting. He was depicted as brandishing a curved sword and cutting off the heads of his adversaries.³

was always assisted by another god, generally by Sît, sometimes by Thot or Anubis.

¹ *Harkhobi, Harûmkhobiû* is the Horus of the marshes (*khobiû*) of the Delta, the lesser Horus the son of Isis, who was also made into the son of Osiris.

² The right reading of the name was given as far back as LEPSIUS. The part played by the god, and the nature of the link connecting him with Shû, have been explained by MASPERO. The Greeks transcribed his name Onouris, and identified him with Ares.

³ Montû preceded Amon as god of the land between Kûs and Gebelên, and he recovered his old position in the Graeco-Roman period after the

Each of the feudal gods naturally cherished pretensions to universal dominion, and proclaimed himself the suzerain, the father of all the gods, as the local prince was the suzerain, the father of all men ; but the effective suzerainty of god or prince really ended where that of his peers ruling

THE HORUS OF HIBONÛ, ON THE BACK OF THE GAZELLE.

over the adjacent nomes began. The goddesses shared in the exercise of supreme power, and had the same right of

destruction of Thebes. Most Egyptologists, and finally BRUGSCH, made him into a secondary form of Amon, which is contrary to what we know of the history of the province. Just as Onû of the south (Erment) preceded Thebes as the most important town in that district, so Montû had been its most honoured god. HERR WIEDEMANN thinks the name related to that of Amon and derived from it, with the addition of the final tû.

inheritance and possession as regards sovereignty that women had in human law.[1] Isis was entitled lady and mistress at Bûto, as Hâthor was at Denderah, and as Nit at Saïs, "the firstborn, when as yet there had been no birth." They enjoyed in their cities the same honours as the male gods in theirs; as the latter were kings, so were they queens, and all bowed down before them. The animal gods, whether entirely in the form of beasts, or having human bodies attached to animal heads, shared omnipotence with those in human form. Horus of Hibonû swooped down upon the back of a gazelle like a hunting hawk, Hâthor of Denderah was a cow, Bastit of Bubastis was a cat or a tigress, while Nekhabit of El Kab was a great bald-headed vulture.[2] Hermopolis worshipped the ibis and cynocephalus of Thot; Oxyrrhynchus the *mormyrus* fish;[3] and Ombos and the Fayûm a crocodile, under the name of Sobkû,[4] sometimes with the epithet of Azaï,

[1] In attempts at reconstituting Egyptian religions, no adequate weight has hitherto been given to the equality of gods and goddesses, a fact to which attention was first called by MASPERO (*Études de Mythologie et d'Archéologie Égyptiennes*, vol. ii. p. 253, et seq.).

[2] Nekhabît, the goddess of the south, is the vulture, so often represented in scenes of war or sacrifice, who hovers over the head of the Pharaohs. She is also shown as a vulture-headed woman.

[3] We have this on the testimony of classic writers, STRABO, book xvii. p. 812, *De Iside et Osiride*, § vii., 1872, PARTHEY's edition, pp. 9, 30, 128; ÆLIANUS, *Hist. anim.*, book x. § 46.

[4] *Sobkû, Sovkû* is the animal's name, and the exact translation of *Sovkû* would be crocodile-god. Its Greek transcription is Σοῦχος. On account of the assonance of the names he was sometimes confounded with *Sivû, Sibû* by the Egyptians themselves, and thus obtained the titles of that god. This was especially the case at the time when Sît having been proscribed, Sovkû the crocodile, who was connected with Sît, shared his evil reputation, and endeavoured to disguise his name or true character as much as possible.

the brigand.[1] We cannot always understand what led the inhabitants of each nome to affect one animal rather than another. Why, towards Græco-Roman times, should they have worshipped the jackal, or even the dog, at Siût?[2] How came Sît to be incarnate in a fennec, or in an imaginary quadruped?[3] Occasionally, however, we can follow the train of thought that determined their choice. The habit of certain monkeys in assembling as it were

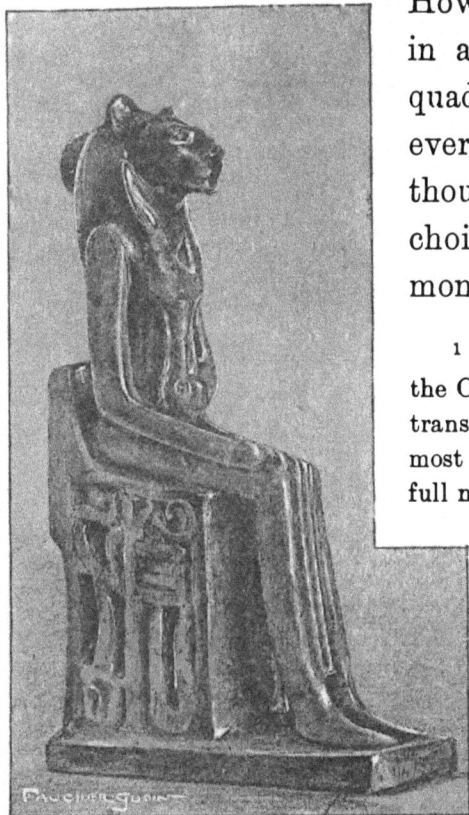

THE CAT-HEADED BAST.[4]

[1] Azaï is generally considered to be the Osiris of the Fayûm, but he was only transformed into Osiris, and that by the most daring process of assimilation. His full name defines him as *Osiri Azai hi hâit To-shît* (*Osiris the Brigand, who is in the Fayûm*), that is to say, as Sovkû identified with Osiris.

[2] Ûapuaîtû, the *guide of the celestial ways*, who must not be confounded with Anubis of the Cynopolite nome of Upper Egypt, was originally the feudal god of Siût. He guided human souls to the paradise of the Oasis, and the sun upon its southern path by day, and its northern path by night.

[3] Champollion, Rosellini, Lepsius, have held that the Typhonian animal was a purely imaginary one, and Wilkinson says that the Egyptians themselves admitted its unreality by representing it along with other fantastic beasts This would rather tend to show that they believed in its actual existence (cf. p. 112 of this *History*). PLEYTE thinks that it may be a degenerated form of the figure of the ass or oryx.

[4] Drawn by Faucher-Gudin, from a green enamelled figure in my possession (Saite period).

in full court, and chattering noisily a little before sunrise and sunset, would almost justify the as yet uncivilized Egyptians

THE FENNEC, SUPPOSED PROTOTYPE OF THE TYPHONIAN ANIMAL.

in entrusting cynocephali with the charge of hailing the god morning and evening as he appeared in the east, or passed

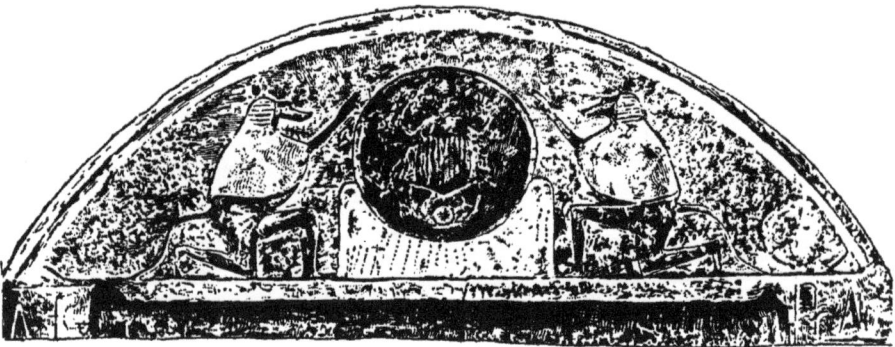

TWO CYNOCEPHALI IN ADORATION BEFORE THE RISING SUN.[1]

away in the west. If Râ was held to be a grasshopper under the Old Empire, it was because he flew far up

[1] Sculptured and painted scene from the tympanum of a stela in the Gizeh Museum. Drawn by Faucher-Gudin, from a photograph by Émil Brugsch-Bey.

in the sky like the clouds of locusts driven from Central
Africa which suddenly fall upon the fields and ravage them.
Most of the Nile-gods, Khnûmû, Osiris, Harshafitû, were
incarnate in the form of a ram or of a buck. Does not the
masculine vigour and procreative rage of these animals
naturally point them out as fitting images of the life-giving
Nile and the overflowing of its waters? It is easy to
understand how the neighbourhood of a marsh or of a
rock-encumbered rapid should have suggested the crocodile
as supreme deity to the inhabitants of the Fayûm or of
Ombos. The crocodiles there multiplied so rapidly as to
constitute a serious danger; there they had the mastery,
and could be appeased only by means of prayers and sacrifices. When instinctive terror had been superseded by
reflection, and some explanation was offered of the origin
of the various cults, the very nature of the animal seemed
to justify the veneration with which it was regarded. The
crocodile is amphibious; and Sobkû was supposed to be a
crocodile, because before the creation the sovereign god
plunged recklessly into the dark waters and came forth to
form the world, as the crocodile emerges from the river
to lay its eggs upon the bank.

Most of the feudal divinities began their lives in solitary
grandeur, apart from, and often hostile to, their neighbours.
Families were assigned to them later.[1] Each appropriated

[1] The existence of the Egyptian triads was discovered and defined by
CHAMPOLLION. These triads have long served as the basis upon which
modern writers have sought to establish their systems of the Egyptian
religion. Brugsch was the first who rightly attempted to replace the triad
by the Ennead, in his book *Religion und Mythologie der alten Ægypter*. The
process of forming local triads, as here set forth, was first pointed out by

two companions and formed a trinity, or as it is generally called, a triad. But there were several kinds of triads. In nomes subject to a god, the local deity was frequently content with one wife and one son; but often he was united to two goddesses, who were at once his sisters and his wives according to the national custom. Thus, Thot of Hermopolis possessed himself of a harem consisting of Seshaît-Safk-hîtâbûi and Nahmâûît. Tûmû divided the homage of the inhabitants of Helio-polis with Nebthôtpît and with Iûsasît. Khnûmû seduced and married the two fairies of the neighbouring cataract—Anûkit the constrainer, who compresses the Nile between its rocks at Philæ and at Syene, and Satît the archeress, who shoots forth the current straight and swift as an arrow.[1] Where a goddess reigned over a nome, the triad was completed by two male deities, a divine

NÎT OF SAÏS.

consort and a divine son. Nît of Saïs had taken for her husband Osiris of Mendes, and borne him a lion's whelp, Ari-hos-nofir.[2] Hâthor of Denderah had com-

MASPERO (*Études de Mythologie et d'Archéologie Égyptiennes*, vol. ii. p. 269, et seq.).

[1] MASPERO, *Études de Mythologie et d'Archéologie Égyptiennes*, vol. ii. p. 273, et seq.

[2] *Arihosnofir* means *the lion whose gaze has a beneficent fascination.* He also goes under the name of *Tûtû*, which seems as though it should be translated "*the bounding*,"—a mere epithet characterizing one gait of the lion-god's.

pleted her household with Haroêris and a younger Horus, with the epithet of Ahi—he who strikes the sistrum.[1] A triad containing two goddesses pro-duced no legitimate offspring, and was unsatisfactory to a people who regarded the lack of progeny as a curse from heaven; one in which the presence of a son promised to ensure the perpetuity of the race was more in keeping with the idea of a blessed and prosperous family, as that of gods should be. Triads of the former kind were there-fore almost everywhere broken up into two new triads, each containing a divine father, a divine mother, and a divine son. Two fruitful households arose from the barren union of Thot with Safkhîtâbûi and Nahmâûît: one composed of Thot, Safkhîtâbûi, and Harnûbi, the golden sparrow-hawk;[3] into the other

IMHOTPÛ.[2]

---

[1] BRUGSCH explains the name of Ahi as meaning *he who causes his waters to rise*, and recognizes this personage as being, among other things, a form of the Nile. The interpretation offered by myself is borne out by the many scenes representing the child of Hâthor playing upon the sistrum and the *mondît*. Moreover, *ahi, ahît* is an invariable title of the priests and priestesses whose office it is, during religious ceremonies, to strike the sistrum, and that other mystic musical instrument, the sounding whip called *mondît*.

[2] Drawn by Faucher-Gudin, from a bronze statuette encrusted with gold, in the Gizeh Museum. The seat is alabaster, and of modern manufacture.

[3] This somewhat rare triad, noted by WILKINSON, is sculptured on the wall of a chamber in the Tûrah quarries.

Nahmâûît and her nursling Nofirhorû entered. The persons united with the old feudal divinities in order to form triads were not all of the same class. Goddesses, especially, were made to order, and might often be described as grammatical, so obvious is the linguistic device to which they owe their being. From Râ, Amon, Horus, Sobkû, female Râs, Amons, Horuses, and Sobkûs were derived, by the addition of the regular feminine affix to the primitive masculine names—Râit, Amonît, Horît, Sobkît.[1] In the same way, detached cognomens of divine fathers were embodied in divine sons. Imhotpû, "he who comes in peace," was merely one of the epithets of Phtah before he became incarnate as the third member of the Memphite triad.[2] In other cases, alliances were contracted between divinities of ancient stock, but natives of different nomes, as in the case of Isis of Bûto and the Mendesian Osiris; of Haroêris of Edfû and Hâthor of Denderah.

NOFIRTÛMÛ.[3]

[1] MASPERO, Études de Mythologie et d'Archéologie Égyptiennes, vol. ii. pp. 7, 8, 256.

[2] Imhotpû, the Imouthes of the Greeks, and by them identified with Æsculapius, was discovered by SALT, and his name was first translated as he who comes with offering. The translation, he who comes in peace, proposed by E. de Rougé, is now universally adopted. Imhotpû did not take form until the time of the New Empire; his great popularity at Memphis and throughout Egypt dates from the Saite and Greek periods.

[3] Drawn by Faucher-Gudin, from a bronze statuette incrusted with gold, in the Gizeh Museum.

In the same manner Sokhît of Letopolis and Bastît of Bubastis were appropriated as wives to Phtah of Memphis, Nofirtûmû being represented as his son by both unions.[1] These improvised connections were generally determined by considerations of vicinity; the gods of conterminous principalities were married as the children of kings of two adjoining kingdoms are married, to form or to consolidate relations, and to establish bonds of kinship between rival powers whose unremitting hostility would mean the swift ruin of entire peoples.

The system of triads, begun in primitive times and continued unbrokenly up to the last days of Egyptian polytheism, far from in any way lowering the prestige of the feudal gods, was rather the means of enhancing it in the eyes of the multitude. Powerful lords as the new-comers might be at home, it was only in the strength of an auxiliary title that they could enter a strange city, and then only on condition of submitting to its religious law. Hâthor, supreme at Denderah, shrank into insignificance before Haroêris at Edfû, and there retained only the somewhat subordinate part of a wife in the house of her husband.[2] On the other hand, Haroêris when at Denderah descended from the supreme rank, and was nothing more than the

[1] Originally, Nofirtûmû appears to have been the son of cat or lioness-headed goddesses, Bastit and Sokhît, and from them he may have inherited the lion's head with which he is often represented. His name shows him to have been in the first place an incarnation of Atûmû, but he was affiliated to the god Phtah of Memphis when that god became the husband of his mothers, and preceded Imhotpû as the third personage in the oldest Memphite triad.

[2] Each year, and at a certain time, the goddess came in high state to spend a few days in the great temple of Edfû, with her husband Haroêris.

almost useless consort of the lady Hâthor. His name came first in invocations of the triad because of his position therein as husband and father; but this was simply a concession to the propriety of etiquette, and even though named in second place, Hâthor was none the less the real chief of Denderah and of its divine family.[1] Thus, the principal personage in any triad was always the one who had been patron of the nome previous to the introduction of the triad: in some places the father-god, and in others the mother-goddess. The son in a divine triad had of himself but limited authority. When Isis and Osiris were his parents, he was generally an infant Horus, naked, or simply adorned with necklaces and bracelets; a thick lock of hair depended from his temple, and his mother squatting on her heels, or else sitting, nursed him upon her knees, offering him

HORUS, SON OF ISIS.[2]

[1] The part played by Haroêris at Denderah was so inconsiderable that the triad containing him is not to be found in the temple. " In all our four volumes of plates, the triad is not once represented, and this is the more remarkable since at Thebes, at Memphis, at Philæ, at the cataracts, at Elephantinê, at Edfû, among all the data which one looks to find in temples, the triad is most readily distinguished by the visitor. But we must not therefore conclude that there was no triad in this case. The triad of Edfû consists of Hor-Hut, Hâthor, and Hor-Sam-ta-ui. The triad of Denderah contains Hâthor, Hor-Hut, and Hor-Sam-ta-ui. The difference is obvious. At Edfû, the male principle, as represented by Hor-Hut, takes the first place, whereas the first person at Denderah is Hâthor, who represents the female principle " (MARIETTE, Dendérah, Texte, pp. 80, 81).

[2] Drawn by Faucher-Gudin from a statuette in the Gizeh Museum (MARIETTE, Album du Musée de Boulaq, pl. 4).

her breast.[1] Even in triads where the son was supposed to have attained to man's estate, he held the
lowest place, and there was enjoined upon him the same
respectful attitude towards his parents as is observed
by children of human race in the presence of theirs.
He took the lowest place at all solemn receptions, spoke
only with his parents' permission, acted only by their
command and as the agent of their will. Occasionally he
was vouchsafed a character of his own, and filled a definite
position, as at Memphis, where Imhotpû was the patron of
science.[2] But, generally, he was not considered as having
either office or marked individuality; his being was but a
feeble reflection of his father's, and possessed neither life
nor power except as derived from him. Two such con-
tiguous personalities must needs have been confused, and,
as a matter of fact, were so confused as to become at length
nothing more than two aspects of the same god, who
united in his own person degrees of relationship mutually
exclusive of each other in a human family. Father,
inasmuch as he was the first member of the triad; son,
by virtue of being its third member; identical with himself
in both capacities, he was at once his own father, his own
son, and the husband of his mother.

Gods, like men, might be resolved into at least two

---

[1] For representations of Harpocrates, the child Horus, see LANZONE,
Dizionario di Mitologia Egizia, pls. ccxxvii., ccxxviii., and particularly pl. cccx.
2, where there is a scene in which the young god, represented as a sparrow-
hawk, is nevertheless sucking the breast of his mother Isis with his beak.

[2] Hence he is generally represented as seated, or squatting, and
attentively reading a papyrus roll, which lies open upon his knees; cf. the
illustration on p. 142.

elements, soul and body;[1] but in Egypt, the conception of the soul varied in different times and in different schools. It might be an insect—butterfly, bee, or praying mantis;[2] or a bird—the ordinary sparrow-hawk, the human-headed sparrow-hawk, a heron or a crane—*bi, baï*—whose wings enabled it to pass rapidly through space;[3] or the black shadow—*khaîbît*—that is attached to every body, but which death sets free, and which thenceforward leads an independent existence, so that it can move about at will, and go out into the open sunlight. Finally, it might be a kind of light shadow, like a reflection from the surface of calm water, or

THE BLACK SHADOW COMING OUT INTO THE SUNLIGHT.[4]

---

[1] In one of the Pyramid texts, Sâhû-Orion, the wild hunter, captures the gods, slaughters and disembowels them, cooks their joints, their haunches, their legs, in his burning cauldrons, and feeds on their souls as well as on their bodies. A god was not limited to a single body and a single soul; we know from several texts that Râ had *seven souls and fourteen doubles.*

[2] Mr. LEPAGE-RENOUF supposes that the soul may have been considered as being a butterfly at times, as in Greece. M. LEFÉBURE thinks that it must sometimes have been incarnate as a wasp—I should rather say a bee or a praying mantis.

[3] The simple sparrow-hawk 🦅 is chiefly used to denote the soul of a god; the human-headed sparrow-hawk 🦅, the heron, or the crane 🦅. is used indifferently for human or divine souls. . It is from HORAPOLLO that we learn this symbolic significance of the sparrow-hawk and the pronunciation of the name of the soul as *baï.*

[4] Drawn by Faucher-Gudin, from NAVILLE's *Das Thebanische Todtenbuch,* vol. i. pl. civ. Pc.

from a polished mirror, the living and coloured projection of the human figure, a double—*ka*—reproducing
in minutest detail the complete image of the object

THE AUGUST SOULS OF OSIRIS AND HORUS IN ADORATION BEFORE THE SOLAR DISK.[1]

[1] Drawn by Faucher-Gudin, from a photograph by DÜMICHEN, of a scene
on the cornice of the front room of Osiris on the terrace of the great temple
of Denderah.   The soul on the left belongs to Horus, that on the right to
Osiris, lord of Amentît.   Each bears upon its head the group of tall feathers
which is characteristic of figures of Anhûri (cf. p. 103).

or the person to whom it belonged.[1] The soul, the shadow, the double of a god, was in no way essentially different from the soul, shadow, or double of a man; his body, indeed, was moulded out of a more rarefied substance, and generally invisible, but endowed with the same qualities, and subject to the same imperfections as ours. The gods, therefore, on the whole, were more ethereal, stronger, more powerful, better fitted to command, to enjoy, and to suffer than ordinary men, but they were still men. They had bones,[2] muscles, flesh, blood; they were hungry and ate, they were thirsty and drank; our passions, griefs, joys, infirmities, were also theirs. The *sa*, a mysterious fluid, circulated throughout their members, and carried with it health, vigour, and life. They were not all equally charged with it; some had more, others less, their energy being in proportion to the amount which they contained. The better supplied willingly gave of their superfluity to those who lacked it, and all could readily transmit it to mankind, this transfusion being easily accomplished in the temples. The king, or any ordinary man who wished to be thus impregnated, presented himself before the statue of the god, and squatted at its feet with his back towards it. The statue then placed its right hand

---

[1] The nature of the double has long been misapprehended by Egyptologists, who had even made its name into a kind of pronominal form. That nature was publicly and almost simultaneously announced in 1878, first by MASPERO, and directly afterwards by LEPAGE-RENOUF.

[2] For example, the text of the *Destruction of Men*, and other documents, teach us that the flesh of the aged sun had become gold, and his bones silver. The blood of Râ is mentioned in the *Book of the Dead*, as well as the blood of Isis and of other divinities.

upon the nape of his neck, and by making passes, caused the fluid to flow from it, and to accumulate in him as in a receiver. This rite was of temporary efficacy only, and required frequent renewal in order that its benefit might be

THE KING AFTER HIS CORONATION RECEIVING THE IMPOSITION OF THE *SA*.[1]

[1] Drawn by Boudier from a photograph by M. Gayet, taken in 1889, of a scene in the hypostyle hall at Lûxor. This illustration shows the relative positions of prince and god. Amon, after having placed the pschent upon the head of the Pharaoh Amenôthes III., who kneels before him, proceeds to *impose the sa.*

maintained. By using or transmitting it the gods them-selves exhausted their *sa* of life; and the less vigorous replenished themselves from the stronger, while the latter went to draw fresh fulness from a mysterious pond in the northern sky, called the "pond of the Sa."[1] Divine bodies, continually recruited by the influx of this magic fluid, preserved their vigour far beyond the term allotted to the bodies of men and beasts. Age, instead of quickly destroying them, hardened and transformed them into precious metals. Their bones were changed to silver, their flesh to gold; their hair, piled up and painted blue, after the manner of great chiefs, was turned into lapis-lazuli.[2] This transformation of each into an animated statue did not altogether do away with the ravages of time. Decrepitude was no less irremediable with them than with men, although it came to them more slowly; when the sun had grown old "his mouth trembled, his drivelling ran down to earth, his spittle dropped upon the ground."

None of the feudal gods had escaped this destiny; for them as for mankind the day came when they must leave

---

[1] It is thus that in the *Tale of the Daughter of the Prince of Bakhtan* we find that one of the statues of the Theban Konsû supplies itself with *sa* from another statue representing one of the most powerful forms of the god. The *pond of Sa*, whither the gods go to draw the magic fluid, is mentioned in the Pyramid texts.

[2] Cf. the text of the *Destruction of Men* (ll. 1, 2) referred to above, where age produces these transformations in the body of the sun. This changing of the bodies of the gods into gold, silver, and precious stones, explains why the alchemists, who were disciples of the Egyptians, often compared the transmutation of metals to the metamorphosis of a genius or of a divinity: they thought by their art to hasten at will that which was the slow work of nature.

the city and go forth to the tomb.[1] The ancients long refused to believe that death was natural and inevitable. They thought that life, once begun, might go on indefinitely : if no accident stopped it short, why should it cease of itself? And so men did not die in Egypt ; they were assassinated. The murderer often belonged to this world, and was easily recognized as another man, an animal, some inanimate object such as a stone loosened from the hillside, a tree which fell upon the passer-by and crushed him. But often too the murderer was of the unseen world, and so was hidden, his presence being betrayed in his malignant attacks only. He was a god, an evil spirit, a disembodied soul who slily insinuated itself into the living man, or fell upon him with irresistible violence—illness being a struggle between the one possessed and the power which possessed him. As soon as the former succumbed he was carried away from his own people, and his place knew him no more. But had all ended for him with the moment in which he had ceased to breathe? As to the body, no one was ignorant of its natural fate. It quickly fell to decay, and a few years sufficed to reduce it to a skeleton. And as for the skeleton, in the lapse of centuries that too was

---

[1] The idea of the inevitable death of the gods is expressed in other places as well as in a passage of the eighth chapter of the *Book of the Dead* (NAVILLE's edition), which has not to my knowledge hitherto been noticed : "I am that Osiris in the West, and Osiris knoweth his day in which he shall be no more ; " that is to say, the day of his death when he will cease to exist. All the gods, Atûmû, Horus, Râ, Thot, Phtah, Khnûmû, are represented under the forms of mummies, and this implies that they are dead. Moreover, their tombs were pointed out in several places in Egypt.

disintegrated and became a mere train of dust, to be blown away by the first breath of wind. The soul might have a longer career and fuller fortunes, but these were believed to be dependent upon those of the body, and commensurate with them. Every advance made in the process of decomposition robbed . the soul of some part of itself; its consciousness gradually faded until nothing was left but a vague and hollow form that vanished altogether when the corpse had entirely disappeared. From an early date the Egyptians had endeavoured to arrest this gradual destruction of the human organism, and their first effort to this end naturally was directed towards the preservation of the body, since without it the existence of the soul could not be ensured. It was imperative that during that last sleep, which for them was fraught with such terrors, the flesh should neither become decomposed nor turn to dust, that it should be free from offensive odour and secure from predatory worms.

They set to work, therefore, to discover how to preserve it. The oldest burials which have as yet been found prove that these early inhabitants were successful in securing the permanence of the body for a few decades only. When one of them died, his son, or his nearest relative, carefully washed the corpse in water impregnated with an astringent or aromatic substance, such as natron or some solution of fragrant gums, and then fumigated it with burning herbs and perfumes which were destined to overpower, at least temporarily, the odour of death.[1] Having

---

[1] This is to be gathered from the various Pyramid texts relating to the purification by water and to fumigation : the pains taken to secure material

taken these precautions, they placed the body in the grave, sometimes entirely naked, sometimes partially covered with its ordinary garments, or sewn up in a closely fitting gazelle skin. The dead man was placed on his left side, lying north and south with his face to the east, in some cases on the bare ground, in others on a mat, a strip of leather or a fleece, in the position of a child in the fœtal state. The knees were sharply bent at an angle of 45° with the thighs, while the latter were either at right angles with the body, or drawn up so as almost to touch the elbows. The hands are sometimes extended in front of the face, sometimes the arms are folded and the hands joined on the breast or neck. In some instances the legs are bent upward in such a fashion that they almost lie parallel with the trunk. The deceased could only be made to assume this position by a violent effort, and in many cases the tendons and the flesh had to be cut to facilitate the operation. The dryness of the ground selected for these burial-places retarded the corruption of the flesh for a long time, it is true, but only retarded it, and so did not prevent the soul from being finally destroyed. Seeing decay could not be prevented, it was determined to accelerate the process, by taking the flesh from the bones before interment. The bodies thus treated are often incomplete; the head is missing, or is detached from the neck and laid in another part of the pit, or, on the other hand, the body is not there, and the head only is found in

cleanliness, described in these formulas, were primarily directed towards the preservation of the bodies subjected to these processes, and further to the perfecting of the souls to which these bodies had been united.

the grave, generally placed apart on a brick, a heap of stones, or a layer of cut flints. The forearms and the hands were subjected to the same treatment as the head. In many cases no trace of them appears, in others they are deposited by the side of the skull or scattered about haphazard. Other mutilations are frequently met with; the ribs are divided and piled up behind the body, the limbs are disjointed or the body is entirely dismembered, and the fragments arranged upon the ground or enclosed together in an earthenware cist.

These precautions were satisfactory in so far as they ensured the better preservation of the more solid parts of the human frame, but the Egyptians felt this result was obtained at too great a sacrifice. The human organism thus deprived of all flesh was not only reduced to half its bulk, but what remained had neither unity, consistency, nor continuity. It was not even a perfect skeleton with its constituent parts in their relative places, but a mere mass of bones with no connecting links. This drawback, it is true, was remedied by the artificial reconstruction in the tomb of the individual thus completely dismembered in the course of the funeral ceremonies. The bones were laid in their natural order; those of the feet at the bottom, then those of the leg, trunk, and arms, and finally the skull itself. But the superstitious fear inspired by the dead man, particularly of one thus harshly handled, and particularly the apprehension that he might revenge himself on his relatives for the treatment to which they had subjected him, often induced them to make this restoration intentionally incomplete. When they had reconstructed the entire skeleton, they refrained from placing the head in position, or else they suppressed one or all of the vertebræ of the spine, so that the deceased should be unable to rise and go forth to bite and harass the living. Having taken this precaution, they nevertheless felt a doubt whether the soul could really enjoy life so long as one half only of the body remained, and the other was lost for ever : they therefore sought to discover the means of preserving the fleshy parts in addition to the bony framework of the body. It had been observed that when a corpse had been buried in the desert, its skin, speedily desiccated and hardened, changed into a case of blackish parchment beneath which the flesh slowly wasted away,[1] and the whole frame thus remained intact, at least in appearance, while its integrity ensured that of the soul. An attempt was made by artificial means to reproduce the conservative action of the sand, and, without mutilating the body, to secure at will that in- corruptibility without which the persistence of the soul was but a useless prolongation of the death-agony. It was the god Anubis—the jackal lord of sepulture—who was supposed to have made this discovery. He cleansed the body of the viscera, those parts which most rapidly decay, saturated it with salts and aromatic substances, protected it first of all with the hide of a beast, and over this laid thick layers of linen. The victory the god had thus gained over corruption was, however, far from

---

[1] Such was the appearance of the bodies of Coptic monks of the sixth, eighth, and ninth centuries, which I found in the convent cemeteries of Contra-Syene, Taûd, and Akhmim, right in the midst of the desert.

being a complete one. The bath in which the dead man was immersed could not entirely preserve the softer parts of the body: the chief portion of them was dissolved, and what remained after the period of saturation was so desiccated that its bulk was seriously diminished.

When any human being had been submitted to this process, he emerged from it a mere skeleton, over which the skin remained tightly drawn: these shrivelled limbs, sunken chest, grinning features, yellow and blackened skin spotted by the efflorescence of the embalmer's salts, were not the man himself, but rather a caricature of what he had been. As nevertheless he was secure against immediate destruction, the Egyptians described him as furnished with his shape; henceforth he had been purged of all that was evil in him, and he could face with tolerable security whatever awaited him in the future. The art of Anubis, transmitted to the embalmers and employed by them from generation to generation, had, by almost eliminating the corruptible part of the body without destroying its outward appearance, arrested decay, if not for ever, at least for an unlimited period of time. If there were hills at hand, thither the mummied dead were still borne, partly from custom, partly because the dryness of the air and of the soil offered them a further chance of preservation. In districts of the Delta where the hills were so distant as to make it very costly to reach them, advantage was taken of the smallest sandy islet rising above the marshes, and there a cemetery was founded. Where this resource failed, the mummy was fearlessly entrusted to the soil itself, but only after being placed within a sarcophagus of hard stone, whose lid and trough, hermetically fastened together with cement, prevented the penetration of any moisture. Reassured on this point, the soul followed the body to the tomb, and there dwelt with it as in its eternal house, upon the confines of the visible and invisible worlds.

Here the soul kept the distinctive character and appearance which pertained to it "upon the earth:" as it had been a "double" before death, so it remained a double after it, able to perform all functions of animal life after its own fashion. It moved, went, came, spoke, breathed, accepted pious homage, but without pleasure, and as it were mechanically, rather from an instinctive horror of annihilation than from any rational desire for immortality. Unceasing regret for the bright world which it had left disturbed its mournful and inert existence. "O my brother, withhold not thyself from drinking and from eating, from drunkenness, from love, from all enjoyment, from following thy desire by night and by day; put not sorrow within thy heart, for what are the years of a man upon earth? The West is a land of sleep and of heavy shadows, a place wherein its inhabitants, when once installed, slumber on in their mummy-forms, never more waking to see their brethren; never more to recognize their fathers or their mothers, with hearts forgetful of their wives and children. The living water, which earth giveth to all who dwell upon it, is for me but stagnant and dead; that water floweth to all who are on earth, while for me it is but liquid putrefaction, this water that is mine. Since I came into this funereal valley I know not where nor what I am. Give me to drink of running water! . . . Let me be placed by the edge of the water with my face to the North, that the breeze may caress me and my heart be refreshed from its sorrow." By day the double remained concealed within the tomb. If it went forth by night, it was from no capricious or sentimental desire to revisit the spots where it had led a happier life. Its organs needed nourishment as formerly did those of its body, and of itself it possessed nothing " but hunger for food, thirst for drink."[1] Want and misery drove it from its retreat, and flung it back among the living. It prowled like a marauder about fields and villages, picking up and greedily devouring whatever it might find on the ground —broken meats which had been left or forgotten, house and stable refuse—and, should these meagre resources fail, even the most revolting dung and excrement.[2] This ravenous sceptre had not the dim and misty form, the long shroud of floating draperies of our modern phantoms, but a precise and definite shape, naked, or clothed in

[1] *Teti*, ll. 74, 75. "Hateful unto Teti is hunger, and he eateth it not; hateful unto Teti is thirst, nor hath he drunk it." We see that the Egyptians made hunger and thirst into two substances or beings, to be swallowed as food is swallowed, but whose effects were poisonous unless counteracted by the immediate absorption of more satisfying sustenance.

[2] King Teti, when distinguishing his fate from that of the common dead, stated that he had abundance of food, and hence was not reduced to so pitiful an extremity. "Abhorrent unto Teti is excrement, Teti rejecteth urine, and Teti abhorreth that which is abominable in him; abhorrent unto him is fæcal matter and he eateth it not, hateful unto Teti is liquid filth." (*Teti*, ll. 68, 69). The same doctrine is found in several places in the *Book of the Dead*.

the garments which it had worn while yet upon earth, and emitting a pale light, to which it owed the name of Luminous—*Khû*, *.Khûû*.[1] The double did not allow its family to forget it, but used all the means at its disposal to remind them of its existence. It entered their houses and their bodies, terrified them waking and sleeping by its sudden apparitions, struck them down with disease or madness,[2] and would even suck their blood like the modern vampire. One effectual means there was, and one only, of escaping or preventing these visitations, and this lay in taking to the tomb all the various provisions of which the double stood in need, and for which it visited their dwellings. Funerary sacrifices and the regular cultus of the dead originated in the need experienced for making provision for the sustenance of the manes after having secured their lasting

---

[1] The name of *luminous* was at first so explained as to make the light wherewith souls were clothed, into a portion of the divine light. In my opinion the idea is a less abstract one, and shows that, as among many other nations, so with the Egyptians the soul was supposed to appear as a kind of pale flame, or as emitting a glow analogous to the phosphorescent halo which is seen by night about a piece of rotten wood, or putrefying fish. This primitive conception may have subsequently faded, and *khû the glorious one*, one of the *mânes*, may have become one of those flattering names by which it was thought necessary to propitiate the dead ; it then came to have that significance of *resplendent with light* which is ordinarily attributed to it.

[2] The incantations of which the Leyden Papyrus published by PLEYTE is full are directed against *dead men* or *dead women* who entered into one of the living to give him the *migraine*, and violent headaches. Another Leyden Papyrus, briefly analyzed by CHABAS, and translated by MASPERO, contains the complaint, or rather the formal act of requisition of a husband whom the *luminous* of his wife returned to torment in his home, without any just cause for such conduct.

existence by the mummification of their bodies.[1] Gazelles and oxen were brought and sacrificed at the door of the tomb chapel; the haunches, heart, and breast of each

SACRIFICING TO THE DEAD IN THE TOMB CHAPEL.[2]

[1] Several chapters of the *Book of the Dead* consist of directions for giving food to that part of man which survives his death, *e.g.* chap. cv., "*Chapter for providing food for the double*" (NAVILLE's edition, pl. cxvii.), and chap. cvi., "*Chapter for giving daily abundance unto the deceased, in Memphis*" (NAVILLE's edition, pl. cxviii.).

[2] Stela of Antûf I., Prince of Thebes, drawn by Faucher-Gudin from a photograph taken by Émil Brugsch-Bey. Below, servants and relations are

Victim being presented and heaped together upon the ground, that there the dead might find them when they began to be hungry. Vessels of beer or wine, great jars of fresh water, purified with natron, or perfumed, were brought to them that they might drink their fill at pleasure, and by such voluntary tribute men bought their good will, as in daily life they bought that of some neighbour too powerful to be opposed.

The gods were spared none of the anguish and none of the perils which death so plentifully bestows upon men. Their bodies suffered change and gradually perished until nothing was left of them. Their souls, like human souls, were only the representatives of their bodies, and gradually became extinct if means of arresting the natural tendency to decay were not found in time. Thus, the same necessity that forced men to seek the kind of sepulture which gave the longest term of existence to their souls, compelled the gods to the same course. At first, they were buried in the hills, and one of their oldest titles describes them as those "who are upon the sand,"[1] safe

bringing the victims and cutting up the ox at the door of the tomb. In the middle is the dead man, seated under his pavilion and receiving the sacrifice : an attendant offers him drink, another brings him the haunch of an ox, a third a basket and two jars ; provisions fill the whole chamber. Behind Antûf stand two servants, the one fanning his master, and the second offering him his staff and sandals. The position of the door, which is in the lowest row of the scenes, indicates that what is represented above it takes place within the tomb.

[1] In the *Book of Knowing that which is in Hades*, for the fourth and fifth hours of the night, we have the description of the sandy realm of Sokaris and of the gods *Hiriů Shâitů-seniů*, who are on their sand. Elsewhere in the same book we have a cynocephalus *upon its sand*, and the gods of the eighth

from putrefaction; afterwards, when the art of embalming had been discovered, the gods received the benefit of the new invention and were mummified. Each nome possessed the mummy and the tomb of its dead god: at Thinis there was the mummy and the tomb of Anhûri, the mummy of Osiris at Mendes, the mummy of Tûmû at Heliopolis.[1] In some of the nomes the gods did not change their names in altering the mode of their existence: the deceased Osiris remained Osiris; Nit and Hâthor when dead were still Nît and Hâthor, at Saïs and at Denderah. But Phtah of Memphis became Sokaris by dying; Ûapûaîtû, the jackal of Siût, was changed into Anubis;[2] and when his disk had disappeared at evening, Anhûri, the sunlit sky of Thinis, was Khontamentît, Lord of the West, until the following day. That bliss which we dream of enjoying in the world to come was not granted to the gods any more than to men. Their bodies were nothing but inert larvæ,

hour are also mysterious gods who are on their sand. Wherever these personages are represented in the vignettes, the Egyptian artist has carefully drawn the ellipse painted in yellow and sprinkled with red, which is the conventional rendering of sand, and sandy districts.

[1] The sepulchres of Tûmû, Khopri, Râ, Osiris, and in each of them the heap of sand hiding the body, are represented in the tomb of Seti I., as also the four rams in which the souls of the god are incarnate. The tombs of the gods were known even in Roman times.

[2] To my mind, at least, this is an obvious conclusion from the monuments of Siût, in which the jackal god is called Ûapûaîtû, as the living god, lord of the city, and Anûpû, master of embalming or of the Oasis, lord of Ra-qrirît, inasmuch as he is god of the dead. Ra-qrirît, *the door of the stone,* was the name which the people of Siût gave to their necropolis and to the infernal domain of their god.

"with unmoving heart,"[1] weak and shrivelled limbs, unable to stand upright were it not that the bandages in which they were swathed stiffened them into one rigid block. Their hands and heads alone were free, and were of the green or black shades of putrid flesh. Their doubles, like those of men, both dreaded and regretted the light. All sentiment was extinguished by the hunger from which they suffered, and gods who were noted for their compassionate kindness when alive, became pitiless and ferocious tyrants in the tomb. When once men were bidden to the presence of Sokarís, Khontamentît, or even of Osiris, "mortals come terrifying their hearts with fear of the god, and none dareth to look him in the face either among gods or men; for him the great are as the small. He spareth not those who love him; he beareth away the child from its mother, and the old man who walketh on his way; full of fear, all creatures

PHTAH AS A MUMMY.[2]

---

[1] This is the characteristic epithet for the dead Osiris, $\hat{U}rd\hat{u}\cdot h\hat{\imath}t$, he whose heart is unmoving, he whose heart no longer beats, and who has therefore ceased to live.

[2] Drawing by Faucher-Gudin of a bronze statuette of the Saïte period, found in the department of Hérault, at the end of a gallery in an ancient mine.

make supplication before him, but he turneth not his face towards them." Only by the unfailing payment of tribute, and by feeding him as though he were a simple human double, could living or dead escape the consequences of his furious temper. The living paid him his dues in pomps and solemn sacrifices, repeated from year to year at regular intervals; but the dead bought more dearly the protection which he deigned to extend to them. He did not allow them to receive directly the prayers, sepulchral meals, or offerings of kindred on feast-days; all that was addressed to them must first pass through his hands. When their friends wished to send them wine, water, bread, meat, vegetables, and fruits, he insisted that these should first be offered and formally presented to himself; then he was humbly prayed to transmit them to such or such a double, whose name and parentage were pointed out to him. He took possession of them, kept part for his own use, and of his bounty gave the remainder to its destined recipient. Thus death made no change in the relative positions of the feudal god and his worshippers. The worshipper who called himself the *amakhû* of the god during life was the subject and vassal of his mummied god even in the tomb;[1] and the god who, while living, reigned

---

[1] The word *amakhû* is applied to an individual who has freely entered the service of king or baron, and taken him for his lord: *amakhû khir nibûf* means *vassal of his lord*. In the same way, each chose for himself a god who became his patron, and to whom he owed *fealty*, *i.e.* to whom he was *amakhû*—vassal. To the god he owed the service of a good vassal—tribute, sacrifices, offerings; and to his vassal the god owed in return the service of a suzerain—protection, food, reception into his dominions and access to his

over the living, after his death continued to reign over the dead.

He dwelt in the city near the prince and in the midst of his subjects : Râ living in Heliopolis along with the prince of Heliopolis; Haroêris in Edfû together with the prince of Edfû ; Nît in Saïs with the prince of Saïs. Although none of the primitive temples have come down to us, the name given to them in the language of the time, shows what they originally were. A temple was considered as the feudal mansion—*hâît*,—the house—*pirû*, *pi*,—of the god, better cared for, and more respected than the houses of men, but not otherwise differing from them. It was built on a site slightly raised above the level of the plain, so as to be safe from the inundation, and where there was no natural mound, the want was supplied by raising a rectangular platform of earth. A layer of sand spread uniformly on the sub-soil provided against settlements or infiltration, and formed a bed for the foundations of the building.[1] This was first of all a single room, circumscribed, gloomy, covered in by a slightly vaulted roof, and having no opening but the doorway, which was framed by two tall masts, whence floated streamers to attract from afar the notice of

---

person. A man might be absolutely *nîb amakhît,* master of fealty, or, relatively to a god, *amakhû khir Osiri,* the vassal of Osiris, *amakhû khir Phtah-Sokari,* the vassal of Phtah-Sokaris.

[1] This custom lasted into Græco-Roman times, and was part of the ritual for laying the foundations of a temple. After the king had dug out the soil on the ground where the temple was to stand, he spread over the spot sand mixed with pebbles and precious stones, and upon this he laid the first course of stone.

worshippers; in front of its façade[1] was a court, fenced in with palisading. Within the temple were pieces of matting, low tables of stone, wood, or metal, a few utensils for cooking the offerings, a few vessels for containing the blood, oil, wine, and water with which the god was every day regaled. As provisions for sacrifice increased, the number of chambers increased with them,

THE 'SACRED BULL, HAPIS OR MNEVIS.[2]

and rooms for flowers, perfumes, stuffs, precious vessels, and food were grouped around the primitive abode; until that which had once constituted the whole temple became no more than its sanctuary. There the god dwelt, not

---

[1] No Egyptian temples of the first period have come down to our time, but HERR ERMAN has very justly remarked that we have pictures of them in several of the signs denoting the word *temple* in texts of the Memphite period.

[2] A sculptor's model from Tanis, now in the Gizeh Museum, drawn by Faucher-Gudin from a photograph by Émil Brugsch-Bey. The sacred marks, as given in the illustration, are copied from those of similar figures on stelæ of the Serapeum.

only in spirit but in body,[1] and the fact that it was incumbent upon him to live in several cities did not prevent his being present in all of them at once. He could divide his double, imparting it to as many separate bodies as he pleased, and these bodies might be human or animal, natural objects or things manufactured—such as statues of stone, metal, or wood.[2] Several of the gods were incarnate in rams : Osiris at Mendes, Harshafitû at Heracleopolis, Khnûmû at Elephantinê. Living rams were kept in their temples, and allowed to gratify any fancy that came into their animal brains. Other gods entered into bulls : Râ at Heliopolis, and, subsequently, Phtah at Memphis, Minû at Thebes, and Montû at Hermonthis. They indicated beforehand by certain marks such beasts as they intended to animate by their doubles, and he who had learnt to recognize these signs was at no loss to find a living god when the time came for seeking one and presenting it to the adoration of worshippers in the temple.[3] And if the statues had not

[1] Thus at Denderah, it is said that the soul of Hâthor likes to leave heaven "in the form of a human-headed sparrow-hawk of lapis-lazuli, accompanied by her divine cycle, to come and unite herself to the statue." "Other instances," adds Mariette, "would seem to justify us in thinking that the Egyptians accorded a certain kind of life to the statues and images which they made, and believed (especially in connection with tombs) that the spirit haunted images of itself."

[2] MASPERO, Études de Mythologie et d'Archéologie Égyptiennes, vol. i. p. 77, et seq. ; Archéologie Égyptienne, pp. 106, 107 ; English edition, pp. 105, 106. This notion of actuated statues seemed so strange and so unworthy of the wisdom of the Egyptians that Egyptologists of the rank of M. DE ROUGÉ have taken in an abstract and metaphorical sense expressions referring to the automatic movements of divine images.

[3] The bulls of Râ and of Phtah, the Mnevis and the Hapis, are known to

the same outward appearance of actual life as the animals, they none the less concealed beneath their rigid exteriors an intense energy of life which betrayed itself on occasion by gestures or by words. They thus indicated, in language which their servants could understand, the will of the gods, or their opinion on the events of the day; they answered questions put to them in accordance with

OPEN-AIR OFFERINGS TO THE SERPENT.[1]

prescribed forms, and sometimes they even foretold the future. Each temple held a fairly large number of statues

us from classic writers. The bull of Minû at Thebes may be seen in the procession of the god as represented on monuments of Ramses II. and Ramses III. Bâkhû (called Bakis by the Greeks), the bull of Hermonthis, is somewhat rare, and mainly represented upon a few later stelæ in the Gizeh Museum; it is chiefly known from the texts. The particular signs distinguishing each of these sacred animals have been determined both on the authority of ancient writers, and from examination of the figured monuments; the arrangement and outlines of some of the black markings of the Hapis are clearly shown in the illustration on p. 167.

[1] Drawn by Faucher-Gudin, from a photograph taken in the tomb of Khopirkerîsonbû. The inscription behind the uræus states that it represents *Ranûit the August, lady of the double granary.*

representing so many embodiments of the local divinity and of the members of his triad. These latter shared, albeit in a lesser degree, all the honours and all the prerogatives of the master; they accepted sacrifices, answered prayers, and, if needful, they prophesied. They occupied either the sanctuary itself, or one of the halls built about the principal sanctuary, or one of the isolated chapels which belonged to them, subject to the suzerainty of the feudal god. The god has his divine court to help him in the administration of his dominions, just as a prince is aided by his ministers in the government of his realm.

This State religion, so complex both in principle and in its outward manifestations, was nevertheless inadequate to express the exuberant piety of the populace. There were casual divinities in every nome whom the people did not love any the less because of their inofficial character; such as an exceptionally high palm tree in the midst of the desert, a rock of curious outline, a spring trickling drop by drop from the mountain to which hunters came to slake their thirst in the hottest hours of the day, or a great serpent believed to be immortal, which haunted a field, a grove of trees, a grotto, or a mountain ravine.[1] The peasants of the district brought it bread, cakes, fruits, and thought that they could call down the blessing of heaven upon their fields by gorging the snake with

---

[1] It was a serpent of this kind which gave its name to the hill of Shêikh Haridi, and the adjacent nome of the Serpent Mountain; and though the serpent has now turned Mussulman, he still haunts the mountain and preserves his faculty of coming to life again every time that he is killed.

offerings. Everywhere on the confines of cultivated ground, and even at some distance from the valley, are fine single sycamores, flourishing as though by miracle amid the sand. Their fresh greenness is in sharp contrast with the surrounding fawn-coloured landscape, and their thick foliage defies the midday sun even in summer. But, on examining the ground in which they grow, we soon find that they drink from water which has infiltrated from the Nile, and whose existence is in no-wise betrayed upon the surface of the soil. They stand as it were with their feet in the river,

THE PEASANT'S OFFERING TO THE SYCAMORE.[1]

though no one about them suspects it. Egyptians of all ranks counted them divine and habitually worshipped them,[2] making them offerings of figs, grapes, cucumbers,

---

[1] Drawn by Faucher-Gudin from a scene in the tomb of Khopirkerîsonbû. The sacred sycamore here stands at the end of a field of corn, and would seem to extend its protection to the harvest.

[2] MASPERO, Études de Mythologie et d'Archéologie Égyptiennes, vol. ii. pp. 224–227. They were represented as animated by spirits concealed within them, but which could manifest themselves on occasion. At such times the head or whole body of the spirit of a tree would emerge from its trunk, and when it returned to its hiding-place the trunk reabsorbed it, or ate it again, according to the Egyptian expression, which I have already had occasion to quote above ; see p. 110, note 3.

vegetables, and water in porous jars daily replenished by good and charitable people. Passers-by drank of the water, and requited the unexpected benefit with a short prayer. There were several such trees in the Memphite nome, and in the Letopolite nome from Dashûr to Gizeh, inhabited, as every one knew, by detached doubles of Nûit and Hâthor. These combined districts were known as the " Land of the Sycamore," a name afterwards extended to the city of Memphis; and their sacred trees are worshipped at the present day both by Mussulman and Christian fellahin.[1] The most famous among them all, the Sycamore of the South—*nûhît rîsit*— was regarded as the living body of Hâthor on earth. Side by side with its human gods and prophetic statues, each nome proudly advanced one or more sacred animals, one or more magic trees. Each family, and almost every individual, also possessed gods and fetishes, which had been pointed out for their worship by some fortuitous meeting with an animal or an object; by a dream, or by sudden intuition. They had a place in some corner of the house, or a niche in its walls; lamps were continually kept burning before them, and small daily offerings were made to them, over and above what fell to their share on solemn feast-days. In return, they became the pro-tectors of the household, its guardians and its counsellors. Appêal was made to them in every exigency of daily life, and their decisions were no less scrupulously carried out

[1] The tree at Matarieh, commonly called the *Tree of the Virgin,* seems to me to be the successor of a sacred tree of Heliopolis in which a goddess, perhaps Hâthor, was worshipped.

by their little circle of worshippers, than was the will of the feudal god by the inhabitants of his principality.

The prince was the great high priest. The whole religion of the nome rested upon him, and originally he himself performed its ceremonies. Of these, the chief was sacrifice,—that is to say, a banquet which it was his duty to prepare and lay before the god with his own

THE SACRIFICE OF THE BULL.—THE OFFICIATING PRIEST LASSOING THE VICTIM.[1]

hands. He went out into the fields to lasso the half-wild bull; bound it, cut its throat, skinned it, burnt part of the carcase in front of his idol and distributed the rest among his assistants, together with plenty of cakes, fruits,

[1] Bas-relief from the temple of Seti I. at Abydos ; drawn by Boudier, from a photograph by M. Daniel Héron. Seti I., second king of the XIXth dynasty, is throwing the lasso ; his son, Ramses II., who is still the crown prince, holds the bull by the tail to prevent its escaping from the slip-knot.

vegetables, and wine.[1] On the occasion, the god was present both in body and double, suffering himself to be clothed and perfumed, eating and drinking of the best that was set on the table before him, and putting aside some of the provisions for future use. This was the time to prefer requests to him, while he was gladdened and disposed to benevolence by good cheer. He was not without suspicion as to the reason why he was so feasted, but he had laid down his conditions beforehand, and if they were faithfully observed he willingly yielded to the means of seduction brought to bear upon him. Moreover, he himself had arranged the ceremonial in a kind of contract formerly made with his worshippers and gradually perfected from age to age by the piety of new generations.[2] Above all things, he insisted on physical cleanliness. The officiating priest must carefully wash—*ûâbû*—his face, mouth, hands, and body; and so necessary was this preliminary purification considered, that from it the professional priest derived his name of *ûîbû*, the washed, the clean.[3] His costume was the archaic dress, modified

[1] This appears from the sacrificial ritual employed in the temples up to the last days of Egyptian paganism ; cf., for instance, the illustration on p. 173, where the king is represented as lassoing the bull. That which in historic times was but an image, had originally been a reality.

[2] The most striking example of the divine institution of religious services is furnished by the inscription relating the history of the destruction of men in the reign of Râ, where the god, as he is about to make his final ascension into heaven, substitutes animal for human sacrifices.

[3] The idea of physical cleanliness comes out in such variants as *ûîbû totûi*, "clean of both hands," found on stelæ instead of the simple title *ûîbû*. We also know; on the evidence of ancient writers, the scrupulous daily care which Egyptian priests took of their bodies. It was only as a secondary matter that the idea of moral purity entered into the conception of a priest.

according to circumstances. During certain services, or at certain points in the sacrifices, it was incumbent upon him to wear sandals, the panther-skin over his shoulder, and the thick lock of hair falling over his right ear; at other times he must gird himself with the loin-cloth having a jackal's tail, and take the shoes from off his feet before proceeding with his office, or attach a false beard to his chin. The species, hair, and age of the victim, the way in which it was to be brought and bound, the manner and details of its slaughter, the order to be followed in opening its body and cutting it up, were all minutely and unchangeably decreed. And these were but the least of the divine exactions, and those most easily satisfied. The formulas accompanying each act of the sacrificial priest contained a certain number of words whose due sequence and harmonies might not suffer the slightest modification whatever, even from the god himself, under penalty of losing their efficacy. They were always recited with the same rhythm, according to a system of chaunting in which every tone had its virtue, combined with movements which confirmed the sense and worked with irresistible effect : one false note, a single discord between the succession of gestures and the utterance of the sacramental words, any hesitation, any awkwardness in the accomplishment of a rite, and the sacrifice was vain.

Worship as thus conceived became a legal transaction,

The Purification Ritual for officiating priests is contained in a papyrus of the Berlin Museum, whose analysis and table of chapters has been published by HERR OSCAR VON LEMM, *Das Ritualbuch des Ammonsdienstes*, p. 4, et seq.

in the course of which the god gave up his liberty in exchange for certain compensations whose kind and value were fixed by law. By a solemn deed of transfer the worshipper handed over to the legal representatives of the contracting divinity such personal or real property as seemed to him fitting payment for the favour which he asked, or suitable atonement for the wrong which he had done. If man scrupulously observed the innumerable conditions with which the transfer was surrounded, the god could not escape the obligation of fulfilling his petition ; [1] but should he omit the least of them, the offering remained with the temple and went to increase the endowments in mortmain, while the god was pledged to nothing in exchange. Hence the officiating priest assumed a formidable responsibility as regarded his fellows : a slip of memory, the slightest accidental impurity, made him a bad priest, injurious to himself and harmful to those worshippers who had entrusted him with their interests before the gods. Since it was vain to expect ritualistic perfections from a prince constantly troubled with affairs of state, the custom was established of associating professional priests with him, personages who devoted all their lives to the study and practice of the thousand formalities whose sum constituted

[1] This obligation is evident from texts where, as in the poem of Pentaûirît, a king who is in danger demands from his favourite god the equivalent in protection of the sacrifices which he has offered to that divinity, and the gifts wherewith he has enriched him. " Have I not made unto thee many offerings ? " says Ramses II. to Amon. " I have filled thy temple with my prisoners, I have built thee a mansion for millions of years. . . . Ah, if evil is the lot of them who insult thee, good are thy purposes towards those who honour thee, O Amon ! "

the local religion. Each temple had its service of priests, independent of those belonging to neighbouring temples, whose members, bound to keep their hands always clean and their voices true, were ranked according to the degrees of a learned hierarchy. At their head was a sovereign pontiff to direct them in the exercise of their functions. In some places he was called the first prophet, or rather the first servant of the god—*hon-nûtir topi*; at Thebes he was the first prophet of Amon, at Thinis he was the first prophet of Anhûri.[1] But generally he bore a title appropriate to the nature of the god whose servant he was. The chief priest of Râ at Heliopolis, and in all the cities which adopted the Heliopolitan form of worship, was called *Oîrû maû*, the master of visions, and he alone besides the sovereign of the nome, or of Egypt, enjoyed the privilege of penetrating into the sanctuary, of " entering into heaven and there beholding the god " face to face. In the same way, the high priest of Anhûri at Sebennytos was entitled the wise and pure warrior—*ahûîti saû uîbu*—because his god went armed with a pike, and a soldier god required for his service a pontiff who should be a soldier like himself.

These great personages did not always strictly seclude themselves within the limits of the religious domain. The gods accepted, and even sometimes solicited, from their worshippers, houses, fields, vineyards, orchards, slaves, and

---

[1] This title of *first prophet* belongs to priests of the less important towns, and to secondary divinities. If we find it employed in connection with the Theban worship, it is because Amon was originally a provincial god, and only rose into the first rank with the rise of Thebes and the great conquests of the XVIIIth and XIXth dynasties.

fishponds, the produce of which assured .their livelihood and the support of their temples. There was no Egyptian who did not cherish the ambition of leaving some such legacy to the patron god of his city, " for a monument to himself," and as an endowment for the priests to institute prayers and perpetual sacrifices on his behalf.[1] In course of time these accumulated gifts at length formed real sacred fiefs—*hotpû-nûtir*—analogous to the *wakfs* of Mussulman Egypt.[2] They were administered by the high priest, who, if necessary, defended them by force against the greed of princes or kings. Two, three, or even four classes of prophets or *hieroduli* under his orders assisted him in performing the offices of worship, in giving religious instruction, and in the conduct of affairs. Women did not hold equal rank with men in the temples of male deities; they there formed a kind of harem whence the god took his mystic spouses, his concubines, his maidservants, the female musicians and dancing women whose duty it was to divert him and to enliven his feasts. But in temples of goddesses they held the chief rank, and were called *hierodules*, or priestesses, *hierodules* of Nît, *hierodules* of Hâthor, *hierodules* of Pakhît.[3] The lower offices in the

---

[1] As regards the Saite period, we are beginning to accumulate many stelæ recording gifts to a god of land or houses, made either by the king or by private individuals.

[2] We know from the *Great Harris Papyrus* to what the fortune of Amon amounted at the end of the reign of Ramses III.; its details may be found in BRUGSCH, *Die Ægyptologie*, pp. 271–274. Cf. in NAVILLE, *Bubastis, Eighth Memoir of the Egyptian Exploration Fund*, p. 61, a calculation as to the quantities of precious metals belonging to one of the least of the temples of Bubastis; its gold and silver were counted by thousands of pounds.

[3] Mariette remarks that priests play but a subordinate part in the

households of the gods, as in princely households, were held by a troop of servants and artisans : butchers to cut the throats of the victims, cooks and pastrycooks, confectioners, weavers, shoemakers, florists, cellarers, water-carriers and milk-carriers. In fact, it was a state within a state, and the prince took care to keep its government in his own hands, either by investing one of his children with tho titles and functions of chief pontiff, or by arrogating them to himself. In that case, he provided against mistakes which would have annulled the sacrifice by associating with himself several masters of the ceremonies, who directed him in the orthodox evolutions before the god and about the victim, indicated the due order of gestures and the necessary changes of costume, and prompted him with the words of each invocation from a book or tablet which they held in their hands.[1]

In addition to its rites and special hierarchy, each of the sacerdotal colleges thus constituted had a theology in accordance with the nature and attributes of its god. Its fundamental dogma affirmed the unity of the nome god, his greatness, his supremacy over all the gods of Egypt

temple of Hâthor. This fact, which surprised him, is adequately explained by remembering that Hâthor being a goddess, women take precedence over men in a temple dedicated to her. At Saïs, the chief priest was a man, the *kharp-kaîtû* ; but the persistence with which women of the highest rank, and even queens themselves, took the title of prophetess of Nît from the times of the Ancient Empire shows that in this city the priestess of the goddess was of equal, if not superior, rank to the priest.

[1] The title of such a personage was *khri-habi*, the man with the roll or tablet, because of the papyrus roll, or wooden tablet containing the ritual, which ho held in his hand.

and of foreign lands[1]—whose existence was nevertheless admitted, and none dreamed of denying their reality or contesting their power. The latter also boasted of their unity, their greatness, their supremacy; but whatever they were, the god of the nome was master of them all—their prince, their ruler, their king. It was he alone who governed the world, he alone kept it in good order, he alone had created it. Not that he had evoked it out of nothing; there was as yet no concept of nothingness, and even to the most subtle and refined of primitive theologians creation was only a bringing of pre-existent elements into play. The latent germs of things had always existed, but they had slept for ages and ages in the bosom of the Nû, of the dark waters. In fulness of time the god of each nome drew them forth, classified them, marshalled them according to the bent of his particular nature, and made his universe out of them by methods peculiarly his own. Nît of Saïs, who was a weaver, had made the world of warp and woof, as the mother of a family weaves her children's linen.

SHÛ UPLIFTING THE SKY.[2]

---

[1] In the inscriptions all local gods bear the titles of *Nûtir ûâ*, only god; *Sûton nûtirû, Sûntirû,* Σουθήρ, king of the gods; of *Nûtir âa nib pît,* the great god, lord of heaven, which show their pretensions to the sovereignty and to the position of creator of the universe.

[2] Drawing by Faucher-Gudin of a green enamelled statuette in my possession. It was from Shû that the Greeks derived their representations, and perhaps their myth of Atlas.

Khnûmû, the Nile-God of the cataracts, had gathered up the mud of his waters and therewith moulded his creatures upon a potter's table. In the eastern cities of the Delta these procedures were not so simple. There it was admitted that in the beginning earth and sky were two lovers lost in the Nû, fast locked in each other's embrace, the god lying beneath the goddess. On the day of creation a new god, Shû, came forth from the primæval waters, slipped between the two, and seizing Nûit with both hands, lifted her above his head with outstretched arms.[1] Though the starry body of the goddess extended in space—her head being to the west and her loins to the east—her feet and hands hung down to the earth. These were the four pillars of the firmament under another form, and four gods of four adjacent principalities were in charge of them. Osiris, or Horus the sparrow-hawk, presided over the southern, and Sît over the northern pillar; Thot over that of the west, and Sapdi, the author of the zodiacal light, over that of the east. They had divided the world among themselves into four regions, or rather into four "houses," bounded by those mountains which surround it, and by the diameters intersecting between the pillars. Each of these houses belonged to one, and to one only; none of the other three, nor even the sun himself, might enter it, dwell there, or even pass through it without having obtained its master's permission. Sibû had not

[1] This was what the Egyptians called *the upliftings of Shû.* The event first took place at Hermopolis, and certain legends added that in order to get high enough the god had been obliged to make use of a staircase or mound situate in this city, and which was famous throughout Egypt.

been satisfied to meet the irruption of Shû by mere passive
resistance. He had tried to struggle, and he is drawn in
the posture of a man who has just awakened out of sleep,
and is half turning on his couch before getting up. One of
his legs is stretched out, the other is bent and partly drawn
up as in the act of rising. The lower part of the body is

SHÛ FORCIBLY SEPARATING SIBÛ AND NÛÎT.[1]

still unmoved, but he is raising himself with difficulty on
his left elbow, while his head droops and his right arm is
lifted towards the sky. His effort was suddenly arrested.
Rendered powerless by a stroke of the creator, Sibû
remained as if petrified in this position, the obvious
irregularities of the earth's surface being due to the painful

[1] Drawn by Fauchẹr-Gudin, from a painting on the mummy-case of
Bûtehamon in the Turin Museum. "Shû, the great god, lord of heaven,"
receives the adoration of two ram-headed souls placed upon his right and
left.

attitude in which he was stricken. His sides have since
been clothed with verdure, generations of men and animals
have succeeded each other upon his back, but without
bringing any relief to his pain ; he suffers evermore from
the violent separation of which he was the victim when
Nûit was torn from him, and his complaint
continues to rise to heaven night and day.

The aspect of the in-
undated plains of the
Delta, of the river by
which they are furrowed
and fertilized, and of the
desert sands by which
they are threatened, had
suggested to the theo-
logians of Mendes and
Bûto an explanation of
the mystery of creation,
in which the feudal di-
vinities of these cities
and of several others in

THE DIDÛ OF OSIRIS.[1]

THE DIDÛ DRESSED.[2]

their neighbourhood, Osiris, Sit, and Isis, played the
principal parts. Osiris first represented the wild and
fickle Nile of primitive times ; afterwards, as those who
dwelt upon his banks learned to regulate his course,

[1] Drawn by Faucher-Gudin from a specimen in blue enamelled pottery,
now in my possession.
[2] Drawn by Faucher-Gudin from a figure frequently found in Theban
mummy-cases of XXIst and XXIInd dynasties (WILKINSON, *Manners and
Customs*. 2nd edit., vol. iii. pl. xxv., No 5).

they emphasized the kindlier side of his character and soon transformed him into a benefactor of humanity, the supremely good being, Ûnnofriû, Onnophris.[1] He was lord of the principality of Didû, which lay along the Sebennytic branch of the river between the coast marshes and the entrance to the Wâdy Tûmilât, but his domain had been divided ; and the two nomes thus formed, namely, the ninth and sixteenth nomes of the Delta in the Pharaonic lists, remained faithful to him, and here he reigned without rival, at Busiris as at Mendes. His most famous idol-form was the Didû, whether naked or clothed, the fetish, formed of four superimposed columns, which had given its name to the principality.[2] They ascribed life to this Didû, and represented it with a somewhat grotesque face, big cheeks, thick lips, a necklace round its throat, a long flowing dress which hid the base of the columns beneath its folds, and two arms bent across the breast, the hands grasping one a whip and the other a crook, symbols of sovereign authority. This, perhaps, was the

---

[1] It has long been a dogma with Egyptologists that Osiris came from Abydos. MASPERO has shown that from his very titles he is obviously a native of the Delta, and more especially of Busiris and Mendes.

[2] The Didû has been very variously interpreted. It has been taken for a kind of nilometer, for a sculptor's or modeller's stand, or a painter's easel, for an altar with four superimposed tables, or a sort of pedestal bearing four door-lintels, for a series of four columns placed one behind another, of which the capitals only are visible, one above the other, etc. The explanation given in the text is that of REUVENS, who recognized the Didû as a symbolic representation of the four regions of the world ; and of MASPERO, Études de Mythologie et d'Archéologie Égyptiennes, vol. ii. p. 359, note 3. According to Egyptian theologians, it represented the spine of Osiris, preserved as a relic in the town bearing the name of Didû, Didît.

most ancient form of Osiris; but they also represented him as a man, and supposed him to assume the shapes of rams

OSIRIS-ONNOPHRIS, WHIP AND CROOK IN HAND.[1]

[1] Drawn by Boudier from a statue in green basalt found at Sakkarah, and now in the Gizeh Museum.

and bulls,[1] or even those of water-birds, such as lapwings, herons, and cranes, which disported themselves about the lakes of that district.[2] The goddess whom we are accustomed to regard as inseparable from him, Isis the cow, or woman with cow's horns, had not always belonged to him. Originally she was an independent deity, dwelling at Bûto in the midst of the ponds of Adhû. She had neither husband nor lover, but had spontaneously conceived and given birth to a son, whom she suckled among the reeds—a lesser Horus who was called Harsiîsît, Horus the son of Isis, to distinguish him from Haroêris. At an early period she was married to her neighbour Osiris, and no marriage could have been better suited to her nature. For she personified the earth —not the earth in general, like Sibu, with its unequal distribution of seas and mountains, deserts and cultivated land; but the black and luxuriant plain of the Delta, where races of men, plants, and animals increase and multiply in ever-succeeding generations. To whom did she owe this inexhaustible productive energy if not to her neighbour Osiris, to the Nile? The Nile rises, overflows, lingers upon the soil; every year it is wedded to the earth, and the earth comes forth green and fruitful from its embraces.

[1] The ram of Mendes is sometimes Osiris, and sometimes the soul of Osiris. The ancients took it for a he-goat, and to them we are indebted for the record of its exploits. According to Manetho, the worship of the sacred ram is not older than the time of King Kaiekhos of the second dynasty. A Ptolemaic necropolis of sacred rams was discovered by Mariette at Tmai el-Amdid, in the ruins of Thmûis, and some of their sarcophagi are now in the Gizeh Museum.

[2] The Bonû, the chief among these birds, is not the phœnix, as has so often been asserted. It is a kind of heron, either the *Ardea cinerea*, which is common in Egypt, or else some similar species.

The marriage of the two elements suggested that of the two divinities; Osiris wedded Isis and adopted the young Horus.

ISIS, WEARING THE COW-HORN HEAD-DRESS.[1]

[1] Drawn by Boudier from a green basalt statue in the Gizeh Museum. From a photograph by Émil Brugsch-Bey.

But this prolific and gentle pair were not representative of all the phenomena of nature. The eastern part of the Delta borders upon the solitudes of Arabia, and although it contains several rich and fertile provinces, yet most of these owe their existence to the arduous labour of the inhabitants, their fertility being dependent on the daily care of man, and on his regular distribution of the water. The moment he suspends the struggle or relaxes his watchfulness, the desert reclaims them and overwhelms them with sterility. Sît was the spirit of the mountain, stone and sand, the red and arid ground as distinguished from the moist black soil of the valley. On the body of a lion or of a dog he bore a fantastic head with a slender curved snout, upright and square-cut ears; his cloven tail rose stiffly behind him, springing from his loins like a fork. He also assumed a human form, or retained the animal head only upon a man's shoulders. He was felt to be cruel and treacherous, always ready to shrivel up the harvest with his burning breath, and to smother Egypt beneath a shroud of shifting sand. The contrast between this evil being and the beneficent couple, Osiris and Isis, was striking. Nevertheless, the theologians of the Delta soon assigned a common origin to these rival divinities of Nile and desert, red land and black. Sîbû had begotten them, Nûit had given birth to them one after another when the demiurge had separated her from her husband; and the days of their birth were the days of creation.[1] At first each of them had kept to his own half

[1] According to one legend which is comparatively old in origin, the four children of Nûit, and Horus her grandson, were born one after another, each on one of the intercalary days of the year. This legend was still current in the Greek period.

of the world. Moreover Sit, who had begun by living alone, had married, in order that he might be inferior to Osiris in nothing. As a matter of fact, his companion, Nephthys, did not manifest any great activity, and was scarcely more

NEPHTHYS, AS A WAILING WOMAN.[1]   THE GOD SÎT, FIGHTING.[2]

[1] Drawn by Faucher-Gudin from a painted wooden statuette in my possession, from a funeral couch found at Akhmim. On her head the goddess bears the hieroglyph for her name; she is kneeling at the foot of the funeral couch of Osiris and weeps for the dead god.

[2] Bronze statuette of the XXth dynasty, encrusted with gold, from the Hoffmann collection : drawn by Faucher-Gudin from a photograph taken by

than an artificial counterpart of the wife of Osiris, a
second Isis who bore no children to her husband;[1] for the
sterile desert brought barrenness to her as to all that

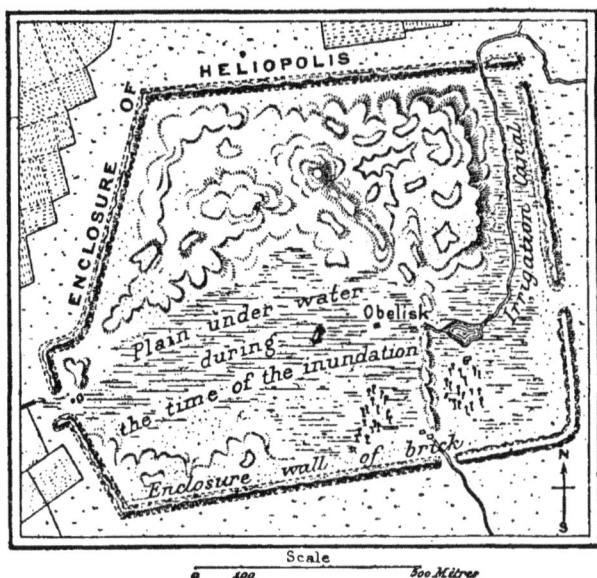

PLAN OF THE RUINS OF HELIOPOLIS.[2]

it touched. Yet she had lost neither the wish nor the
power to bring forth, and sought fertilization from another

Legrain in 1891. About the time when the worship of Sît was proscribed,
one of the Egyptian owners of this little monument had endeavoured to alter
its character, and to transform it into a statuette of the god Khnûmû. He
took out the upright ears, replacing them with ram's horns, but made no other
change. In the drawing I have had the later addition of the curved horns
removed, and restored the upright ears, whose marks may still be seen upon
the sides of the head-dress.

[1] The impersonal character of Nephthys, her artificial origin, and her
derivation from Isis, have been pointed out by MASPERO (*Études de Mythologie
et d'Archéologie Égyptiennes*, vol. ii. pp. 362-364). The very name of the
goddess, which means *the lady* (*nibît*) of the *mansion* (*hâit*), confirms this
view.

[2] Drawn by Thuillier, from the *Description de l'Égypte* (Atlas, Ant., vol.
v. pl. 26, 1).

source.   Tradition had it that she had made Osiris drunken, drawn him to her arms without his knowledge, and borne him a son; the child of this furtive union was the jackal Anubis.   Thus when a higher Nile overflows lands not usually covered by the inundation, and lying unproductive for lack of moisture, the soil eagerly absorbs the water, and the germs which lay concealed in the ground burst forth into life.   The gradual invasion of the domain of Sît by Osiris marks the beginning of the strife.   Sît rebels against the wrong of which he is the victim, involuntary though it was;   he surprises and treacherously slays his brother, drives Isis into temporary banishment among her marshes, and reigns over the kingdom of Osiris as well as over his own.   But his triumph is short-lived.   Horus, having grown up, takes arms against him, defeats him in many encounters, and banishes him in his turn.   The creation of the world had brought the destroying and the life-sustaining gods face to face: the history of the world is but the story of their rivalries and warfare.

None of these conceptions alone sufficed to explain the whole mechanism of creation, nor the part which the various gods took in it.   The priests of Heliopolis appropriated them all, modified some of their details and eliminated others, added several new personages, and thus finally constructed a complete cosmogony, the elements of which were learnedly combined so as to correspond severally with the different operations by which the world had been evoked out of chaos and gradually brought to its present state.   Heliopolis was never directly involved in the great revolutions of political history; but no city ever originated so many mystic ideas and consequently exercised so great an influence upon the development of civilization.[1] It was a small town built on the plain not far from the Nile at the

HORUS, THE AVENGER OF HIS FATHER, AND ANUBIS ĈAPĈAÎTÔ.[2]

apex of the Delta, and surrounded by a high wall of mud bricks whose remains could still be seen at the beginning

[1] By its inhabitants it was accounted older than any other city of Egypt

[2] Drawn by Faucher Gudin, from a photograph by Béato of a bas-relief in the temple of Seti I. at Abydos The two gods are conducting King Ramses II., here identified with Osiris towards the goddess Hâthor

of the century, but which have now almost completely disappeared. One obelisk standing in the midst of the open plain, a few waste mounds of débris, scattered blocks, and two or three lengths of crumbling wall, alone mark the place where once the city stood. Râ was worshipped there, and the Greek name of Heliopolis is but the translation of that which was given to it by the priests—Pi-râ, City of the Sun. Its principal temple, the " Mansion of the Prince," rose from about the middle of the enclosure, and sheltered, together with the god himself, those animals in which he became incarnate : the bull Mnevis, and sometimes the Phœnix. According to an old legend, this

THE SUN SPRINGING FROM AN OPENING LOTUS-FLOWER IN THE FORM OF THE CHILD HORUS.[1]

[1] Drawn by Faucher-Gudin. The open lotus-flower, with a bud on either side, stands upon the usual sign for any water-basin. Here the sign represents the Nû, that dark watery abyss from which the lotus sprang on the morning of creation, and whereon it is still supposed to bloom.

wondrous bird appeared in Egypt only once in five hundred years. It is born and lives in the depths of Arabia, but when its father dies it covers the body with a layer of myrrh, and flies at utmost speed to the temple of Heliopolis, there to bury it.[1] In the beginning, Râ was the sun

THE PLAIN AND MOUNDS OF HELIOPOLIS FIFTY YEARS AGO.[2]

[1] The Phœnix is not the Bonû (cf. p. 186, note 2), but a fabulous bird derived from the golden sparrow-hawk, which was primarily a form of Haroêris, and of the sun-gods in second place only. On the authority of his Heliopolitan guides, Herodotus tells us (ii. 83) that in shape and size the phœnix resembled the eagle, and this statement alone should have sufficed to prevent any attempt at identifying it with the Bonû, which is either a heron or a lapwing.

[2] Drawn by Faucher-Gudin, from a water-colour published by LEPSIUS, Denkm., i. 56. The view is taken from the midst of the ruins at the foot of the obelisk of Ûsirtasen. A little stream runs in the foreground, and passes

itself, whose fires appear to be lighted every morning in the east and to be extinguished at evening in the west; and to the people such he always remained. Among the theologians there was considerable difference of opinion on the point. Some held the disk of the sun to be the body which the god assumes when presenting himself for the adoration of his worshippers. Others affirmed that it rather represented his active and radiant soul. Finally, there were many who defined it as one of his forms of being—*khopriû*—one of his self-manifestations, without presuming to decide whether it was his body or his soul which he deigned to reveal to human eyes; but whether soul or body, all agreed that the sun's disk had existed in the Nû before creation. But how could it have lain beneath the primordial ocean without either drying up the waters or being extinguished by them? At this stage the identification of Râ with Horus and his right eye served the purpose of the theologians admirably: the god needed only to have closed his eyelid in order to prevent his fires from coming in contact with the water.[1] He was also said to have shut up his disk within a lotus-bud, whose folded petals had safely protected it. The flower had opened on the morning of the first day, and from it the god had sprung suddenly as a child wearing the solar disk upon his head. But all

through a muddy pool ; to right and left are mounds of ruins, which were then considerable, but have since been partially razed. In the distance Cairo rises against the south-west.

[1] This is clearly implied in the expression so often used by the sacred writers of Ancient Egypt in reference to the appearance of the sun and his first act at the time of creation : " *Thou openest the two eyes*, and earth is flooded with rays of light."

theories led the theologians to distinguish two periods, and as it were two beings in the existence of supreme deity: a pre-mundane sun lying inert within the bosom of the dark waters, and our living and life-giving sun.

One division of the Heliopolitan school retained the use of traditional terms and images in reference to these Sun-

HARMAKHÛÎTI-HARMAKHIS, THE GREAT GOD.[1]

gods. To the first it left the human form, and the title of Râ, with the abstract sense of creator, deriving the name from the verb râ, which means to give. For the second it kept the form of the sparrow-hawk and the name of Harma-khûîti—Horus in the two horizons—which clearly denoted

[1] Drawn by Boudier, from a photograph by Insinger of an outer wall of the Hypostyle Hall at Karnak. Harmakhis grants years and festivals to the Pharaoh Seti I., who kneels before him, and is presented by the lioness-headed goddess Sokhît, here described as a magician—Oîrît hikaû.

his function ;[1] and it summed up the idea of the sun as a whole in the single name of Râ-Harmakhûîti, and in a single image in which the hawk-head of Horus was grafted upon the human body of Râ. The other divisions of the school invented new names for new conceptions. The sun existing before the world they called Creator—*Tûmû, Atûmû*[2]—and our earthly sun they called *Khopri*—He who is. Tûmû was a man crowned and clothed with the insignia of supreme power, a true king of gods, majestic and impassive as the Pharaohs who succeeded each other upon the throne of Egypt. The conception of Khopri as a disk enclosing a scarabæus, or a man with a scarabæus upon his head, or a scarabæus-headed mummy, was suggested by the accidental alliteration of his name and that of *Khopirrû,* the scarabæus. The difference between the possible forms of the god was so slight as to be eventually lost altogether. His names were grouped by twos and threes in every

---

[1] Harmakhûîti is Horus, the sky of the two horizons ; *i.e.* the sky of the daytime, and the night sky. When the celestial Horus was confounded with Râ, and became the sun (cf. p. 133), he naturally also became the sun of the two horizons, the sun by day, and the sun by night.

[2] E. DE ROUGÉ, *Études sur le Rituel funéraire,* p. 76 : " His name may be connected with two radicals. *Tem* is a negation ; it may be taken to mean *the Inapproachable One, the Unknown* (as in Thebes, where *Amûn* means mystery). Atûm is, in fact, described as ' existing alone in the abyss,' before the appearance of light. It was in this time of darkness that Atûm performed the first act of creation, and this allows of our also connecting his name with the Coptic TAMIO, *creare.* Atûm was also the prototype of man (in Coptic TME, *homo*), and becomes a perfect ' *tûm* ' after his resurrection." BRUGSCH would rather explain *Tûmû* as meaning *the Perfect One, the Complete.* E. DE ROUGÉ's philological derivations are no longer admissible ; but his explanation of the name corresponds so well with the part played by the god that I fail to see how that can be challenged.

conceivable way, and the scarabæus of Khopri took its place upon the head of Râ, while the hawk headpiece was transferred from the shoulders of Harmakhûîti to those of Tûmû. The complex beings resulting from these combinations, Râ-Tûmû, Atûmû-Râ, Râ-Tûmû-Khopri, Râ-Harmakhûîti-Tûmû, Tûm-Harmakhûîti-Khopri, never attained to any pronoûnced individuality. They were as a rule simple dupli-

KHOPRI, THE SCARABÆUS GOD, IN HIS BARK.

cates of the feudal god, names rather than persons, and though hardly taken for one another indiscriminately, the distinctions between them had reference to mere details of their functions and attributes. Hence arose the idea of making these gods into embodiments of the main phases in the life of the sun during the day and throughout the year. Râ symbolized the sun of springtime and before sunrise, Harmakhûîti the summer and the morning sun, Atûmû the sun of autumn and of afternoon, Khopri that of winter and of night. The people of Heliopolis accepted the new names and the new forms presented for their worship, but always subordinated them to their beloved Râ. For them Râ never ceased to be the god of the nome; while Atûmû remained the god of the theologians, and was invoked by them, the people preferred Râ. At Thinis and at Sebennytos Anhûri incurred the same fate as befell Râ at Heliopolis. After he had been identified with the sun, the similar identification of Shû inevitably followed. Of old, Anhûri and Shû were twin gods, incarnations of sky and earth. They were soon but one god in two persons—the god Anhûri-Shû, of which the one half under the title of Anhûri represented, like Atûmû, the primordial being; and Shû, the other half, became, as his name indicates, the creative sun-god who upholds (*shû*) the sky.

Tûmû then, rather than Râ, was placed by the Heliopolitan priests at the head of their cosmogony as supreme creator and governor. Several versions were current as to how he had passed from inertia into action, from the personage of Tûmû into that of Râ. According to the version most widely received, he had suddenly cried across the waters, " Come unto me !"[1] and immediately the mysterious lotus had unfolded its petals, and Râ had appeared at the edge of its open cup as a disk, a newborn child, or a disk-crowned sparrow-hawk; this was probably a refined form of a ruder and earlier tradition, according to which it was upon Râ himself that the office had devolved of

---

[1] It was on this account that the Egyptians named the first day of the year the *Day of Come-unto-me !*

separating Sibû from Nûît, for the purpose of constructing the heavens and the earth. But it was doubtless felt that so unseemly an act of intervention was beneath the dignity even of an inferior form of the suzerain god; Shû was therefore borrowed for the purpose from the kindred cult of Anhûri, and at Heliopolis, as at Sebennytos, the office was entrusted to him of seizing the sky-goddess and raising her with outstretched arms. The violence suffered by Nûit at the hands of Shû led to a connexion of the Osirian dogma of Mendes with the solar dogma of Sebennytos, and thus the tradition describing the creation of the world was completed by another, explaining its division into deserts and fertile lands. Sibû, hitherto concealed beneath the body of his wife, was now exposed to the sun; Osiris and Sit, Isis and Nephthys, were born, and, falling from the sky, their mother, on to the earth, their father, they shared the surface of the latter among themselves. Thus the Heliopolitan doctrine recognized three principal events in the creation of the universe: the dualization of the supreme god and the breaking forth of light, the raising of the sky and the laying bare of the earth, the birth of the Nile and the allotment of the soil of Egypt, all expressed as the manifestations of successive deities. Of these deities, the latter ones already constituted a family of father, mother, and children, like human families. Learned theologians availed themselves of this example to effect analogous relationships between the rest of the gods, combining them all into one line of descent. As Atûmû-Râ could have no fellow, he stood apart in the first rank, and it was decided that Shû should be his son, whom he had formed out of himself alone, on the first day of creation, by the simple intensity of his own virile energy. Shû, reduced to the position of divine son, had in his turn begotten Sibû and Nûît, the two deities which he separated. Until then he had not been supposed to have any wife, and he also might have himself brought his own progeny into being; but lest a power of spontaneous generation equal to that of the demiurge should be ascribed to him, he was married, and the wife found for him was Tafnûît, his twin sister, born in the same

THE TWIN LIONS, SHÛ AND TAFNÛÎT.[1]

way as he was born. This goddess, invented for the occasion, was never fully alive, and remained, like Nephthys, a theological entity rather than a real person. The texts describe her as the pale reflex of her husband. Together with him she upholds the sky, and every morning receives

[1] Drawn by Faucher-Gudin from a vignette in the papyrus of Ani in the British Museum, published by LEPAGE-RENOUF in the *Proceedings of the Society of Biblical Archæology*, vol. xi., 1889-90, pp. 26-28. The inscription above the lion on the right reads *safû*, "yesterday;" the other, *dúaú*, "this morning."

the newborn sun as it emerges from the mountain of the east; she is a lioness when Shû is a lion, a woman when he is a man, a lioness-headed woman if he is a lion-headed man; she is angry when he is angry, appeased when he is appeased; she has no sanctuary wherein he is not worshipped. In short, the pair made one being in two bodies, or, to use the Egyptian expression, "one soul in its two twin bodies."

Hence we see that the Heliopolitans proclaimed the creation to be the work of the sun-god, Atûmû-Râ, and of the four pairs of deities who were descended from him. It was really a learned variant of the old doctrine that the universe was composed of a sky-god, Horus, supported by his four children and their four pillars: in fact, the four sons of the Heliopolitan cosmogony, Shû and Sibû, Osiris and Sît, were occasionally substituted for the four older gods of the "houses" of the world. This being premised, attention must be given to the important differences between the two systems. At the outset, instead of appearing contemporaneously upon the scene, like the four children of Horus, the four Heliopolitan gods were deduced one from another, and succeeded each other in the order of their birth. They had not that uniform attribute of supporter, associating them always with one definite function, but each of them felt himself endowed with faculties and armed with special powers required by his condition. Ultimately they took to themselves goddesses, and thus the total number of beings working in different ways at the organization of the universe was brought up to nine. Hence they were called by the collective name

of the Ennead, the Nine gods—*paûit nûtîrû*,[1]—and the god
at their head was entitled *Paûiti*, the god of the Ennead.
When creation was completed, its continued existence was
ensured by countless agencies with whose operation the
persons of the Ennead were not at leisure to concern themselves, but had ordained auxiliaries to preside over each
of the functions essential to the regular and continued
working of all things. The theologians of Heliopolis
selected eighteen from among the inumerable divinities
of the feudal cults of Egypt, and of these they formed two
secondary Enneads, who were regarded as the offspring of
the Ennead of the creation. The first of the two
secondary Enneads, generally known as the Minor Ennead,
recognized as chief Harsiesis, the son of Osiris. Harsiesis
was originally an earth-god who had avenged the assassina-
tion of his father and the banishment of his mother by Sît ;
that is, he had restored fulness to the Nile and fertility to
the Delta. When Harsiesis was incorporated into the solar
religions of Heliopolis, his filiation was left undisturbed as
being a natural link between the two Enneads, but his

---

[1] The first Egyptologists confounded the sign used in writing *paûit* with
the sign *kh*, and the word *khet, other*. E. de Rougé was the first to determine its phonetic value : "it should be read *Paû*, and designates a body of
gods." Shortly afterwards BRUGSCH proved that "the group of gods invoked
by E. de' Rougé must have consisted of nine "—of an Ennead. This explanation was not at first admitted either by LEPSIUS or by MARIETTE, who had
proposed a mystic interpretation of the word in his *Mémoire sur la mère
d'Apis*, or by E. DE ROUGÉ, or by CHABAS. The interpretation a *Nine*, an
Ennead, was not frankly adopted until later, and more especially after the
discovery of the Pyramid texts ; to-day, it is the only meaning admitted. Of
course the Egyptian Ennead has no other connection than that of name with
the Enneads of the Neo-Platonists.

personality was brought into conformity with the new surroundings into which he was transplanted. He was identified with Râ through the intervention of the older Horus, Haroêris-Harmakhis, and the Minor Ennead, like the Great Ennead, began with a sun-god. This assimilation was not pushed so far as to invest the younger Horus with the same powers as his fictitious ancestor : he was the sun of earth, the everyday sun, while Atûmû-Râ was still the sun pre-mundane and eternal. Our knowledge of the

THE FOUR FUNERARY GENII, KHADSONÛF, TIÛMAÛTF, HÂPI, AND AMSÎT.[1]

eight other deities of the Minor Ennead is very imperfect. We see only that these were the gods who chiefly protected the sun-god against its enemies and helped it to follow its regular course. Thus Harhûditi, the Horus of Edfû, spear in hand, pursues the hippopotami or serpents which haunt the celestial waters and menace the god. The progress of the Sun-bark is controlled by the incantations of Thot, while Uapûaîtû, the dual jackal-god of Siût, guides, and occasionally tows it along the sky from south to north. The third Ennead would seem to have included among its

[1] Drawn by Faucher-Gudin, from WILKINSON's *Manners and Customs*, 2nd edit., vol. iii. p. 221, pl. xlviii.

members Anubis the jackal, and the four funerary genii, the children of Horus—Hapi, Amsît, Tiûmaûtf, Kabhsonûf; it further appears as though its office was the care and defence of the dead sun, the sun by night, as the second Ennead had charge of the living sun. Its functions were so obscure and apparently so insignificant as compared with those exercised by the other Enneads, that the theologians did not take the trouble either to represent it or to enumerate its persons. They invoked it as a whole, after the two others, in those formulas in which they called into play all the creative and preservative forces of the universe; but this was rather as a matter of conscience and from love of precision than out of any true deference. At the initial impulse of the lord of Heliopolis, the three combined Enneads started the world and kept it going, and gods whom they had not incorporated were either enemies to be fought with, or mere attendants.

The doctrine of the Heliopolitan Ennead acquired an immediate and a lasting popularity. It presented such a clear scheme of creation, and one whose organization was so thoroughly in accordance with the spirit of tradition, that the various sacerdotal colleges adopted it one after another, accommodating it to the exigencies of local patriotism. Each placed its own nome-god at the head of the Ennead as "god of the Nine," "god of the first time," creator of heaven and earth, sovereign ruler of men, and lord of all action. As there was the Ennead of Atûmû at Heliopolis, so there was that of Anhûri at Thinis and at Sebennytos; that of Minû at Coptos and at Panopolis; that of Haroêris at Edfû; that of Sobkhû at Ombos; and, later, that of Phtah at Memphis and of Amon at Thebes. Nomes which worshipped a goddess had no scruples whatever in ascribing to her the part played by Atûmû, and in crediting her with the spontaneous maternity of Shû and Tafnûît. Nit was the source and ruler of the

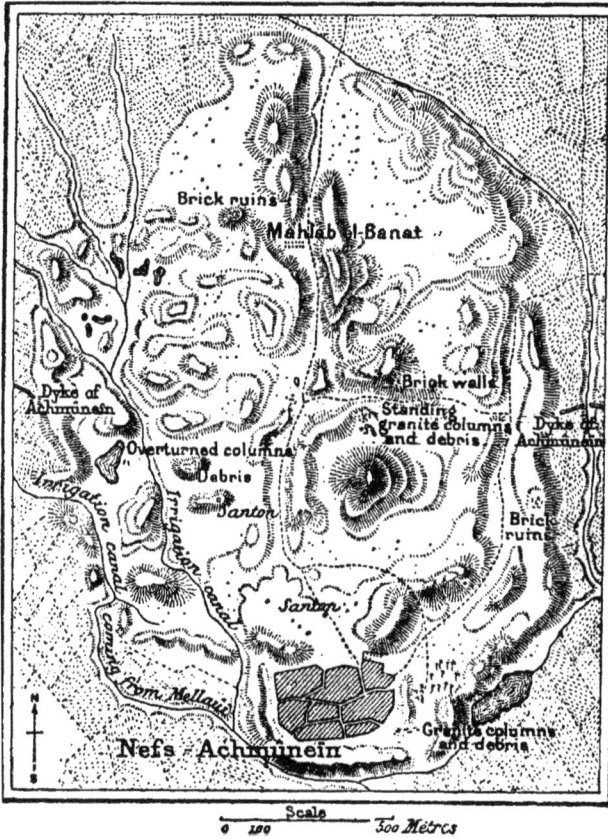

PLAN OF THE RUINS OF HERMOPOLIS MAGNA.[1]

Ennead of Saïs, Isis of that of Bûto, and Hâthor of that of Denderah.[2] Few of the sacerdotal colleges went beyond

---

[1] Plan drawn by Thuillier, from the *Description de l' Égypte*, Ant., vol. iv. pl. 50.

[2] On the Ennead of Hâthor at Denderah, see MARIETTE, *Denderah*, p. 80,

the substitution of their own feudal gods for Atûmû. Provided that the god of each nome held the rank of supreme lord, the rest mattered little, and the local theologians made no change in the order of the other agents of creation, their vanity being unhurt even by the lower offices assigned by the Heliopolitan tradition to such powers as Osiris, Sibû, and Sit, who were known and worshipped throughout the whole country. The theologians of Hermopolis alone declined to borrow the new system just as it stood, and in all its parts. Hermopolis had always been one of the ruling cities of Middle Egypt. Standing alone in the midst of the land lying between the Eastern and Western Niles, it had established upon each of the two great arms of the river a port and a custom-house, where all boats travelling either up or down stream paid toll on passing. Not only the corn and natural products of the valley and of the Delta, but also goods from distant parts of Africa brought to Siût by Soudanese caravans, helped to fill the treasury of Hermopolis. Thot, the god of the city, represented as ibis or baboon, was essentially a moon-god, who measured time, counted the days, numbered the months, and recorded the years. Lunar divinities, as we know, are everywhere supposed to exercise the most varied powers: they command the mysterious forces of the universe; they know the sounds,

et seq., of the text. The fact that Nît, Isis, and, generally speaking, all the feudal goddesses, were the chiefs of their local Enneads, is proved by the epithets applied to them, which represent them as having independent creative power by virtue of their own unaided force and energy, like the god at the head of the Heliopolitan Ennead.

words, and gestures by which those forces are put in
motion, and not content with using them for their own
benefit, they also teach to their worshippers the art of
employing them. Thot formed no
exception to this rule. He was
lord of the voice, master of words
and of books, possessor or inventor
of those magic writings which

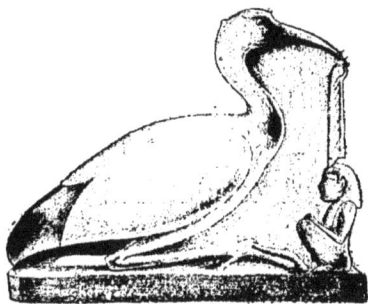

THE IBIS THOT.[1]   THE CYNOCEPHALOUS THOT.[2]

nothing in heaven, on earth, or in Hades can withstand.[3]

[1] Drawn by Faucher-Gudin from an enamelled pottery figure from Coptos,
now in my possession. Neck, feet, and tail are in blue enamel, the rest is
in green. The little personage represented as squatting beneath the beak is
Mâit, the goddess of truth, and the ally of Thot. The ibis was furnished
with a ring for suspending it; this has been broken off, but traces of it may
still be seen at the back of the head.

[2] Drawn by Faucher-Gudin from a green enamelled pottery figure in my
possession (Saite period).

[3] Cf. in the tale of Satni (MASPERO, Contes populaires de l'Ancienne Égypte,
2nd edit., p. 175) the description of " the book which Thot has himself written
with his own hand," and which makes its possessor the equal of the gods.
" The two formulas which are written therein, if thou recitest the first thou
shalt charm heaven, earth, Hades, the mountains, the waters ; thou shalt
know the birds of the sky and the reptiles, how many soever they be ; thou
shalt see the fish of the deep, for a divine power will cause them to rise to
the surface of the water. If thou readest the second formula, even although

He had discovered the incantations which evoke and control the gods; he had transcribed the texts and noted the melodies of these incantations; he recited them with that true intonation—*mâ khrôû*—which renders them all-powerful, and every one, whether god or man, to whom he imparted them, and whose voice he made true—*smâ khrôû* —became like himself master of the universe. He had accomplished the creation not by muscular effort to which the rest of the cosmogonical gods primarily owed their birth, but by means of formulas, or even of the voice alone, "the first time" when he awoke in the Nû. In fact, the articulate word and the voice were believed to be the most potent of creative forces, not remaining immaterial on issuing from the lips, but condensing, so to speak, into tangible substances; into bodies which were themselves animated by creative life and energy; into gods and goddesses who lived or who created in their turn. By a very short phrase Tûmû had called forth the gods who order all things; for his "Come unto me!" uttered with a loud voice upon the day of creation, had evoked the sun from within the lotus. Thot had opened his lips, and the voice which proceeded from him had become an entity; sound had solidified into matter, and by a simple emission of voice the four gods who preside over the four houses of the world had come forth alive from his mouth without bodily effort on his part, and without spoken evocation. Creation by the voice is almost as

thou shouldest be in the tomb, thou shalt again take the form which was thine upon earth; thou shalt even see the sun rising in heaven, and his cycle of gods, and the moon in the form wherein it appeareth.

great a refinement of thought as the substitution of creation by the word for creation by muscular effort. In fact, sound bears the same relation to words that the whistle of a quartermaster bears to orders for the navigation of a ship transmitted by a speaking trumpet; it simplifies speech, reducing it as it were to a pure abstraction. At first it was believed that the creator had made the world with a word, then that he had made it by sound; but the further conception of his having made it by thought does not seem to have occurred to the theologians. It was narrated at Hermopolis, and the legend was ultimately universally accepted, even by the Heliopolitans, that the separation of Nûît and Sibû had taken place at a certain spot on the site of the city where Sibû had ascended the mound on which the feudal temple was afterwards built, in order that he might better sustain the goddess and uphold the sky at the proper height. The conception of a Creative Council of five gods had so far prevailed at Hermopolis that from this fact the city had received in remote antiquity the name of the "House of the Five;" its temple was called the "Abode of the Five" down to a late period in Egyptian history, and its prince, who was the hereditary high priest of Thot, reckoned as the first of his official titles that of "Great One of the House of the Five."

The four couples who had helped Atûmû were identified with the four auxiliary gods of Thot, and changed the council of Five into a Great Hermopolitan Ennead, but at the cost of strange metamorphoses. However artificially they had been grouped about Atûmû, they had all preserved such distinctive characteristics as prevented their being confounded one with another. When the universe which they had helped to build up was finally seen to be the result of various operations demanding a considerable manifestation of physical energy, each god was required to preserve the individuality necessary for the production of such effects as were expected of him. They could not have existed and carried on their work without conforming to the ordinary conditions of humanity; being born one of another, they were bound to have paired with living goddesses as capable of bringing forth their children as they were of begetting them. On the other hand, the four auxiliary gods of Hermopolis exercised but one means of action—the voice. Having themselves come forth from the master's mouth, it was by voice that they created and perpetuated the world. Apparently they could have done without goddesses had marriage not been imposed upon them by their identification with the corresponding gods of the Heliopolitan Ennead; at any rate, their wives had but a show of life, almost destitute of reality. As these four gods worked after the manner of their master, Thot, so they also bore his form and reigned along with him as so many baboons. When associated with the lord of Hermopolis, the eight divinities of Heliopolis assumed the character and the appearance of the four Hermopolitan gods in whom they were merged. They were often represented as eight baboons surrounding the supreme baboon, or as four pairs of gods and goddesses without either characteristic attributes or features; or, finally, as four pairs of gods and goddesses, the gods being

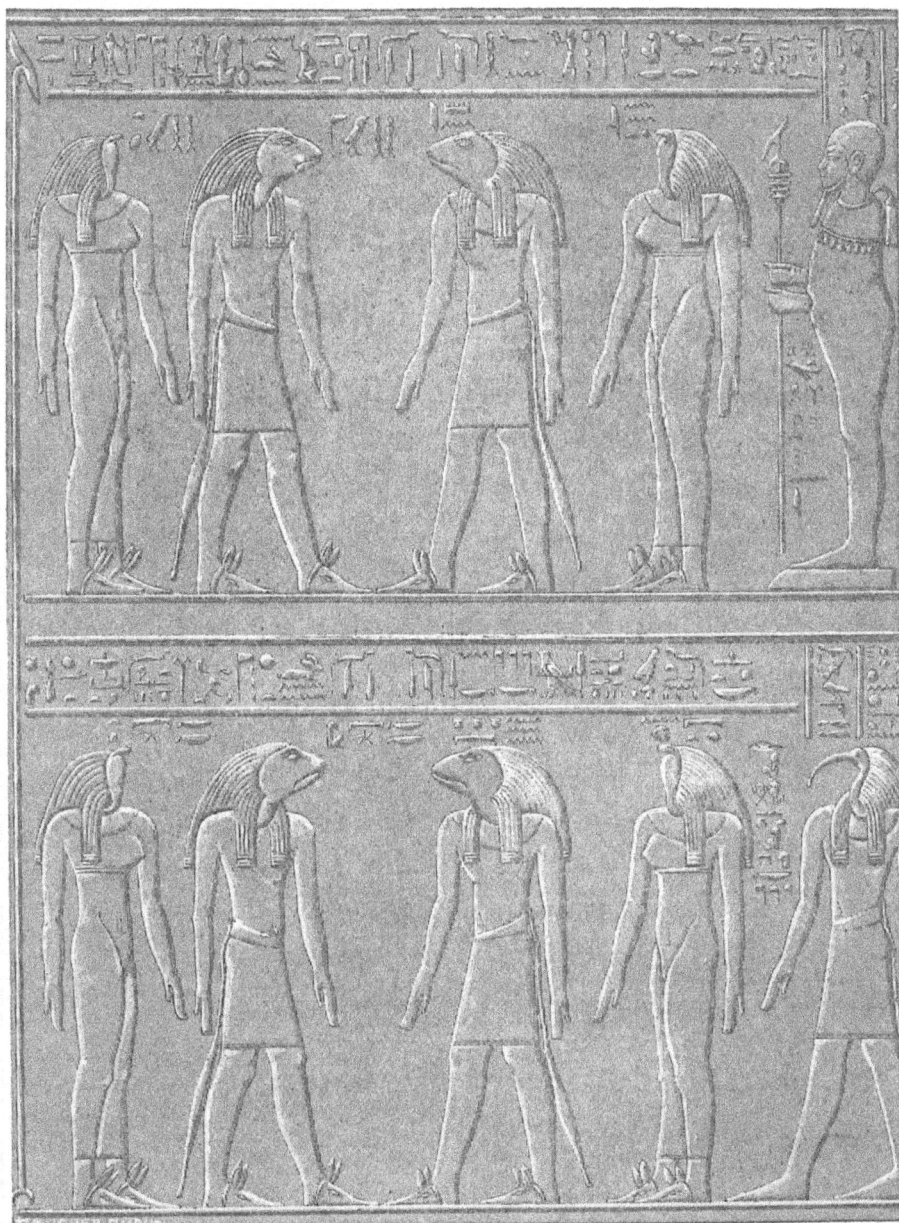

THE HERMOPOLITAN OGDOAD.[1]

[1] Drawn by Faucher-Gudin from a photograph by Béato. Cf. LEPSIUS, *Denkm.*, iv. pl. 66 c. In this illustration I have combined the two extremities of a great scene at Philæ, in which the *Eight*, divided into two groups of four,

frog-headed men, and the goddesses serpent-headed women. Morning and evening do they sing; and the mysterious hymns wherewith they salute the rising and the setting sun ensure the continuity of his course. Their names did not survive their metamorphoses; each pair had no longer more than a single name, the termination of each name varying according as a god or a goddess was intended: —Nû and Nûit, Hehû and Hehît, Kakû and Kakît, Ninû and Ninît. As far as we are able to judge, the couple Nû-Nûit answers to Shû-Tafnûît; Hahû-Hehît to Sibû and Nûit; Kakû-Kakît to Osiris and Isis; Ninû-Ninit to Sit and Nephthys. There was seldom any occasion to invoke them separately; they were addressed collectively as the Eight—*Khmûnû*—and it was on their account that Hermopolis was named *Khmûnû*, the City of the Eight. Ultimately they were deprived of the little individual life still left to them, and were fused into a single being to whom the texts refer as Khomninû, the god Eight. By degrees the Ennead of Thot was thus reduced to two terms:

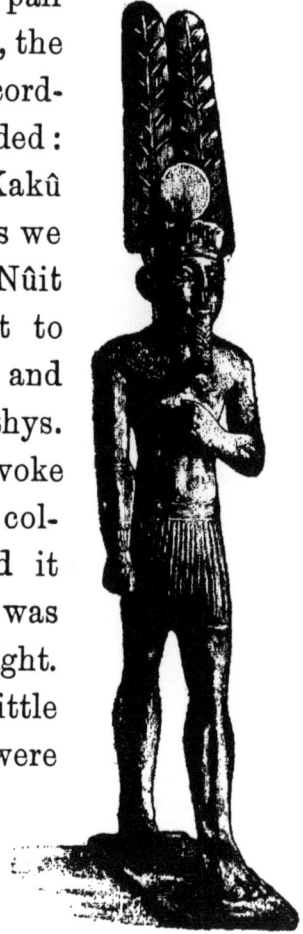

AMON.[1]

take part in the adoration of the king. According to a custom common towards the Græco-Roman period, the sculptor has made the feet of his gods like jackals' heads; it is a way of realizing the well-known metaphor which compares a rapid runner to the jackal roaming around Egypt.

[1] Drawn by Faucher-Gudin from a bronze statuette found at Thebes, and now in my possession.

the god One and the god Eight, the Monad and the Ogdoad. The latter had scarcely more than a theoretical existence, and was generally absorbed into the person of the former. Thus the theologians of Hermopolis gradually disengaged the unity of their feudal god from the multiplicity of the cosmogonic deities.

As the sacerdotal colleges had adopted the Heliopolitan doctrine, so they now generally adopted that of Hermopolis: Amon, for instance, being made to preside indifferently over the eight baboons and over the four independent couples of the primitive Ennead. In both cases the process of adaptation was absolutely identical, and would have been attended by no difficulty whatever, had the divinities to whom it was applied only been without family; in that case, the one needful change for each city would have been that of a single name in the Heliopolitan list, thus leaving the number of the Ennead unaltered. But since these deities had been turned into triads they could no longer be primarily regarded as simple units, to be combined with the elements of some one or other of the Enneads without preliminary arrangement. The two companions whom each had chosen had to be adopted also, and the single Thot, or single Atûmû, replaced by the three patrons of the nome, thus changing the traditional nine into eleven. Happily, the constitution of the triad lent itself to all these adaptations. We have seen that the father and the son became one and the same personage, whenever it was thought desirable. We also know that one of the two parents always so far predominated as almost to efface the other. Sometimes it was the goddess

who disappeared behind her husband ; sometimes it was the
god whose existence merely served to account for the offspring of the goddess, and whose only title to his position
consisted in the fact that he was her husband. Two
personages thus closely connected were not long in blending
into one, and were soon defined as being two faces, the
masculine and feminine aspects of a single being. On the
one hand, the father was one with the son, and on the
other he was one with the mother. Hence the mother was
one with the son as with the father, and the three gods of

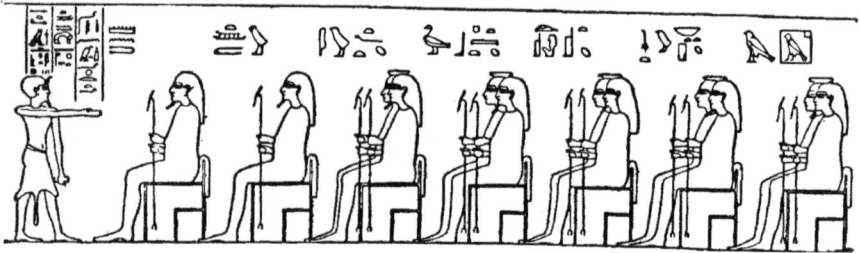

THE THEBAN ENNEAD.[1]

the triad were resolved into one god in three persons.
Thanks to this subterfuge, to put a triad at the head of an
Ennead was nothing more than a roundabout way of placing
a single god there : the three persons only counted as one,
and the eleven names only amounted to the nine canonical
divinities. Thus, the Theban Ennead of Amon-Mant-
Khonsû, Shû, Tafnûît, Sibû, Nûit, Osiris, Isis, Sît, and
Nephthys, is, in spite of its apparent irregularity, as correct
as the typical Ennead itself. In such Enneads Isis is
duplicated by goddesses of like nature, such as Hâthor,

[1] This Ennead consists of fourteen members—Montû, duplicating Atûmû ;
the four usual couples ; then Horus, the son of Isis and Osiris, together with
his associate deities, Hâthor, Tanu, and Anit.

Selkît, Taninît, and yet remains but one, while Osiris brings in his son Horus, who gathers about himself all such gods as play the part of divine son in other triads. The theologians had various methods of procedure for keeping the number of persons in an Ennead at nine, no matter how many they might choose to embrace in it. Supernumeraries were thrown in like the "shadows" at Roman suppers, whom guests would bring without warning to their host, and whose presence made not the slightest difference either in the provision for the feast, or in the arrangements for those who had been formally invited.

Thus remodelled at all points, the Ennead of Heliopolis was readily adjustable to sacerdotal caprices, and even profited by the facilities which the triad afforded for its natural expansion. In time the Heliopolitan version of the origin of Shû-Tafnûît must have appeared too primitively barbarous. Allowing for the licence of the Egyptians during Pharaonic times, the concept of the spontaneous emission whereby Atûmû had produced his twin children was characterized by a superfluity of coarseness which it was at least unnecessary to employ, since by placing the god in a triad, this double birth could be duly explained in conformity with the ordinary laws of life. The solitary Atûmû of the more ancient dogma gave place to Atûmû the husband and father. He had, indeed, two wives, Iûsâsît and Nebthotpît, but their individualities were so feebly marked that no one took the trouble to choose between them; each passed as the mother of Shû and Tafnûît. This system of combination, so puerile in its ingenuity, was fraught with the gravest consequences to the history of Egyptian religions. Shû having been transformed into the divine son of the Heliopolitan triad, could henceforth be assimilated with the divine sons of all those triads which took the place of Tûmû at the heads of provincial Enneads. Thus we find that Horus the son of Isis at Bûto, Arihosnofir the son of Nit at Saïs, Khnûmû the son of Hâthor at Esneh, were each in turn identified with Shû the son of Atûmû, and lost their individualities in his. Sooner or later this was bound to result in bringing all the triads closer together, and in their absorption into one another. Through constant reiteration of the statement that the divine sons of the triads were identical with Shû, as being in the second rank of the Ennead, the idea arose that this was also the case in triads unconnected with Enneads; in other terms, that the third person in any family of gods was everywhere and always Shû under a different name. It having been finally admitted in the sacerdotal colleges that Tûmû and Shû, father and son, were one, all the divine sons were, therefore, identical with Tûmû, the father of Shû, and as each divine son was one with his parents, it inevitably followed that these parents themselves were identical with Tûmû. Reasoning in this way, the Egyptians naturally tended towards that conception of the divine oneness to which the theory of the Hermopolitan Ogdoad was already leading them. In fact, they reached it, and the monuments show us that in comparatively early times the theologians were busy uniting in a single person the prerogatives which their ancestors had ascribed to many different beings. But this conception of deity towards which their ideas were converging has nothing in common with the conception of the God of our modern religions and philosophies. No god of the Egyptians was ever spoken of simply as God. Tûmû was the "one and only god"— *nûtir ûâû ûâiti*—at Heliopolis; Anhûri-Shû was also the "one and only god" at Sebennytos and at Thinis. The unity of Atûmû did not interfere with that of Anhûri-Shû, but each of these gods, although the "sole" deity in his own domain, ceased to be so in the domain of the other. The feudal spirit, always alert and jealous, prevented the higher dogma which was dimly apprehended in the temples from triumphing over local religions and extending over the whole land. Egypt had as many "sole" deities as she had large cities, or even important temples; she never accepted the idea of the sole God, "beside whom there is none other."

THE
LEGENDARY HISTORY OF EGYPT

——◆◆——

THE DIVINE DYNASTIES: RÂ, SHÛ, OSIRIS, SÎT, HORUS—THOT, AND THE
INVENTION OF SCIENCES AND WRITING—MENES, AND THE THREE FIRST
HUMAN DYNASTIES.

· *The Egyptians claim to be the most ancient of peoples : traditions concerning
the creation of man and of animals—The Heliopolitan Enneads the framework
of the divine dynasties—Râ, the first King of Egypt, and his fabulous history :
he allows himself to be duped and robbed by Isis, destroys rebellious men, and
ascends into heaven.*

*The legend of Shû and Sibû—The reign of Osiris Onnophris and of Isis :
they civilize Egypt and the world—Osiris, slain by Sît, is entombed by Isis and
avenged by Horus—The wars of Typhon and of Horus : peace, and the division
of Egypt between the two gods.*

*The Osirian embalmment : the kingdom of Osiris opened to the followers of
Horus—The Book of the Dead—The journeying of the soul in search of the*

fields of Ialû—The judgment of the soul, the negative confession—The privileges and duties of Osirian souls—Confusion between Osirian and Solar ideas as to the state of the dead : the dead in the bark of the Sun—The going forth by day —The campaigns of Harmakhis against Sît.

Thot, the inventor : he reveals all sciences to men—Astronomy, stellar tables ; the year, its subdivisions, its defects, influence of the heavenly bodies and the days upon human destiny—Magic arts ; incantations, amulets—Medicine : the vitalizing spirits, diagnosis, treatment — Writing : ideographic, syllabic, alphabetic.

The history of Egypt as handed down by tradition : Manetho, the royal lists, main divisions of Egyptian history—The beginnings of its early history vague and uncertain : Menes, and the legend of Memphis—The first three human dynasties, the two Thinite and the Memphite—Character and origin of the legends concerning them—The famine stela—The earliest monuments : the step pyramid of Saqqârah.

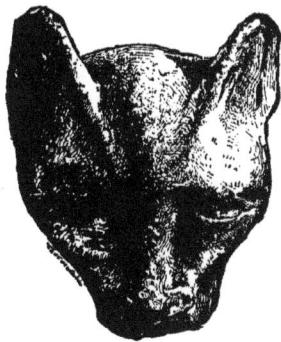

ISIS, HAVING FLED TO THE MARSHES, SUCKLES HORUS UNDER THE PROTECTION OF THE GODS.[1]

CHAPTER III

THE LEGENDARY HISTORY OF EGYPT

The divine dynasties : Râ, Shû, Osiris, Sît, Horus—Thot, and the invention of sciences and writing—Menes, and the three first human dynasties.

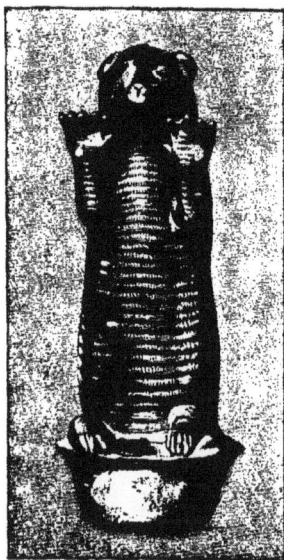

THE building up and diffusion of the doctrine of the Ennead, like the formation of the land of Egypt, demanded centuries of sustained effort, centuries of which the inhabitants themselves knew neither the number nor the authentic history. When questioned as to the remote past of their race, they proclaimed themselves the most ancient of mankind, in comparison with whom all other races were but a mob of young children; and they

[1] Bas-relief at Philæ; drawn by Faucher-Gudin, from a photograph by Béato. The vignette, also drawn by Faucher-Gudin, represents an ichneumon,

looked upon nations which denied their pretensions with
such indulgence and pity as we feel for those who doubt a
well-known truth. Their forefathers had appeared upon the
banks of the Nile even before the creator had completed
his work, so eager were the gods to behold their birth.
No Egyptian disputed the reality of this right of the
firstborn, which ennobled the whole race; but if they were
asked the name of their divine father, then the harmony
was broken, and each advanced the claims of a different
personage.[1] Phtah had modelled man with his own hands;[2]
Khnûmû had formed him on a potter's table.[3] Râ at his
first rising, seeing the earth desert and bare, had flooded

or Pharaoh's rat, sitting up on its haunches, with paws uplifted in adoration.
It has been variously interpreted. I take it to be the image of an animal
spontaneously generated out of the mud, and giving thanks to Râ at the
very moment of its creation. The original is of bronze, and in the Gizeh
Museum.

[1] We know the words which Plato puts into the mouth of an Egyptian
priest : "O Solon, Solon, you Greeks are always children, and there is no old
man who is a Greek! You are all young in mind ; there is no opinion or
tradition of knowledge among you which is white with age." Other nations
disputed their priority—the Phrygians, the Medes, or rather the tribe of the
Magi among the Medes, the Ethiopians, the Scythians. A cycle of legends
had gathered about this subject, giving an account of the experiments
instituted by Psamtik, or other sovereigns, to find out which were right,
Egyptians or foreigners.

[2] At Philæ and at Denderah, Phtah is represented as piling upon his
potter's table the plastic clay from which he is about to make a human body,
and which is somewhat wrongly called the egg of the world. It is really the
lump of earth from which man came forth at his creation.

[3] At Philæ, Khnûmû calls himself "the potter who fashions men, the
modeller of the gods." He there moulds the members of Osiris, the
husband of the local Isis, as at Erment he forms the body of Harsamtaûi, or
rather that of Ptolemy Cæsarion, the son of Julius Cæsar and the celebrated
Cleopatra, identified with Harsamtaûi.

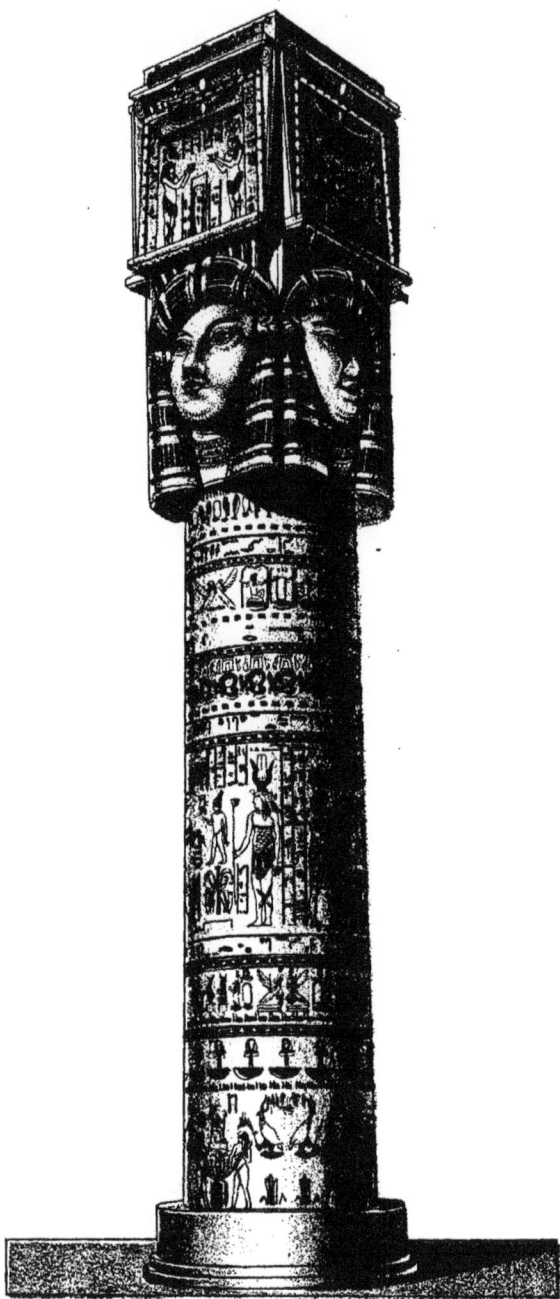

COLUMN OF THE TEMPLE OF DENDERAK.

it with his rays as with a flood of tears; all living things, vegetable and animal, and man himself, had sprung pell-mell from his eyes, and were scattered abroad with the light over the surface of the world.[1] Sometimes the facts were presented under a less poetic aspect. The mud of the Nile, heated to excess by the burning sun, fermented and brought forth the various races of men and animals by spontaneous generàtion, having moulded itself into a thousand living forms. Then its procreative power became weakened to the verge of exhaustion. Yet on the banks of the river, in the height of summer, smaller animals might still be found whose condition showed what had once taken place in the case of the larger kinds. Some appeared as already fully formed, and struggling to free themselves from the oppressive mud; others, as yet imperfect, feebly stirred their heads and fore feet, while their hind quarters were completing their articulation and taking shape within the matrix of earth.[2] It was not Râ alone whose tears were

[1] With reference to the substances which proceeded from the eye of Râ, see the remarks of BIRCH, Sur un papyrus magique du Musée Britannique. By his tears (romîtû) Horus, or his eye as identified with the sun, had given birth to all men, Egyptians (romîtû, rotû), Libyans, and Asiatics, excepting only the negroes. The latter were born from another part of his body by the same means as those employed by Atûmû in the creation of Shû and Tafnûît.

[2] The same story is told, but with reference to rats only, by PLINY, by DIODORUS, by ÆLIANUS, by MACROBIUS, and by other Greek or Latin writers. Even in later times, and in Europe, this pretended phenomenon met with a certain degree of belief, as may be seen from the curious work of MARCUS FREDERICUS WENDELINUS, Archi-palatinus, Admiranda Nili, Franco-furti, MDCXXIII., cap. xxi. pp. 157-183. In Egypt all the fellahin believe in the spontaneous generation of rats as in an article of their creed. They have spoken to me of it at Thebes, at Denderah, and on the plain of Abydos; and

endowed with vitalizing power. All divinities whether beneficent or malevolent, Sit as well as Osiris or Isis, could give life by weeping; and the work of their eyes, when once it had fallen upon earth, flourished and multiplied as vigorously as that which came from the eyes of Râ. The individual character of the creator was not without bearing upon the nature of his creatures; good was the necessary outcome of the good gods, evil of the evil ones ; and herein lay the explanation of the mingling of things excellent and things execrable, which is found everywhere

KHNÛMÛ MODELLING MAN UPON A POTTER'S TABLE.[1]

Major Brown has lately noted the same thing in the Fayûm. The variant which he heard from the lips of the notables is curious, for it professes to explain why the rats who infest the fields in countless bands during the dry season, suddenly disappear at the return of the inundation ; born of the mud and putrid water of the preceding year, to mud they return, and as it were dissolve at the touch of the new waters.

[1] Drawn by Boudier, from a photograph by Gayet. The scene is taken from bas-reliefs in the temple of Luxor, where the god Khnûmû is seen completing his modelling of the future King Amenôthes III. and his double, represented as two children wearing the side-lock and large necklace. The first holds his finger to his lips, while the arms of the second swing at his sides.

throughout the world. Voluntarily or involuntarily, Sît and his partisans were the cause and origin of all that is harmful. Daily their eyes shed upon the world those juices by which plants are made poisonous, as well as malign influences, crime, and madness. Their saliva, the foam which fell from their mouths during their attacks of rage, their sweat, their blood itself, were all no less to be feared. When any drop of it touched the earth, straightway it germinated, and produced something strange and baleful—a serpent, a scorpion, a plant of deadly nightshade or of henbane. But, on the other hand, the sun was all goodness, and persons or things which it cast forth into life infallibly partook of its benignity. Wine that maketh man glad, the bee who works for him in the flowers secreting wax and honey, the meat and herbs which are his food, the stuffs that clothe him, all useful things which he makes for himself, not only emanated from the Solar Eye of Horus, but were indeed nothing more than the Eye of Horus under different aspects, and in his name they were presented in sacrifice. The devout generally were of opinion that the first Egyptians, the sons and flock of Râ, came into the world happy and perfect;[1] by degrees their descendants had fallen from that native felicity into their present state. Some, on the contrary, affirmed that their

---

[1] In the tomb of Seti I., the words *flock of the Sun, flock of Râ*, are those by which the god Horus refers to men. Certain expressions used by Egyptian writers are in themselves sufficient to show that the first generations of men were supposed to have lived in a state of happiness and perfection. To the Egyptians *the times of Râ, the times of the god*—that is to say, the centuries immediately following on the creation—were the ideal age, and no good thing had appeared upon earth since then.

ancestors were born as so many brutes, unprovided with
the most essential arts of gentle life. They knew nothing
of articulate speech, and expressed themselves by cries
only, like other animals, until the day when Thot taught
them both speech and writing.

These tales sufficed for popular edification; they provided but meagre fare for the intelligence of the learned.
The latter did not confine their ambition to the possession
of a few incomplete and contradictory details concerning
the beginnings of humanity. They wished to know the
history of its consecutive development from the very first;
what manner of life had been led by their fathers; what
chiefs they had obeyed and the names or adventures of
those chiefs; why part of the nations had left the blessed
banks of the Nile and gone to settle in foreign lands; by
what stages and in what length of time those who had not
emigrated rose out of native barbarism into that degree
of culture to which the most ancient monuments bore
testimony. No efforts of imagination were needful for the
satisfaction of their curiosity: the old substratum of indigenous traditions was rich enough, did they but take the
trouble to work it out systematically, and to eliminate its
most incongruous elements. The priests of Heliopolis took
this work in hand, as they had already taken in hand
the same task with regard to the myths referring to the
creation; and the Enneads provided them with a ready-
made framework. They changed the gods of the Ennead
into so many kings, determined with minute accuracy the
lengths of their reigns, and compiled their biographies from
popular tales. The duality of the feudal god supplied an

admirable expedient for connecting the history of the world with that of chaos. Tûmû was identified with Nû, and relegated to the primordial Ocean : Râ was retained, and proclaimed the first king of the world. He had not established his rule without difficulty. The " Children of Defeat," beings hostile to order and light, engaged him in fierce battles; nor did he succeed in organizing his kingdom until he had conquered them in nocturnal combat at Hermopolis, and even at Heliopolis itself.[1] Pierced with wounds, Apôpi the serpent sank into the depths of Ocean at the very moment when the new year began. The secondary members of the Great Ennead, together with the Sun, formed the first dynasty, which began with the dawn of the first day, and ended at the coming of Horus, the son of Isis. The local schools of theology welcomed this method of writing history as readily as they had welcomed the principle of the Ennead itself. Some of them retained the Heliopolitan demiurge, and hastened to associate him with their own ; others completely eliminated him in favour of the feudal divinity,—Amon at Thebes

[1] The *Children of Defeat*, in Egyptian *Mosû batashû*, or *Mosû batashît*, are often confounded with the followers of Sît, the enemies of Osiris. From the first they were distinct, and represented beings and forces hostile to the sun, with the dragon Apôpi at their head. Their defeat at Hermopolis corresponded to the moment when Shû, raising the sky above the sacred mound in that city, substituted order and light for chaos and darkness. This defeat is mentioned in chap. xvii. of the *Book of the Dead* (NAVILLE's edition, vol. i. pl. xxiii. l. 3, et seq.), in which connexion E. DE ROUGÉ first explained its meaning. In the same chapter of the *Book of the Dead* (NAVILLE's edition, vol. i. pls. xxiv., xxv., ll. 54–58), reference is also made to the battle by night, in Heliopolis, at the close of which Râ appeared in the form of a cat or lion, and beheaded the great serpent.

Thot at Hermopolis, Phtah at Memphis,—keeping the rest of the dynasty absolutely unchanged.[1] The gods in no way compromised their prestige by becoming incarnate and descending to earth. Since they were men of finer nature, and their qualities, including that of miracle-working, were human qualities raised to the highest pitch of intensity, it was not considered derogatory to them personally to have watched over the infancy and childhood of primeval man. The raillery in which the Egyptians occasionally indulged with regard to them, the good-humoured and even ridiculous *rôles* ascribed to them in certain legends, do not prove that they were despised, or that zeal for them had cooled. The greater the respect of believers for the objects of their worship, the more easily do they tolerate the taking of such liberties, and the condescension of the members of the Ennead, far from lowering them in the eyes of generations who came too late to live with them upon familiar terms, only enhanced the love and reverence in which they were held.

Nothing shows this better than the history of Râ. His world was ours in the rough ; for since Shû was yet non-existent, and Nûît still reposed in the arms of Sibû, earth and sky were but one.[2] Nevertheless in this first attempt

[1] Thot is the chief of the Hermopolitan Ennead, and the titles ascribed to him by inscriptions maintaining his supremacy show that he also was considered to have been the first king. One of the Ptolemies said of himself that he came " as the Majesty of Thot, because he was the equal of Atûmû, hence the equal of Khopri, hence the equal of Râ." Atûmû-Khopri-Râ being the first earthly king, it follows that the *Majesty of Thot*, with whom Ptolemy identifies himself, comparing himself to the three forms of the God Râ, is also the first earthly king.

[2] This conception of the primitive Egyptian world is clearly implied in

at a world there was vegetable, animal, and human life. Egypt was there, all complete, with her two chains of mountains, her Nile, her cities, the people of her nomes, and the nomes themselves. Then the soil was more generous; the harvests, without the labourer's toil, were higher and more abundant; [1] and when the Egyptians of Pharaonic times wished to mark their admiration of any person or thing, they said that the like had never been known since the time of Râ. It is an illusion common to all peoples; as their insatiable thirst for happiness is never assuaged by the present, they fall back upon the remotest past in search of an age when that supreme felicity which is only known to them as an ideal was actually enjoyed by their ancestors. Râ dwelt in Heliopolis, and the most ancient portion of the temple of the city, that known as the "Mansion of the Prince"—*Hâît Sarû*,—passed for having been his palace. His court was mainly composed of gods and goddesses, and they as well as he were visible to men. It contained also men who filled minôr offices

the very terms employed by the author of *The Destruction of Men*. Nûît does not rise to form the sky until such time as Râ thinks of bringing his reign to an end; that is to say, after Egypt had already been in existence for many centuries. In chap. xvii. of the *Book of the Dead* (NAVILLE's edition, vol. i. pl. xxiii. ll. 3–5) it is stated that the reign of Râ began *in the times when the upliftings had not yet taken place;* that is to say, before Shû had separated Nûît from Sibû, and forcibly *uplifted* her above the body of her husband.

[2] This is an ideal in accordance with the picture drawn of the fields of Ialû in chap. cx. of the *Book of the Dead* (NAVILLE's edition, vol. i. pls. cxxi.–cxxiii.). As with the Paradise of most races, so the place of the Osirian dead still possessed privileges which the earth had enjoyed during the first years succeeding the creation; that is to say, under the direct rule of Râ.

about his person, prepared his food, received the offerings of his subjects, attended to his linen and household affairs. It was said that the *oîrû maû*—the high priest of Râ, the *hankistît*—his high priestess, and generally speaking all the servants of the temple of Heliopolis, were either directly descended from members of this first household

AT THE FIRST HOUR OF THE DAY THE SUN EMBARKS FOR HIS JOURNEY THROUGH EGYPT.[1]

establishment of the god, or had succeeded to their offices in unbroken succession. In the morning he went forth with his divine train, and, amid the acclamations of the crowd, entered the bark in which he made his accustomed circuit of the world, returning to his home at the end of twelve hours after the accomplishment of his journey. He

[1] Drawn by Faucher-Gudin, from one of the scenes represented upon the architraves of the pronaos at Edfû (ROSELLINI, *Monumenti del Culto*, pl. xxxviii. No. 1).

visited each province in turn, and in each he tarried for an hour, to settle all disputed matters, as the final judge of appeal. He gave audience to both small and great, he decided their quarrels and adjudged their lawsuits, he granted investiture of fiefs from the royal domains to those who had deserved them, and allotted or confirmed to every family the income needful for their maintenance. He pitied the sufferings of his people, and did his utmost to alleviate them; he taught to all comers potent formulas against reptiles and beasts of prey, charms to cast out evil spirits, and the best recipes for preventing illness. His incessant bounties left him at length with only one of his talismans: the name given to him by his father and mother at his birth, which they had revealed to him alone, and which he kept concealed within his bosom lest some sorcerer should get possession of it to use for the furtherance of his evil spells.

But old age came on, and infirmities followed; the body of Râ grew bent, "his mouth trembled, his slaver trickled down to earth and his saliva dropped upon the ground." Isis, who had hitherto been a mere woman-servant in the household of the Pharaoh, conceived the project of stealing his secret from him, " that she might possess the world and make herself a goddess by the name of the august god." Force would have been unavailing; all enfeebled as he was by reason of his years, none was strong enough to contend successfully against him. But Isis "was a woman more knowing in her malice than millions of men, clever among millions of the gods, equal to millions of spirits, to whom as unto

Râ nothing was unknown either in heaven or upon earth." She contrived a most ingenious stratagem. When man or god was struck down by illness, the only chance of curing him lay in knowing his real name, and thereby adjuring the evil being that tormented him. Isis determined to cast a terrible malady upon Râ, concealing its cause from him; then to offer her services as his nurse, and by means of his sufferings to extract from him the mysterious word indispensable to the success of the exorcism. She gathered up mud impregnated with the divine saliva, and moulded of it a sacred serpent which she hid in the dust of the road. Suddenly bitten as he was setting out upon his daily round, the god cried out aloud, "his voice ascended into heaven and his Nine called: 'What is it? what is it?' and his gods: 'What is the matter? what is the matter?' but he could make them no answer so much did his lips tremble, his limbs shake, and the venom take hold upon his flesh as the Nile seizeth upon the land which it invadeth." Presently he came to himself, and succeeded in describing his sensations. "Something painful hath stung me; my heart perceiveth it, yet my two eyes see it not; my hand hath not wrought it, nothing that I have made knoweth it what it is, yet have I never tasted suffering like unto it, and there is no pain that may overpass it. . . . Fire it is not, water it is not, yet is my heart in flames, my flesh trembleth, all my members are full of shiverings born of breaths of magic. Behold! let there be brought unto me children of the gods of beneficent words, who know the power of their mouths, and whose science reacheth unto heaven." They came, these children of the gods, all with their books of magic. There came Isis with her sorcery, her mouth full of life-giving breaths, her recipe for the destruction of pain, her words which pour life into breathless throats, and she said: "What is it? what is it, O father of the gods? May it not be that a serpent hath wrought this suffering in thee; that one of thy children hath lifted up his head against thee? Surely he shall be over-thrown by beneficent incantations, and I will make him to retreat at the sight of thy rays." On learning the cause of his torment, the Sun-god is terrified, and begins to lament anew: "I, then, as I went along the ways, travelling through my double land of Egypt and over my mountains, that I might look upon that which I ·have made, I was bitten by a serpent that I saw not. Fire it is not, water it is not, yet am I colder than water, I burn more than fire, all my members stream with sweat, I tremble, mine eye is not steady, no longer can I discern the sky, drops roll from my face as in the season of summer." Isis proposes her remedy, and cautiously asks him his ineffable name. But he divines her trick, and tries to evade it by an enumeration of his titles. He takes the universe to witness that he is called "Khopri in the morning, Râ at noon, Tûmû in the evening." The poison did not recede, but steadily advanced, and the great god was not eased. Then Isis said to Râ: "Thy name was not spoken in that which thou hast said. Tell it to me and the poison will depart; for he liveth upon whom a charm is pronounced in his own name." The poison glowed like fire, it was strong as the burning of flame, and the Majesty of Râ said, "I grant thee leave that thou shouldest search within me, O mother Isis! and that my name pass from my bosom into thy bosom." In truth, the all-powerful name was hidden within the body of the god, and could only be extracted thence by means of a surgical operation similar to that practised upon a corpse which is about to be mummified. Isis undertook it, carried it through successfully, drove out the poison, and made herself a goddess by virtue of the name. The cunning of a mere woman had deprived Râ of his last talisman.

In course of time men perceived his decrepitude. They took counsel against him: "Lo! his Majesty waxeth old, his bones are of silver, his flesh is of gold, his hair of lapis-lazuli." As soon as his Majesty perceived that which they were saying to each other, his Majesty said to those who were of his train, "Call together for me my Divine Eye, Shû, Tafnûît, Sibû, and Nûît, the father and the mother gods who were with me when I was in the Nû, with the god Nû. Let each bring his cycle along with him; then, when thou shalt have brought them in secret, thou shalt take them to the great mansion that they may lend me their counsel and their consent, coming hither from the Nû into this place where I have manifested myself." So the family council comes together : the ancestors of Râ, and his posterity still awaiting amid the primordial waters the time of their manifestation—his children Shû and Tafnûît, his grandchildren Sibû and Nûît. They place themselves,

according to etiquette, on either side his throne, prostrate, with their foreheads to the ground, and thus their
conference begins : " O Nû, thou the eldest of the gods,
from whom I took my being, and ye the ancestor-
gods, behold! men who are the emanation of mine eye
have taken counsel together against me! Tell me what
ye would do, for I have bidden you here before I slay
them, that I may hear what ye would say thereto."
Nû, as the eldest, has the right to speak first, and
demands that the guilty shall be brought to judgment
and formally condemned. " My son Râ, god greater
than the god who made him, older than the gods who
created him, sit thou upon thy throne, and great shall
be the terror when thine eye shall rest upon those who
plot together against thee!" But Râ not unreasonably
fears that when men see the solemn pomp of royal
justice, they may suspect the fate that awaits them,
and "flee into the desert, their hearts terrified at that
which I have to say to them." The desert was even
then hostile to the tutelary gods of Egypt, and offered
an almost inviolable asylum to their enemies. The con-
clave admits that the apprehensions of Râ are well
founded, and pronounces in favour of summary execution; the Divine Eye is to be the executioner. " Let
it go forth that it may smite those who have devised
evil against thee, for there is no Eye more to be feared
than thine when it attacketh in the form of Hâthor."
So the Eye takes the form of Hâthor, suddenly falls
upon men, and slays them right and left with great
strokes of the knife. After some hours, Râ, who would

chasten but not destroy his children, commands her to cease from her carnage; but the goddess has tasted blood, and refuses to obey him. "By thy life," she replies, "when I slaughter men then is my heart right joyful!" That is why she was afterwards called Sokhît the slayer, and represented under the form of a fierce lioness. Night-fall stayed her course in the neighbourhood of Heracleopolis; all the way from Heliopolis she had trampled through blood. As soon as she had fallen asleep, Râ hastily took effectual measures to prevent her from beginning her work again on the morrow. "He said: 'Call on my behalf mes-sengers agile and swift, who go like the wind.' When these messengers were straightway brought to him, the Majesty of the god said: 'Let them run to Elephantinê and bring me mandragora in plenty.'[2] When they had brought him the mandragora, the Majesty of this great god summoned

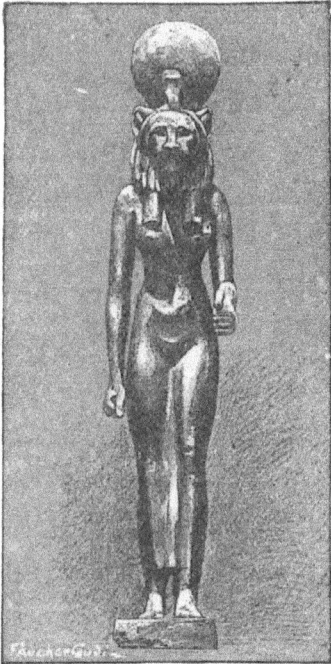

SOKHÎT, THE LIONESS-HEADED.[1]

[1] Drawn by Faucher-Gudin from a bronze statuette of the Saïte period in the Gizeh Museum (MARIETTE, *Album photographique du Musée de Boulaq*, pl. 6).

[2] The mandragora of Elephantinê was used in the manufacture of an intoxicating and narcotic drink employed either in medicine or in magic. In a special article, BRUGSCH has collected particulars preserved by the texts as to the uses of this plant. It was not as yet credited with the human form and the peculiar kind of life ascribed to it by western sorcerers.

the miller which is in Heliopolis that he might bray it;
and the women-servants having crushed grain for the
beer, the mandragora, and also human blood, were
mingled with the liquor, and thereof was made in all
seven thousand jars of beer." Râ himself examined
this delectable drink, and finding it to possess the
wished-for properties: "'It is well,' said he; 'therewith shall I save men from the goddess;' then, address-
ing those of his train: 'Take these jars in your arms,
and carry them to the place where she has slaughtered
men.' Râ, the king, caused dawn to break at midnight,
so that this philtre might be poured down upon the
earth; and the fields were flooded with it to the depth
of four palms, according as it pleased the souls of his
Majesty." In the morning the goddess came, "that
she might return to her carnage, but she found that all
was flooded, and her countenance softened; when she
had drunken, it was her heart that softened; she went
away drunk, without further thought of men." There
was some fear lest her fury might return when the
fumes of drunkenness were past, and to obviate this
danger Râ instituted a rite, partly with the object of
instructing future generations as to the chastisement
which he had inflicted upon the impious, partly to console Sokhît for her discomfiture. He decreed that "on
New Year's Day there should be brewed for her as many
jars of philtre as there were priestesses of the sun. That
was the origin of all those jars of philtre, in number
equal to that of the priestesses, which, at the feast of
Hâthor, all men make from that day forth."

Peace was re-established, but could it last long? Would not men, as soon as they had recovered from their terror, betake themselves again to plotting against the god? Besides, Râ now felt nothing but disgust for our race. The ingratitude of his children had wounded him deeply; he foresaw ever-renewed rebellions as his feebleness became more marked, and he shrank from having to order new massacres in which mankind would perish altogether. " By my life," says he to the gods who accompanied him, "my heart is too weary for me to remain with mankind, and slay them until they are no more: annihilation is not of the gifts that I love to make." And the gods exclaim in surprise : " Breathe not a word of thy weariness at a time when thou dost triumph at thy pleasure." But Râ does not yield to their representations; he will leave a kingdom wherein they murmur against him, and turning towards Nû he says : " My limbs are decrepit for the first time; I will not go to any place where I can be reached." It was no easy matter to find him an inaccessible retreat owing to the imperfect state in which the universe had been left by the first effort of the demiurge. Nû saw no other way out of the difficulty than that of setting to work to complete the creation. Ancient tradition had imagined the separation of earth and sky as an act of violence exercised by Shû upon Sibû and Nûît. History presented facts after a less brutal fashion, and Shû became a virtuous son who devoted his time and strength to upholding Nûît, that he might thereby do his father a service. Nûît, for her part, showed herself

to be a devoted daughter whom there was no need to
treat roughly in order to teach her her duty; of herself
she consented to leave her husband, and place her
beloved ancestor beyond reach. "The Majesty of Nû
said: 'Son Shû, do as thy father Râ shall say; and
thou, daughter Nûît, place him upon thy back and
hold him suspended above the earth!' Nûît said:
'And how then, my father Nû?' Thus spake Nûît,
and she did that which Nû commanded her; she
changed herself into a cow, and placed the Majesty of
Râ upon her back. When those men who had not been
slain came to give thanks to Râ, behold! they found
him no longer in his palace; but a cow stood there,
and they perceived him upon the back of the cow."
They found him so resolved to depart that they did
not try to turn him from his purpose, but only desired
to give him such a proof of their repentance as should
assure them of the complete pardon of their crime.
"They said unto him: 'Wait until the morning, O
Râ! our lord, and we will strike down thine enemies
who have taken counsel against thee.' So his Majesty
returned to his mansion, descended from the cow, went
in along with them, and earth was plunged into darkness. But when there was light upon earth the next
morning, the men went forth with their bows and
their arrows, and began to shoot at the enemy. Where-
upon the Majesty of this god said unto them: 'Your
sins are remitted unto you, for sacrifice precludes the
execution of the guilty.' And this was the origin upon
earth of sacrifices in which blood was shed."

Thus it was that when on the point of separating for ever, the god and men came to an understanding as to the terms of their future relationship. Men offered to the god the life of those who had offended him. Human sacrifice was in their eyes the obligatory sacrifice, the only one which could completely atone for the wrongs committed against the godhead; man alone was worthy to wash away with his blood the sins of men.[1] For this one time the god accepted the expiation just as it was offered to him; then the repugnance which he felt to killing his children overcame him, he substituted beast for man, and decided that oxen, gazelles, birds, should henceforth furnish the material for sacrifice.[2] This point settled, he again mounted the cow, who rose, supported on her four legs as on so many pillars; and her belly,

---

[1] This legend, which seeks to explain the discontinuance of human sacrifices among the Egyptians, affords direct proof of their existence in primitive times. This is confirmed by many facts. We shall see that *ûashbîti* laid in graves were in place of the male or female slaves who were originally slaughtered at the tombs of the rich and noble that they might go to serve their masters in the next world. Even in Thebes, under the XIXth dynasty, certain rock-cut tombs contain scenes which might lead us to believe that occasionally at least human victims were sent to doubles of distinction. During this same period, moreover, the most distinguished hostile chiefs taken in war were still put to death before the gods. In several towns, as at Eilithyia and at Heliopolis, or before certain gods, such as Osiris or Kronos-Sibû, human sacrifice lasted until near Roman times. But generally speaking it was very rare. Almost everywhere cakes of a particular shape, and called πέμματα, or else animals, had been substituted for man.

[2] It was asserted that the partisans of Apôpi and of Sît, who were the enemies of Râ, Osiris, and the other gods, had taken refuge in the bodies of certain animals. Hence, it was really human or divine victims which were offered when beasts were slaughtered in sacrifice before the altars.

stretched out above the earth like a ceiling, formed the sky. He busied himself with organizing the new world which he found on her back; he peopled it with many beings, chose two districts in which to establish his abode, the Field of Reeds—*Sokhît Ialû*—and the Field of Rest —*Sokhît Hotpît*—and suspended the stars which were to give light by night. All this is related with many plays upon words, intended, according to Oriental custom, as explanations of the names which the legend assigned to the different regions of heaven. At sight of a plain whose situation pleased him, he cried: "The Field rests in the distancé!"—and that was the origin of the Field of Rest. He added: "There will I gather plants!"—and from this the Field of Reeds took its name. While he gave himself up to this philological pastime, Nûit, suddenly transported to unaccustomed heights, grew frightened, and cried for help: "For pity's sake give me supports to sustain me!" This was the origin of the support-gods. They came and stationed themselves by each of her four legs, steadying these with their hands, and keeping constant watch over them. As this was not enough to reassure the good beast, "Râ said, 'My son Shû, place thyself beneath my daughter Nûit, and keep watch on both sides over the supports, who live in the twilight; hold thou her up above thy head, and be her guardian!'" Shû obeyed; Nûît composed herself, and the world, now furnished with the sky which it had hitherto lacked, assumed its present symmetrical form.

Shû and Sibû succeeded Râ, but did not acquire so lasting a popularity as their great ancestor. Nevertheless

they had their annals, fragments of which have come
down to us. Their power also extended over the whole
universe: "The Majesty of Shû was the excellent king
of the sky, of the earth, of Hades, of the water, of the
winds, of the inundation, of the two chains of mountains,

NÛÎT, THE COW, SUSTAINED ABOVE THE EARTH BY SHÛ AND THE SUPPORT-GODS.[1]

of the sea, governing with a true voice according to the
precepts of his father Râ-Harmakhis." Only "the children
of the serpent Apôpi, the impious ones who haunt the
solitary places and the deserts," disavowed his authority.
Like the Bedawin of later times, they suddenly streamed

[1] Drawn by Faucher-Gudin.

in by the isthmus routes, went up into Egypt under cover of night, slew and pillaged, and then hastily returned to their fastnesses with the booty which they had carried off. From sea to sea Râ had fortified the eastern frontier against them. He had surrounded the principal cities with walls, embellished them with temples, and placed within them those mysterious talismans more powerful for defence than a garrison of men. Thus Aitnobsû, near the mouth of the Wady-Tûmilât, possessed one of the rods of the Sun-god, also the living uræus of his crown whose breath consumes all that it touches, and, finally, a lock of his hair, which, being cast into the waters of a lake, was changed into a hawk-headed crocodile to tear the invader in pieces.[1] The employment of these talismans was dangerous to those unaccustomed to use them, even to the gods themselves. Scarcely was Sibû enthroned as the successor of Shû, who, tired of reigning, had reascended into heaven in a nine days' tempest, before he began his inspection of the eastern marches, and caused the box in which was kept the uræus of Râ to be opened. "As soon as the living viper had breathed its breath against the Majesty of Sibû there was a great disaster— great indeed, for those who were in the train of the god perished, and his Majesty himself was burned in that day. When his Majesty had fled to the north of Aît-nobsû,

[1] Egyptians of all periods never shrank from such marvels. One of the tales of the Theban empire tells us of a piece of wax which, on being thrown into the water, changed into a living crocodile capable of devouring a man. The talismans which protected Egypt against invasion are mentioned by the Pseudo-Callisthenes, who attributes their invention to Nectanebo. Arab historians often refer to them.

pursued by the fire of this magic uræus, behold! when he came to the fields of henna, the pain of his burn was not yet assuaged, and the gods who were behind him said unto him: 'O Sire! let them take the lock of Râ which is there, when thy Majesty shall go to see it and its mystery, and his Majesty shall be healed as soon as it shall be placed upon thee.' So the Majesty of Sibû

THREE OF THE DIVINE AMULETS PRESERVED IN THE TEMPLE OF AÎT-NOBSÛ AT THE ROMAN PERIOD.[1]

caused the magic lock to be brought to Piarît, — the lock for which was made that great reliquary of hard stone which is hidden in the secret place of Piarît, in the district of the divine lock of the Lord Râ, — and behold! this fire departed from the members of the Majesty of Sibû. And many years afterwards, when this lock, which had thus belonged to Sibû, was brought back to Piarît in Ait-nobsû, and cast into the great lake of Piarît

[1] Drawn by Faucher-Gudin, from a sketch by GRIFFITH. The three talismans here represented are two crowns, each in a naos, and the burning fiery uræus.

whose name is *Aît-tostesı̂*, the dwelling of waves, that it might be purified, behold! this lock became a crocodile : it flew to the water and became Sobkû, the divine crocodile of Ait-nobsû." In this way the gods of the solar dynasty from generation to generation multiplied talismans and enriched the sanctuaries of Egypt with relics.

Were there ever duller legends and a more senile phantasy! They did not spring spontaneously from the lips of the people, but were composed at leisure by priests desirous of enhancing the antiquity of their cult, and augmenting the veneration of its adherents in order to increase its importance. Each city wished it to be understood that its feudal sanctuary was founded upon the very day of creation, that its privileges had been extended or confirmed during the course of the first divine dynasty, and that these pretensions were supported by the presence of objects in its treasury which had belonged to the oldest of the king-gods. Such was the origin of tales in which the personage of the beneficent Pharaoh is often depicted in ridiculous fashion. Did we possess all the sacred archives, we should frequently find them quoting as authentic history more than one document as artificial as the chronicle of Ait-nobsû. When we come to the later members of the Ennead, there is a change in the character and in the form of these tales. Doubtless Osiris and Sît did not escape unscathed out of the hands of the theologians; but even if sacerdotal interference spoiled the legend concerning them, it did not altogether disfigure it. Here and there in it is still noticeable a sincerity of feeling and liveliness of imagination such as are never found in those of Shû and of Sibû. This arises from the fact that the functions of these gods left them strangers, or all but strangers, to the current affairs of the world. Shû was the stay, Sibû the material foundation of the world; and so long as the one bore the weight of the firmament without bending, and the other continued to suffer the tread of human generations upon his back, the devout took no more thought of them than they themselves took thought of the devout. The life of Osiris, on the other hand, was intimately mingled with that of the Egyptians, and his most trivial actions immediately reacted upon their fortunes. They followed the movements of his waters; they noted the turning-points in his struggles against drought; they registered his yearly decline, yearly compensated by his aggressive returns and his intermittent victories over Typhon; his proceedings and his character were the subject of their minute study. If his waters almost invariably rose upon the appointed day and extended over the black earth of the valley, this was no mechanical function of a being to whom the consequences of his conduct are indifferent; he acted upon reflection, and in full consciousness of the service that he rendered. He knew that by spreading the inundation he prevented the triumph of the desert; he was life, he was goodness—*Onnofriû*—and Isis, as the partner of his labours, became like him the type of perfect goodness. But while Osiris developed for the better, Sît was transformed for the worse, and increased in wickedness as his brother gained in purity and moral elevation. In proportion as the person of Sît grew more defined, and stood out more clearly, the evil within him contrasted more markedly with the innate goodness of Osiris, and what had been at first an instinctive struggle between two beings somewhat vaguely defined — the desert and the Nile, water and drought—was changed into conscious and deadly enmity. No longer the conflict of two elements, it was war between two gods ; one labouring to produce abundance, while the other strove to do away with it; one being all goodness and life, while the other was evil and death incarnate.

A very ancient legend narrates that the birth of Osiris and his brothers took place during the five additional days at the end of the year ; a subsequent legend explained how Nûit and Sibû had contracted marriage against the express wish of Râ, and without his knowledge. When he became aware of it he fell into a violent rage, and cast a spell over the goddess to prevent her giving birth to her children in any month of any year whatever. But Thot took pity upon her, and playing at draughts with the moon won from it in several games one seventy-second part of its fires, out of which he made five whole days ; and as these were not included in the ordinary calendar, Nûit could then bring forth her five children, one after another: Osiris, Haroêris, Sit, Isis, and Nephthys. Osiris was beautiful of face, but with a dull and black complexion ; his height exceeded five and a half yards.[1] He was born at Thebes, in the first of

---

[1] As a matter of fact, Osiris is often represented with black or green hands and face, as is customary for gods of the dead ; it was probably this peculiarity which suggested the popular idea of his black complexion. A magic papyrus of Ramesside times fixes the stature of the god at seven

the additional days, and straightway a mysterious voice announced that the lord of all—*nibû-r-zarû*—had appeared. The good news was hailed with shouts of joy, followed by tears and lamentations when it became known with what evils he was menaced.[1] The echo reached Râ in his far-off dwelling, and his heart rejoiced, notwithstanding the curse which he had laid upon Nûît. He commanded the presence of his great-grandchild in Xois, and unhesitatingly acknowledged him as the heir to his throne. Osiris had married his sister Isis, even, so it was said, while both of them were still within their mother's womb;[2] and when he became king he made her queen regnant and the partner of all his undertakings. The Egyptians were as yet but half civilized; they were cannibals, and though occasionally they lived upon the fruits of the earth, they did not know how to cultivate them. Osiris taught them the art of making agricultural implements—the plough and the

cubits, and a phrase in a Ptolemaic inscription places it at eight cubits, six palms, three fingers.

[1] One variant of the legend told that a certain Pamylis of Thebes having gone to draw water had heard a voice proceeding from the temple of Zeus, which ordered him to proclaim aloud to the world the birth of the great king, the beneficent Osiris. He had received the child from the hands of Kronos, brought it up to youth, and to him the Egyptians had consecrated the feast of Pamylies, which resembled the Phallophoros festival of the Greeks.

[2] *De Iside et Osiride*, LEEMANS' edition, § 12, pp. 20, 21. Haroêris, the Apollo of the Greeks, was supposed to be the issue of a marriage consummated before the birth of his parents while they were still within the womb of their mother Rhea-Nûit. This was a way of connecting the personage of Haroêris with the Osirian myths by confounding him with the homonymous Harsiêsis, the son of Isis, who became the son of Osiris through his mother s marriage with that god.

hoe,—field labour, the rotation of crops, the harvesting of wheat and barley,[1] and vine culture. Isis weaned them from cannibalism, healed their diseases by means of medicine or of magic, united women to men in legitimate marriage, and showed them how to grind grain between two flat stones and to prepare bread for the household. She invented the loom with the help of her sister Nephthys, and was the first to weave and bleach linen. There was no worship of the gods before Osiris established it, appointed the offerings, regulated the order of ceremonies, and composed the texts and melodies of the liturgies. He built cities, among them Thebes itself, according to some; though others declared that he was born there. As he had been the model of a just and pacific king, so did he desire to be that of a victorious conqueror of nations; and, placing the regency in the hands of Isis, he went forth to war against Asia, accompanied by Thot the ibis and the jackal Anubis. He made little or no use of force and arms, but he attacked men by gentleness and persuasion, softened them with songs in which voices were accompanied by instruments, and taught them also the arts which he had made known to the Egyptians. No country escaped his beneficent action, and he did not return to the banks of the Nile until he had traversed and civilized the world from one horizon to the other.

---

[1] DIODORUS even ascribes to him the discovery of barley and of wheat; this is consequent upon the identification of Isis with Demeter by the Greeks. According to the historian, Leo of Pella, the goddess twined herself a crown of ripe ears and placed it upon her head one day when she was sacrificing to her parents.

Sit-Typhon was red-haired and white-skinned, of violent, gloomy, and jealous temper.[1] Secretly he aspired to the crown, and nothing but the vigilance of Isis had kept him from rebellion during the absence of his brother. The rejoicings which celebrated the king's return to Memphis provided Sit with his opportunity for seizing the throne. He invited Osiris to a banquet along with seventy-two officers whose support he had ensured, made a wooden chest of cunning workmanship and ordered that it should be brought in to him, in the midst of the feast. As all admired its beauty, he sportively promised to present it to any one among the guests whom it should exactly fit. All of them tried it, one after another, and all unsuccessfully; but when Osiris lay down within it, immediately

THE OSIRIAN TRIAD HORUS, OSIRIS, ISIS.[2]

---

[1] The colour of his hair was compared with that of a red-haired ass, and on that account the ass was sacred to him. As to his violent and jealous disposition, see the opinion of DIODORUS SICULUS, book i. 21, and the picture drawn by SYNESIUS in his pamphlet Ægyptius. It was told how he tore his mother's bowels at birth, and made his own way into the world through her side.

[2] Drawing by Boudier of the gold group in the Louvre Museum. The drawing is made from a photograph which belonged to M. de Witte, before the monument was acquired by E. de Rougé in 1871. The little square pillar of lapis-lazuli, upon which Osiris squats, is wrongly set up, and the names and titles of King Osorkon, the dedicator of the triad, are placed upside down.

the conspirators shut to the lid, nailed it firmly down, sol-
dered it together with melted lead, and then threw it into
the Tanitic branch of the Nile, which carried it to the sea.
. The news of the crime spread terror on all sides. The
gods friendly to Osiris feared the fate of their master, and
hid themselves within the bodies of animals to escape the
malignity of the new king. Isis cut off her hair, rent her
garments, and set out in search of the chest. She found it
aground near the mouth of the river [1] under the shadow of a
gigantic acacia, deposited it in a secluded place where no
one ever came, and then took refuge in Bûto, her own
domain and her native city, whose marshes protected her
from the designs of Typhon even as in historic times they
protected more than one Pharaoh from the attacks of his
enemies. There she gave birth to the young Horus,
nursed and reared him in secret among the reeds, far from
the machinations of the wicked one.[2] But it happened that
Sît, when hunting by moonlight, caught sight of the chest,
opened it, and recognizing the corpse, cut it up into

[1] At this point the legend of the Saïte and Greek period interpolates
a whole chapter, telling how the chest was carried out to sea and cast upon
the Phœnician coast near to Byblos. The acacia, a kind of heather or
broom in this case, grew up enclosing the chest within its trunk. This
addition to the primitive legend must date from the XVIIIth to the XXth
dynasties, when Egypt had extensive relations with the peoples of Asia.
No trace of it whatever has hitherto been found upon Egyptian monuments
strictly so called; not even on the latest.

[2] The opening illustration of this chapter (p. 221) is taken from a
monument at Philæ, and depicts Isis among the reeds. The representation
of the goddess as squatting upon a mat probably gave rise to the legend of
the floating isle of Khemmis, which HECATÆUS OF MILETUS had seen upon
the lake of Bûto, but whose existence was denied by HERODOTUS notwithstanding the testimony of Hecatæus.

fourteen pieces, which he scattered abroad at random.
Once more Isis set forth on her woeful pilgrimage. She
recovered all the parts of the body excepting one only,
which the oxyrhynchus had greedily devoured;[1] and with
the help of her sister Nephthys, her son Horus, Anubis,
and Thot, she joined together and embalmed them, and
made of this collection of his remains an imperishable
mummy, capable of sustaining for ever the soul of a god.
On his coming of age, Horus called together all that were
left of the loyal Egyptians and formed them into an
army.[2] His "Followers"—*Shosûû Horû*— defeated the
"Accomplices of Sit"—*Samiû Sit*—who were now driven
in their turn to transform themselves into gazelles,
crocodiles and serpents,—animals which were henceforth
regarded as unclean and Typhonian. For three days the
two chiefs had fought together under the forms of men and
of hippopotami, when Isis, apprehensive as to the issue of
the duel, determined to bring it to an end. "Lo! she

---

[1] This part of the legend was so thoroughly well known, that by the
time of the XIXth dynasty it suggested incidents in popular literature.
When Bitiû, the hero of *The Tale of the Two Brothers*, mutilated himself
to avoid the suspicion of adultery, he cast his bleeding member into the
water, and *the Oxyrhynchus devoured it.*

[2] Towards the Grecian period there was here interpolated an account
of how Osiris had returned from the world of the dead to arm his son and
train him to fight. According to this tale he had asked Horus which of all
animals seemed to him most useful in time of war, and Horus chose the
horse rather than the lion, because the lion avails for the weak or cowardly
in need of help, whereas the horse is used for the pursuit and destruction
of the enemy. Judging from this reply that Horus was ready to dare all,
Osiris allowed him to enter upon the war. The mention of the horse affords
sufficient proof that this episode is of comparatively late origin (cf. p. 41,
for the date at which the horse was acclimatized in Egypt).

caused chains to descend upon them, and made them to drop upon Horus. Thereupon Horus prayed aloud, saying: 'I am thy son Horus!' Then Isis spake unto the fetters, saying; 'Break, and unloose yourselves from my son Horus!' She made other fetters to descend, and let them fall upon her brother Sît. Forthwith he lifted up his voice and cried out in pain, and she spake unto the fetters and said unto them: 'Break!' Yea, when Sit prayed unto her many times, saying: 'Wilt thou not have pity upon the brother of thy son's mother?" then her heart was filled with compassion, and she cried to the fetters: 'Break, for he is my eldest brother!' and the fetters unloosed themselves from him, and the two foes again stood face to face like two men who will not come to terms. "Horus, furious at seeing his mother deprive him of his prey, turned upon her like a panther of the South. She fled before him on that day when battle was waged with Sit the Violent, and he cut off her head. But Thot transformed her by his enchantments and made a cow's head for

ISIS-HÂTHOR, COW-HEADED. [1]

her," thereby identifying her with her companion, Hâthor. The war went on, with all its fluctuating fortunes, till the gods at length decided to summon both rivals before their tribunal. According to a very ancient tradition, the

[1] Drawn by Faucher-Gudin, from a bronze statuette of Saïte period in the Gizeh Museum (MARIETTE, Album photographique du musée de Boulaq, pl. 5, No. 167).

combatants chose the ruler of a neighbouring city, Thot, lord of Hermopolis Parva, as the arbitrator of their quarrel. Sit was the first to plead, and he maintained that Horus was not the son of Osiris, but a bastard, whom Isis had conceived after the death of her husband. Horus triumphantly vindicated the legitimacy of his birth ; and Thot condemned Sît to restore, according to some, the whole of the inheritance which he had wrongly retained,— according to others, part of it only. The gods ratified the sentence, and awarded to the arbitrator the title of *Ûapirahûhûi*: he who judges between two parties. A legend of more recent origin, and circulated after the worship of Osiris had spread over all Egypt, affirmed that the case had remained within the jurisdiction of Sibû, who was father to the one, and grandfather to the other party. Sibû, however, had pronounced the same judgment as Thot, and divided the kingdom into halves—*poshûi*; Sit retained the valley from the neighbourhood of Memphis to the first cataract, while Horus entered into possession of the Delta. Egypt henceforth consisted of two distinct kingdoms, of which one, that of the North, recognized Horus, the son of Isis, as its patron deity ; and the other, that of the South, placed itself under the protection of Sît Nûbîti, the god of Ombos.[1] The moiety of Horus, added to that of Sit, formed

---

[1] Another form of the legend gives the 27th Athyr as the date of the judgment, assigning Egypt to Horus, and to Sît Nubia, or *Doshirît*, the red land. It must have arisen towards the age of the XVIIIth dynasty, at a time when their piety no longer allowed the devout to admit that the murderer of Osiris could be the legitimate patron of half the country. So *the half* belonging to Sît was then placed either in Nubia or in the western desert, which had, indeed, been reckoned as his domain from earliest times.

the kingdom which Sibû had inherited; but his children failed to keep it together, though it was afterwards reunited under Pharaohs of human race.

The three gods who preceded Osiris upon the throne had ceased to reign, but not to live. Râ had taken refuge in heaven, disgusted with his own creatures; Shû had disappeared in the midst of a tempest; and Sibû had quietly retired within his palace when the time of his sojourning upon earth had been fulfilled. Not that there was no death, for death, too, together with all other things and beings, had come into existence in the beginning, but while cruelly persecuting both man and beast, had for a while respected the gods. Osiris was the first among them to be struck down, and hence to require funeral rites. He also was the first for whom family piety sought to provide a happy life beyond the tomb. Though he was king of the living and the dead at Mendes by virtue of the rights of all the feudal gods in their own principalities, his sovereignty after death exempted him no more than the meanest of his subjects from that painful torpor into which all mortals fell on breathing their last. But popular imagination could not resign itself to his remaining in that miserable state for ever. What would it have profited him to have Isis the great Sorceress for his wife, the wise Horus for his son, two master-magicians —Thot the Ibis and the jackal Anubis—for his servants, if their skill had not availed to ensure him a less gloomy and less lamentable after-life than that of men. Anubis had long before invented the art of mummifying, and his mysterious science had secured the everlasting existence of the flesh ; but at what a price ! For the breathing, warm, fresh-coloured body, spontaneous in movement and

THE OSIRIAN MUMMY PREPARED AND LAID UPON THE FUNERARY COUCH BY THE JACKAL ANUBIS.[1]

[1] Drawn by Faucher-Gudin, from ROSELLINI, *Monumenti Civili*, pl. cxxxiv. 2. While Anubis is stretching out his hands to lay out the mummy on its couch, the soul is hovering above its breast, and holding to its nostrils the sceptre, and the wind-filled sail which is the emblem of breath and of the new life.

function, was substituted an immobile, cold and blackish mass, a sufficient basis for the mechanical continuity of the double, but which that double could neither raise nor guide; whose weight paralysed and whose inertness condemned it to vegetate in darkness, without pleasure and almost without consciousness of existence. Thot, Isis, and Horus applied themselves in the case of Osiris to ameliorating the discomfort and constraint entailed by the more primitive embalmment. They did not dispense with

THE RECEPTION OF THE MUMMY BY ANUBIS AT THE DOOR OF THE TOMB, AND THE OPENING OF THE MOUTH.[1]

the manipulations instituted by Anubis, but endued them with new power by means of magic. They inscribed the principal bandages with protective figures and formulas; they decorated the body with various amulets of specific efficacy for its different parts; they drew numerous scenes of earthly existence and of the life beyond the tomb upon the boards of the coffin and upon the walls of the sepulchral chamber. When the body had been made imperishable,

[1] Drawn by Faucher-Gudin, from a painting in the tomb of a king in the Theban necropolis.

they sought to restore one by one all the faculties of which their previous operations had deprived it. The mummy was set up at the entrance to the vault; the statue representing the living person was placed beside it, and semblance was made of opening the mouth, eyes, and ears, of loosing the arms and legs, of restoring breath to the throat and movement to the heart. The incantations by which these acts were severally accompanied were so powerful that the god spoke and ate, lived and heard, and could use his limbs as freely as though he had never been steeped in the bath of the embalmer. He might have returned to his place among men, and various legends prove that he did occasionally appear to his faithful adherents. But, as his ancestors before him, he preferred to leave their towns and withdraw into his own domain. The cemeteries of the inhabitants of Busiris and of Mendes were called *Sokhît Ialû*, the Meadow of Reeds, and *Sokhît Hotpû*, the Meadow of Rest. They were secluded amid the marshes, in small archipelagoes of sandy islets where the dead bodies, piled together, rested in safety from the inundations. This was the first kingdom of the dead Osiris, but it was soon placed elsewhere, as the nature of the surrounding districts and the geography of the adjacent countries became better known; at first perhaps on the Phoenician shore beyond the sea, and then in the sky, in the Milky Way, between the North and the East, but nearer to the North than to the East. This kingdom was not gloomy and mournful like that of the other dead gods, Sokaris or Khontamentît, but was lighted by sun and moon; the heat of the day was tempered by the steady breath of the north wind, and its crops grew and throve abundantly. Thick walls served as fortifications against the attacks of Sît and evil genii; a palace like that of the Pharaohs stood in the midst of delightful gardens; and there, among his own people, Osiris led a

OSIRIS IN HADES, ACCOMPANIED BY ISIS, AMENTÎT, AND NEPHTHYS, RECEIVES THE HOMAGE OF TRUTH.[1]

tranquil existence, enjoying in succession all the pleasures of earthly life without any of its pains.

The goodness which had gained him the title of Onnophris while he sojourned here below, inspired him

[1] Drawn by Faucher-Gudin, from a photograph by Daniel Héron, taken in 1881 in the temple of Seti I. at Abydos.

with the desire and suggested the means of opening the gates of his paradise to the souls of his former subjects. Souls did not enter into it unexamined, nor without trial. Each of them had first to prove that during its earthly life it had belonged to a friend, or, as the Egyptian texts have it, to a vassal of Osiris—*amakhû khir Osiri*—one of those who had served Horus in his exile and had rallied to his banner from the very beginning of the Typhonian wars. These were those followers of Horus—*Shosûû Horû*—so often referred to in the literature of historic times.[1] Horus, their master, having loaded them with favours during life, decided to extend to them after death the same privileges which he had conferred upon his father. He convoked around the corpse the gods who had worked with him at the embalmment of Osiris : Anubis and Thot, Isis and Nephthys, and his four children—Hâpi, Qabhsonûf,

THE DECEASED CLIMBING THE SLOPE OF THE MOUNTAIN OF THE WEST.[2]

---

[1] Cf. p. 252. The *Followers of Horus*, i.e. those who had followed Horus during the Typhonian wars, are mentioned in a Turin fragment of the Canon of the Kings, in which the author summarizes the chronology of the divine period. Like the reign of Râ, the time in which the followers of Horus were supposed to have lived was for the Egyptians of classic times the ultimate point beyond which history did not reach.

[2] Drawn by Faucher-Gudin, from NAVILLE *Das Ægyptische Todtenbuch*, vol. i. pl. cxxviii. A*i*.

Amsît, and Tiûmaûtf—to whom he had entrusted the charge of the heart and viscera. They all performed their functions exactly as before, repeated the same ceremonies, and recited the same formulas at the same stages of the operations, and so effectively that the dead man became a real Osiris under their hands, having a true voice, and henceforth combining the name of the god with his own. He had been Sakhomka or Menkaûrî; he became the Osiris Sakhomka, or the Osiris Menkaûrî, true of voice. Horus and his companions then celebrated the rites consecrated to the "Opening of the Mouth and the Eyes:" animated the statue of the deceased, and placed the mummy in the tomb, where Anubis received it in his arms. Recalled to life and movement, the double reassumed, one by one, all the functions of being, came and went and took part in the ceremonies of the worship

THE MUMMY OF SÛTIMOSÛ CLASPING HIS SOUL IN HIS ARMS.[1]

---

[1] Drawn by Faucher-Gudin, from GUIEYSSE-LEFÉBURE, Le Papyrus de Soutimès, pl. viii. The outlines of the original have unfortunately been restored and enfeebled by the copyist.

which was rendered to him in his tomb. There he might be seen accepting the homage of his kindred, and clasping to his breast his soul under the form of a great human-headed bird with features the counterpart of his own. After being equipped with the formulas and amulets wherewith his prototype, Osiris, had been furnished, he set forth to seek the "Field of Reeds." The way was long and arduous, strewn with perils to which he must have succumbed at the very first stages had he not been carefully warned beforehand and armed against them. A papyrus placed with the mummy in its coffin contained the needful topographical directions and passwords, in order that he might neither stray nor perish by the way. The wiser Egyptians copied out the principal chapters for themselves, or learned them by heart while yet in life,

CYNOCEPHALI DRAWING THE NET IN WHICH SOULS ARE CAUGHT.[1]

[1] Drawn by Faucher-Gudin, from a facsimile by Déveria (E. DE ROUGÉ, Études sur le Rituel Funéraire, pl. iv. No. 4). Ignorant souls fished for by the cynocephali are here represented as fish; but the soul of Nofirûbnû, instructed in the protective formulas, preserves its human form.

in order to be prepared for the life beyond. Those who had not taken this precaution studied after death the copy with which they were provided; and since few Egyptians could read, a priest, or relative of the deceased, preferably his son, recited the prayers in the mummy's ear, that he might learn them before he was carried away to the cemetery. If the double obeyed the prescriptions of the "Book of the Dead" to the letter, he reached his goal without fail.[1] On leaving the tomb he turned his back on the valley, and staff in hand climbed the hills which bounded it on the west, plunging boldly into the desert, where some bird, or even a kindly insect such as a praying mantis, a grasshopper, or a butterfly, served as his guide. Soon he came to one of those sycamores which grow in the sand far away from the Nile, and are regarded as magic trees by the fellahin. Out of the foliage a goddess—Nûît, Hâthor, or Nît—half emerged, and offered him a dish of fruit, loaves of bread, and a jar of water.

---

[1] Manuscripts of this work represent about nine-tenths of the papyri hitherto discovered. They are not all equally full; complete copies are still relatively scarce, and most of those found with mummies contain nothing but extracts of varying length. The book itself was studied by CHAMPOLLION, who called it the *Funerary Ritual;* Lepsius afterwards gave it the less definite name of *Book of the Dead,* which seems likely to prevail. It has been chiefly known from the hieroglyphic copy at Turin, which LEPSIUS traced and had lithographed in 1841, under the title of *Das Todtenbuch der Ægypter.* In 1865, E. DU ROUGÉ began to publish a hieratic copy in the Louvre, but since 1886 there has been a critical edition of manuscripts of the Theban period most carefully collated by E. NAVILLE, *Das Ægyptische Todtenbuch der XVIII bis XX Dynastie,* Berlin, 1886, 2 vols. of plates in folio, and 1 vol. of Introduction in 4to. On this edition see MASPERO, *Études de Mythologie et d'Archéologie Égyptiennes,* vol. i. pp. 325–387.

By accepting these gifts he became the guest of the
goddess, and could never more retrace his steps[1] without
special permission. Beyond the sycamore were lands of

THE DECEASED AND HIS WIFE SEATED IN FRONT OF THE SYCAMORE OF NÛÎT AND
RECEIVING THE BREAD AND WATER OF THE NEXT WORLD.[2]

[1] MASPERO, Études de Mythologie et d'Archéologie Égyptiennes, vol. ii.
pp. 224–227. It was not in Egypt alone that the fact of accepting food
offered by a god of the dead constituted a recognition of suzerainty, and
prevented the human soul from returning to the world of the living.
Traces of this belief are found everywhere, in modern as in ancient times,
and E. B. TYLOR has collected numerous examples of the same in Primitive
Culture, 2nd edit., vol. ii. pp. 47, 51, 52.
[2] Drawn by Faucher-Gudin, from a coloured plate in ROSELLINI,
Monumenti civili., pl. cxxxiv. 3.

terror, infested by serpents and ferocious beasts, furrowed by torrents of boiling water, intersected by ponds and marshes where gigantic monkeys cast their nets. Ignorant souls, or those ill prepared for the struggle, had no easy work before them when they imprudently entered upon it. Those who were not overcome by hunger and thirst at the outset were bitten by a uræus, or horned viper, hidden with evil intent below the sand, and perished in convulsions from the poison; or crocodiles seized as many of them as they could lay hold of at the fords of rivers; or cynocephali netted and devoured them indiscriminately along with the fish into which the partisans of Typhon were transformed. They came safe and sound out of one peril only to fall into another, and infallibly succumbed before they were half through their journey. But, on the other hand, the double who was equipped and instructed, and armed with the true voice, confronted each foe with the phylactery and the incantation by which his enemy was held in check. As soon as he caught sight of one of them he recited the appropriate chapter from his book, he loudly proclaimed himself Râ, Tûmû, Horus, or Khopri—that god whose name and attributes were best fitted to repel the immediate danger—and flames withdrew at his voice, monsters fled or sank paralysed, the most cruel of genii drew in their claws and lowered their arms before him. He compelled crocodiles to turn away their heads; he transfixed serpents with his lance; he supplied himself at pleasure with all the provisions that he needed, and gradually ascended the mountains which surround the world, sometimes alone, and fighting his way step by step, sometimes escorted by beneficent divinities. Halfway up the slope was the good cow Hâthor, the lady of the West, in meadows of tall plants where every evening she received the sun at his setting. If the dead man knew how to ask it according to the prescribed rite, she would take him upon her shoulders[1] and carry him across the accursed countries at full speed. Having reached the North, he paused at the edge of an immense lake, the lake of Kha, and saw in the far distance the outline of the Islands of the Blest. One tradition, so old as to have been almost forgotten in Ramesside times, told how Thot the ibis there awaited him, and bore him away on his wings;[3] another, no less ancient but of more lasting popularity, declared that a ferry-boat plied regularly between the solid earth and the shores

THE DECEASED PIERCING A SERPENT WITH HIS LANCE.[2]

[1] Coffins of the XXth and XXIst dynasties, with a yellow ground, often display this scene. Generally the scene is found beneath the feet of the dead, at the lower end of the cartonage, and the cow is represented as carrying off at a gallop the mummy who is lying on her back.

[2] Drawn by Faucher-Gudin, from a sketch by NAVILLE (*Das Ægyptische Todtenbuch*, vol. i. pl. iii. P *b*). The commonest enemies of the dead were various kinds of serpents.

[3] It is often mentioned in the Pyramid texts, and inspired one of the. most obscure chapters among them (*Teti*, ll. 185–200 ; cf. *Recueil de Travaux*, vol. v. pp. 22, 23). It seems that the ibis had to fight with Sît for right of passage.

of paradise. The god who directed it questioned the dead, and the bark itself proceeded to examine them before they were admitted on board; for it was a magic bark. "Tell me my name," cried the mast; and the travellers replied: He who guides the great goddess on her way is thy name." "Tell me my name," repeated the braces. "The Spine of the Jackal Ûapûaîtû is thy name." "Tell me my name," proceeded the mast-head.

THE GOOD COW HÁTHOR CARRYING THE DEAD MAN AND HIS SOUL.[1]

"The Neck of Amsît is thy name." "Tell me my name," asked the sail. "Nûît is thy name." Each part of the hull and of the rigging spoke in turn and questioned the applicant regarding its name, this being generally a mystic phrase by which it was identified either with some divinity as a whole, or else with some part of his body.

[1] Drawn by Faucher-Gudin, from a coloured facsimile published by LEEMANS, *Monuments Égyptiens du Musée d'Antiquités des Pays-Bas à Leyden*, part iii. pl. xii.

When the double had established his right of passage by
the correctness of his answers, the bark consented to
receive him and to carry him to the further shore.
There he was met by the gods and goddesses of the
court of Osiris : by Anubis, by Hâthor the lady of the
cemetery, by Nit, by the two Mâîts who preside over justice

ANUBIS AND THOT WEIGHING THE HEART OF THE DECEASED IN THE SCALES OF TRUTH.[1]

and truth, and by the four children of Horus stiff-sheathed
in their mummy wrappings. They formed as it were a
guard of honour to introduce him and his winged guide into
an immense hall, the ceiling of which rested on light graceful columns of painted wood. At the further end of the

[1] Drawn by Faucher-Gudin, from pl. cxxxvi. Ag of NAVILLE's *Das
Thebanische Todtenbuch.*

hall Osiris was seated in mysterious twilight within a shrine through whose open doors he might be seen wearing a red necklace over his close-fitting case of white bandaging, his green face surmounted by the tall white diadem flanked by two plumes, his slender hands grasping flail and crook, the emblems of his power.   Behind him stood Isis and Neph-

THE DECEASED IS BROUGHT BEFORE THE SHRINE OF OSIRIS THE JUDGE
BY HORUS, THE SON OF ISIS.

thys watching over him with uplifted hands, bare bosoms, and bodies straitly cased in linen.   Forty-two jurors who had died and been restored to life like their lord, and who had been chosen, one from each of those cities of Egypt which recognized his authority, squatted right and left, and motionless, clothed in the wrappings of the dead, silently waited until they were addressed.   The soul first advanced to the foot of the throne, carrying on its outstretched hands the image of its heart or of its eyes, agents and accomplices of its sins and virtues. It humbly " smelt the earth," then arose, and with uplifted hands recited its profession of faith, " Hail unto you, ye lords of Truth ! hail to thee, great god, lord of Truth and Justice ! I have come before thee, my master; I have been brought to see thy beauties. For I know thee, I know thy name, I know the names of thy forty-two gods who are with thee in the Hall of the Two Truths, living on the remains of sinners, gorging themselves with their blood, in that day when account is rendered before Onnophris, the true of voice. Thy name which is thine is ' the god whose two twins are the ladies of the two Truths ; ' and I, I know you, ye lords of the two Truths, I bring unto you Truth, I have destroyed sins for you. I have not committed iniquity against men ! I have not oppressed the poor ! I have not made defalcations in the necropolis ! I have not laid labour upon any free man beyond that which he wrought for himself ! I have not transgressed, I have not been weak, I have not defaulted, I have not committed that which is an abomination to the gods. I have not caused the slave to be ill-treated of his master ! I have not starved any man, I have not made any to weep, I have not assassinated any man, I have not caused any man to be treacherously assassinated, and I have not committed treason against any ! I have not in aught diminished the supplies of temples ! I have not spoiled the shrewbread of the gods ! I have not taken away the loaves and the wrappings of the dead ! I have done no carnal act within the sacred enclosure of the

temple! I have not blasphemed! I have in nought cur-
tailed the sacred revenues! I have not pulled down the
scale of the balance! I have not falsified the beam of the
balance! I have not taken away the milk from the mouths
of sucklings! I have not lassoed cattle on their pastures!
I have not taken with nets the birds of the gods! I have
not fished in their ponds! I have not turned back the
water in its season! I have not cut off a water-channel in
its course! I have not put out the fire in its time! I
have not defrauded the Nine Gods of the choice part of
victims! I have not ejected the oxen of the gods! I have
not turned back the god at his coming forth! I am pure!
I am pure! I am pure! I am pure! Pure as. this Great
Bonû of Heracleopolis is pure! . . . There is no crime
against me in this land of the Double Truth! Since I
know the names of the gods who are with thee in the Hall
of the Double Truth, save thou me from them!" He then
turned towards the jury and pleaded his cause before them.
They had been severally appointed for the cognizance of
particular sins, and the dead man took each of them by
name to witness that he was innocent of the sin which that
one recorded. His plea ended, he returned to the supreme
judge, and repeated, under what is sometimes a highly
mystic form, the ideas which he had already advanced in
the first part of his address. "Hail unto you, ye gods who
are in the Great Hall of the Double Truth, who have no
falsehood in your bosoms, but who live on Truth in Aûnû,
and feed your hearts upon it before the Lord God who
dwelleth in his solar disc! Deliver me from the Typhon
who feedeth on entrails, O chiefs! in this hour of supreme

judgment;—grant that the deceased may come unto you, he who hath not sinned, who hath neither lied, nor done evil, nor committed any crime, who hath not borne false witness, who hath done nought against himself, but who liveth on truth, who feedeth on truth. He hath spread joy on all sides; men speak of that which he hath done, and the gods rejoice in it. He hath reconciled the god to him by his love; he hath given bread to the hungry, water to the thirsty, clothing to the naked; he hath given a boat to the shipwrecked; he hath offered sacrifices to the gods, sepulchral meals unto the manes. Deliver him from himself, speak not against him before the Lord of the Dead, for his mouth is pure, and his two hands are pure!" In the middle of the Hall, however, his acts were being weighed by the assessors. Like all objects belonging to the gods, the balance is magic, and the genius which animates it sometimes shows its fine and delicate little human head on the top of the upright stand which forms its body. Everything about the balance recalls its superhuman origin: a cynocephalus, emblematic of Thot, sits perched on the upright and watches the beam; the cords which suspend the scales are made of alternate *cruces ansatœ* and *tats*. Truth squats upon one of the scales; Thot, ibis-headed, places the heart on the other, and always merciful, bears upon the side of Truth that judgment may be favourably inclined. He affirms that the heart is light of offence, inscribes the result of the proceeding upon a wooden tablet, and pronounces the verdict aloud. "Thus saith Thot, lord of divine discourse, scribe of the Great Ennead, to his father Osiris, lord of eternity, ' Behold the deceased in this Hall

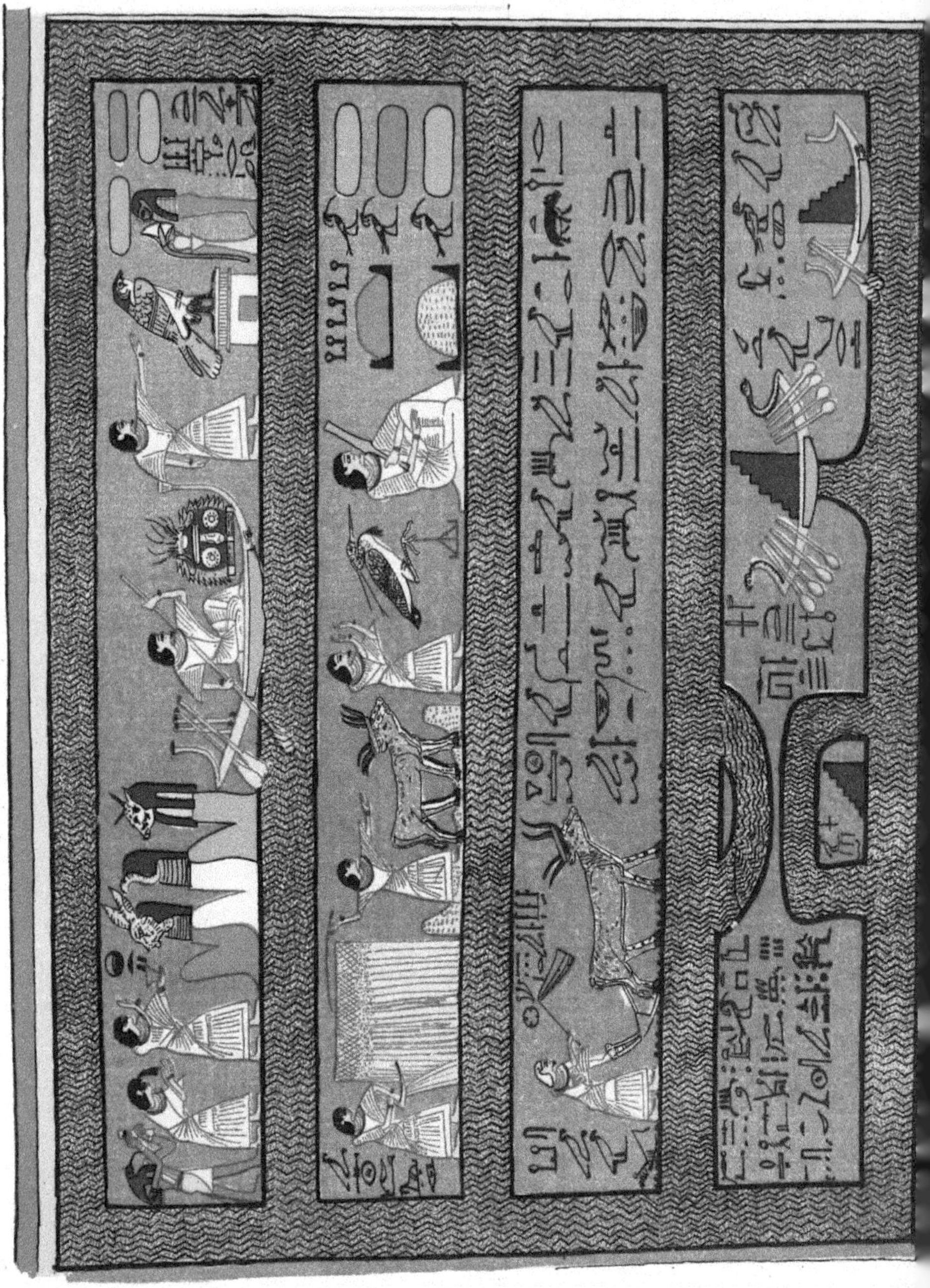

of the Double Truth, his heart hath been weighed in the balance in the presence of the great genii, the lords of Hades, and been found true. No trace of earthly impurity hath been found in his heart. Now that he leaveth the tribunal true of voice, his heart is restored to him, as well as his eyes and the material cover of his heart, to be put back in their places each in its own time, his soul in heaven, his heart in the other world, as is the custom of the "Followers of Horus." Henceforth let his body lie in the hands of Anubis, who presideth over the tombs; let him receive offerings at the cemetery in the presence of Onnophris; let him be as one of those favourites who follow thee; let his soul abide where it will in the necropolis of his city, he whose voice is true before the Great Ennead.' "

In this "Negative Confession," which the worshippers of Osiris taught to their dead, all is not equally admirable. The material interests of the temple were too prominent, and the crime of killing a sacred goose or stealing a loaf from the bread offerings was considered as abominable as calumny or murder. But although it contains traces of priestly cupidity, yet how many of its precepts are untarnished in their purity by any selfish ulterior motive! In it is all our morality in germ, and with refinements of delicacy often lacking among peoples of later and more advanced civilizations. The god does not confine his favour to the prosperous and the powerful of this world; he bestows it also upon the poor. His will is that they be fed and clothed, and exempted from tasks beyond their strength; that they be not oppressed, and that unnecessary tears be spared them. If this does not amount to the love of our neighbour as our religions preach it, at least it represents the careful solicitude due from a good lord to his vassals. His pity extends to slaves; not only does he command that no one should ill-treat them himself, but he forbids that their masters should be led to ill-treat them. This profession of faith, one of the noblest bequeathed us by the old world, is of very ancient origin. It may be read in scattered fragments upon the monuments of the first dynasties, and the way in which its ideas are treated by the compilers of. these inscriptions proves that it was not then regarded as new, but as a text so old and so well known that its formulas were current in all mouths, and had their prescribed places in epitaphs.[1] Was it composed in Mendes, the god's own home, or in Heliopolis, when the theologians of that city appropriated the god of Mendes and incorporated him in their Ennead? In conception it certainly belongs to the Osirian priesthood, but it can only have been diffused over the whole of Egypt after the general adoption of the Heliopolitan Ennead throughout the cities.

As soon as he was judged, the dead man entered into the possession of his rights as a pure soul. On high he received from the Universal Lord all that kings and princes here below bestowed upon their followers—rations of food,[2]

---

[1] For instance, one of the formulas found in Memphite tombs states that the deceased had been the friend of his father, the beloved of his mother, sweet to those who lived with him, gracious to his brethren, loved of his servants, and that he had never sought wrongful quarrel with any man; briefly, that he spoke and did that which is right here below.

[2] The formula of the pyramid times is: " Thy thousand of oxen, thy thousand of geese, of roast and boiled joints from the larder of the gods, of bread, and plenty of the good things presented in the hall of Osiris."

and a house, gardens, and fields to be held subject to the usual conditions of tenure in Egypt, *i.e.* taxation, military service, and the *corvée*. If the island was attacked by the partisans of Sît, the Osirian doubles hastened in a body to repulse them, and fought bravely in its defence. Of the revenues sent to him by his kindred on certain days and by means of sacrifices, each gave tithes to the heavenly storehouses. Yet this was but the least part of the burdens laid upon him by the laws of the country, which

THE MANES TILLING THE GROUND AND REAPING IN THE FIELDS OF IALÛ.[1]

did not suffer him to become enervated by idleness, but obliged him to labour as in the days when he still dwelt in Egypt. He looked after the maintenance of canals and dykes, he tilled the ground, he sowed, he reaped, he garnered the grain for his lord and for himself. Yet to those upon whom they were incumbent, these posthumous obligations, the sequel and continuation of feudal service, at length seemed too heavy, and theologians exercised their ingenuity to find means of lightening the burden. They authorized the manes to look to their servants for the

---

[1] Drawn by Faucher-Gudin, from a vignette in the funerary papyrus of Nebhopît in Turin.

discharge of all manual labour which they ought to have performed themselves. Rarely did a dead man, no matter how poor, arrive unaccompanied at the eternal cities; he brought with him a following proportionate to his rank and fortune upon earth. At first they were real doubles, those of slaves or vassals killed at the tomb, and who had departed along with the double of the master to serve him beyond the grave as they had served him here. A number of statues and images, magically endued with activity and intelligence, was afterwards substituted for this retinue of victims. Originally of so large a size that only the rich or noble could afford them, they were reduced little by little to the height of a few inches. Some were carved out of alabaster, granite, diorite, fine limestone, or moulded out of fine clay and delicately modelled; others had scarcely any human resemblance. They were endowed with life by means of a formula recited over them at the time of their manufacture, and afterwards traced upon their legs. All were possessed of the same faculties. When the god who called the Osirians to the *corvée* pronounced the name of the dead man to whom the figures belonged, they arose and answered for him; hence their designation of " Respondents "—*Ûashbti*. Equipped for agricultural labour, each grasping a hoe and carrying a

ÛASHBÎTI.[1]

---

[1] Drawn by Faucher-Gudin from a painted limestone statuette from the tomb of *Sonnozmû* at Thebes, dating from the end of the XXth dynasty.

seed-bag on his shoulder, they set out to work in their appointed places, contributing the required number of days of forced labour. Up to a certain point they thus compensated for those inequalities of condition which death itself did not efface among the vassals of Osiris; for the figures were sold so cheaply that even the poorest could always

THE DEAD MAN AND HIS WIFE PLAYING AT DRAUGHTS IN THE PAVILION.[1]

afford some for themselves, or bestow a few upon their relations; and in the Islands of the Blest, fellah, artisan, and slave were indebted to the *Ûashbiti* for release from their old routine of labour and unending toil. While the

---

[1] Drawn by Faucher-Gudin, from a vignette in No. 4 Papyrus, Dublin (NAVILLE, *Das Ægyptische Todtenbuch*, vol. i. pl. xxvii. *Da*). The name of *draughts* is not altogether accurate; a description of the game may be found in FALKNER, *Games Ancient and Oriental and how to play them*, pp. 9–101.

little peasants of stone or glazed ware dutifully toiled and tilled and sowed, their masters were enjoying all the delights of the Egyptian paradise in perfect idleness. They sat at ease by the water-side, inhaling the fresh north breeze, under the shadow of trees which were always green. They fished with lines among the lotus-plants; they embarked in their boats, and were towed along by their servants, or they would sometimes deign to paddle themselves slowly about the canals. They went fowling

THE DEAD MAN SAILING IN HIS BARK ALONG THE CANALS OF THE FIELDS OF IALÛ.[1]

among the reed-beds, or retired within their painted pavilions to read tales, to play at draughts, to return to their wives who were for ever young and beautiful.[2] It was but an ameliorated earthly life, divested of all suffering

[1] Drawn by Faucher-Gudin, from the Papyrus of Nebhopît, in Turin. This drawing is from part of the same scene as the illustration on p. 275.
[2] Gymnastic exercises, hunting, fishing, sailing, are all pictured in Theban tombs. The game of draughts is mentioned in the title of chap. xvii. of the *Book of the Dead* (NAVILLE's edition, vol. i. pl. xxiii. l. 2), and the women's pavilion is represented in the tomb of Rakhmirî. That the dead were supposed to read tales is proved from the fact that broken ostraca bearing long fragments of literary works are found in tombs; they were broken to kill them and to send on their doubles to the dead man in the next world.

under the rule and by the favour of the true-voiced Onnophris.

The feudal gods promptly adopted this new mode of life. Each of their dead bodies, mummified, and afterwards reanimated in accordance with the Osirian myth, became

BOAT OF A FUNERARY FLEET ON ITS WAY TO ABIDOS.[1]

an Osiris as did that of any ordinary person. Some carried the assimilation so far as to absorb the god of Mendes, or

[1] Drawn by Faucher-Gudin, from a photograph by Émil Brugsch-Bey. The original was found in the course of M. de Morgan's excavations at Mêîr, and is now at Gizeh. The dead man is sitting in the cabin, wrapped in his cloak. As far as I know, this is the only boat which has preserved its original rigging. It dates from the XIth or XIIth dynasty.

to be absorbed in him. At Memphis Phtah-Sokaris became Phtah-Sokar-Osiris, and at Thinis Khontamentît became Osiris Khontamentît. The sun-god lent himself to this process with comparative ease because his life is more like a man's life, and hence also more like that of Osiris, which is the counterpart of a man's life. Born in the morning, he ages as the day de-clines, and gently passes away at evening. From the time of his entering the sky to that of his leaving it, he reigns above as he reigned here below in the beginning; but when he has left the sky and sinks into Hades, he becomes as one of the dead, and is, as they are, subjected to Osirian embalmment. The same dangers that menace their human souls threaten his soul also; and when he has vanquished them, not in his own strength, but by the power of amulets and magical formulas, he enters into the fields of Ialû, and ought to dwell there for ever under the rule of Onnophris. He did nothing of the kind, however, for daily the sun was to be seen reappearing in the east twelve hours after it had sunk into the darkness of the west. Was it a new orb each time, or did the same sun shine every day? In either case the result was pre-cisely the same; the god came forth from death and

THE SOLAR BARK INTO WHICH THE DEAD MAN IS ABOUT TO ENTER.[1]

---

[1] Drawn by Faucher-Gudin, from a vignette in the Papyrus of Nebqadû, in Paris.

re-entered into life. Having identified the course of the sun-god with that of man, and Râ with Osiris for a first day and a first night, it was hard not to push the matter further, and identify them for all succeeding days and nights, affirming that man and Osiris might, if they so wished, be born again in the morning, as Râ was, and together with him. If the Egyptians had found the prospect of quitting the darkness of the tomb for the bright meadows of Ialû a sensible alleviation of their lot, with what joy must they have been filled by the conception which allowed them to substitute the whole realm of the sun for a little archipelago in an out-of-the-way corner of the universe. Their first consideration was to obtain entrance into the divine bark, and this was the object of all the various practices and prayers, whose text, together with that which already contained the Osirian formulas, ensured the unfailing protection of Râ to their possessor. The soul desirous of making use of them went straight from his tomb to the very spot where the god left earth to descend into Hades. This was somewhere in the immediate neighbourhood of Abydos, and was reached through a narrow gorge or "cleft" in the Libyan range, whose "mouth" opened in front of the temple of Osiris Khontamentît, a little to the north-west of the city. The soul was supposed to be carried thither by a small flotilla of boats, manned by figures representing friends or priests, and laden with food, furniture, and statues. This flotilla was placed within the vault on the day of the funeral, and was set in motion by means of incantations recited over it during one of the first nights of the year, at the annual feast of the dead. The bird or insect which had previously served as guide to the soul upon its journey now took the helm to show the fleet the right way, and under this command the boats left Abydos and mysteriously passed through the "cleft" into that western sea which is inaccessible to the living, there to await the daily coming of the dying sun-god. As soon as his bark appeared at

THE SOLAR BARK PASSING INTO THE MOUNTAIN OF THE WEST.[1]

the last bend of the celestial Nile, the cynocephali, who guarded the entrance into night, began to dance and gesticulate upon the banks as they intoned their accustomed hymn. The gods of Abydos mingled their shouts of joy with the chant of the sacred baboons, the bark lingered for a moment upon the frontiers of day, and

---

[1] Drawn by Faucher-Gudin, from a very small photograph published in the Catalogue of the Minutoli Sale.

THE GOING FORTH OF SOULS BY DAY 283

initiated souls seized the occasion to secure their recognition and their reception on board of it.[1] Once admitted,
they took their share in the management of the boat, and
in the battles with hostile deities; but they were not all
endowed with the courage or equipment needful to withstand the perils and terrors of the voyage. Many stopped
short by the way in one of the regions which it traversed,
either in the realm of Khontamentît, or in that of Sokaris,
or in those islands where the good Osiris welcomed them
as though they had duly arrived in the ferry-boat, or upon
the wing of Thot. There they dwelt in colonies under the
suzerainty of local gods, rich, and in need of nothing, but
condemned to live in darkness, excepting for the one brief
hour in which the solar bark passed through their midst,
irradiating them with beams of light.[2] The few persevered,
feeling that they had courage to accompany the sun
throughout, and these were indemnified for their sufferings
by the most brilliant fate ever dreamed of by Egyptian
souls. Born anew with the sun-god and appearing with
him at the gates of the east, they were assimilated to him,
and shared his privilege of growing old and dying, only to
be ceaselessly rejuvenated and to live again with ever-
renewed splendour. They disembarked where they

---

[1] This description of the embarkation and voyage of the soul is composed
from indications given in one of the vignettes of chap. xvi. of the *Book of the
Dead* (NAVILLE's edition, vol. i. pl. xxii.), combined with the text of a
formula which became common from the times of the XIth and XIIth
dynasties (MASPERO, *Études de Mythologie et d'Archéologie Égyptiennes*, vol. i.
pp. 14–18, and *Études Égyptiennes*, vol. i. pp. 122, 123).

[2] MASPERO, *Études de Mythologie et d'Archéologie Égyptiennes*, vol. ii. pp.
44, 45.

pleased, and returned at will into the world. If now and then they felt a wish to revisit all that was left of their earthly bodies, the human-headed sparrow-hawk descended the shaft in full flight, alighted upon the funeral couch, and, with hands softly laid upon the spot where the heart had been wont to beat, gazed upwards at the impassive mask of the mummy. This was but for a moment, since nothing compelled these perfect souls to be imprisoned within the tomb like the doubles of earlier times, because they feared the light. They " went forth by day,'" and dwelt in those places where they had lived; they walked in their gardens by their ponds of running water; they perched like so many birds on the branches of the trees which they had planted, or enjoyed the fresh air under the shade of their sycamores; they ate and drank at pleasure ; they travelled by hill and dale ; they embarked in the boat of Râ, and disembarked

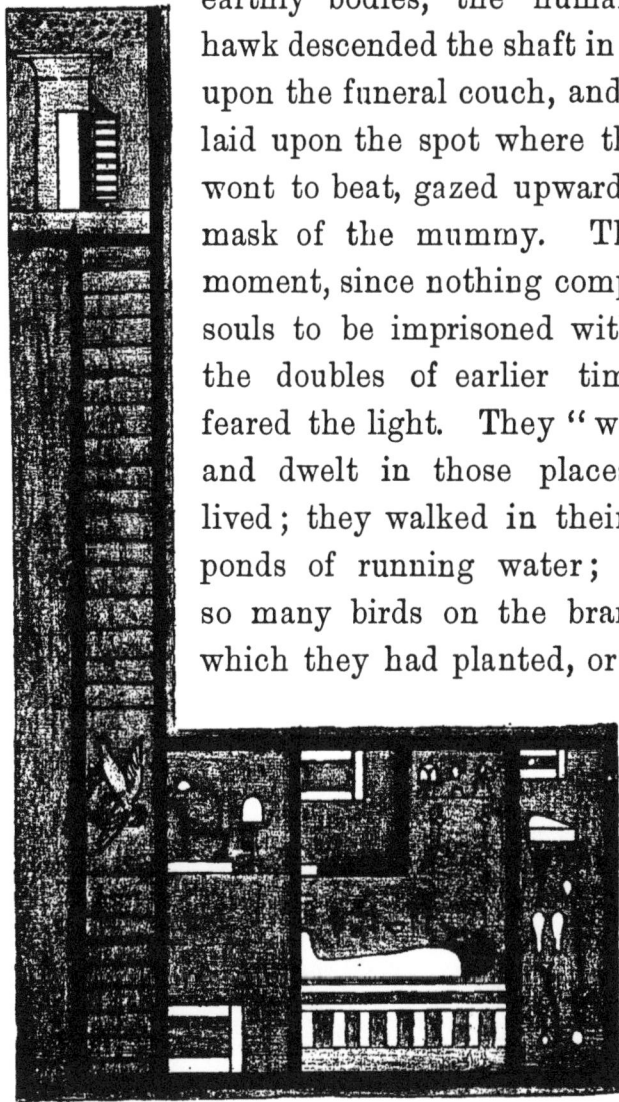

THE SOUL DESCENDING THE SEPULCHRAL SHAFT ON ITS WAY TO REJOIN THE MUMMY.[1]

without weariness, and without distaste for the same perpetual round.

[1] Drawn by Faucher-Gudin, from DÉVÉRIA.

This conception, which was developed somewhat late, brought the Egyptians back to the point from which they had started when first they began to speculate on the life to come. The soul, after having left the place of its incarnation to which in the beginning it clung, after having ascended into heaven and there sought congenial asylum in vain, forsook all havens which it had found

THE SOUL ON THE EDGE OF THE FUNERAL COUCH, WITH ITS HANDS ON THE HEART OF THE MUMMY.[1]

above, and unhesitatingly fell back upon earth, there to lead a peaceful, free, and happy life in the full light of day, and with the whole valley of Egypt for a paradise.

The connection, always increasingly intimate between Osiris and Râ, gradually brought about a blending of the previously separate myths and beliefs concerning each.

[1] Drawn by Faucher-Gudin, from a photograph by Émil Brugsch-Bey, reproducing the miniature sarcophagus of the scribe Râ (MASPERO, Guide du Visiteur, pp. 130, 131, No. 1621).

The friends and enemies of the one became the friends
and enemies of the other, and from a mixture of the
original conceptions of the two deities, arose new personalities, in which contradictory elements were blent
together, often without true fusion. The celestial Horuses
one by one were identified with Horus, son of Isis, and
their attributes were given to him, as his in the same way
became theirs. Apopi and the monsters — the hippopotamus, the crocodile, the wild boar—who lay in wait
for Râ as he sailed the heavenly ocean, became one with
Sît and his accomplices. Sit still possessed his half of
Egypt, and his primitive brotherly relation to the celestial
Horus remained unbroken, either on account of their
sharing one temple, as at Nûbît, or because they were
worshipped as one in two neighbouring nomes, as, for
example, at Oxyrrhynchos and at Heracleopolis Magna.
The repulsion with which the slayer of Osiris was regarded did not everywhere dissociate these two cults :
certain small districts persisted in this double worship
down to the latest times of paganism. It was, after all,
a mark of fidelity to the oldest traditions of the race,
but the bulk of the Egyptians, who had forgotten these,
invented reasons taken from the history of the divine
dynasties to explain the fact. The judgment of Thot or
of Sibû had not put an end to the machinations of Sît :
as soon as Horus had left the earth, Sît resumed them,
and pursued them, with varying fortune, under the divine
kings of the second Ennead. Now, in the year 363 of
Harmakhis, the Typhonians reopened the campaign.
Beaten at first near Edfû, they retreated precipitately

northwards, stopping to give battle wherever their partisans predominated,—at Zatmît in the Theban nome,[1] at Khaîtnûtrît to the north-east of Denderah, and at Hibonû in the principality of the Gazelle. Several bloody combats, which took place between Oxyrrhynchos and

THE SOUL GOING FORTH INTO ITS GARDEN BY DAY [2]

Heracleopolis Magna, were the means of driving them finally out of the Nile Valley; they rallied for the last

---

[1] Zatmît appears to have been situate at some distance from Bayadîyéh, on the spot where the map published by the Egyptian Commission marks the ruins of a modern village. There was a necropolis of considerable extent there, which furnishes the Luxor dealers with antiquities, many of which belong to the first Theban empire.

[2] Copied by Faucher-Gudin from the survey-drawings of the tomb of Anni by Boussac, member of the *Mission française* in Egypt (1891). The inscription over the arbour gives the list of the various trees in the garden of Anni during his lifetime.

time in the eastern provinces of the Delta, were beaten at Zalû, and giving up all hope of success on land, they embarked at the head of the Gulf of Suez, in order to return to the Nubian Desert, their habitual refuge in times of distress. The sea was the special element of Typhon, and upon it they believed themselves secure. Horus, however, followed them, overtook them near Shashirit, routed them, and on his return to Edfû, celebrated his victory by a solemn festival. By degrees, as he made himself master of those localities which owed allegiance to Sît, he took energetic measures to establish in them the authority of Osiris and of the solar cycle. In all of them he built, side by side with the sanctuary of the Typhonian divinities, a temple to himself, in which he was enthroned under the particular form he was obliged to assume in order to vanquish his enemies. Metamorphosed into a hawk at the battle of Hibonû, we next see him springing on to the back of Sît under the guise of a hippopotamus; in his shrine at Hibonû he is represented as a hawk perching on the back of a gazelle, emblem of the nome where the struggle took place. Near to Zalû he became incarnate as a human-headed lion, crowned with the triple diadem, and having feet armed with claws which cut like a knife; it was under the form, too, of a lion that he was worshipped in the temple at Zalû. The correlation of Sît and the celestial Horus was not, therefore, for these Egyptians of more recent times a primitive religious fact; it was the consequence, and so to speak the sanction, of the old hostility between the two gods. Horus had treated his enemy in the same

fashion that a victorious Pharaoh treated the barbarians conquered by his arms : he had constructed a fortress to keep his foe in check, and his priests formed a sort of garrison as a precaution against the revolt of the rival priesthood and the followers of the rival deity. In this manner the battles of the gods were changed into human struggles, in which, more than once, Egypt was deluged with blood. The hatred of the followers of Osiris to those of Typhon was perpetuated with such implacability, that the nomes which had persisted in adhering to the worship of Sît, became odious to the rest of the population : the image of their master on the monuments was mutilated, their names were effaced from the geographical lists, they were assailed with insulting epithets, and to pursue and slay their sacred animals was reckoned a pious act. Thus originated those skirmishes which developed into actual civil wars, and were continued down to Roman times. The adherents of Typhon only became more confirmed in their veneration for the accursed god ; Christianity alone overcame their obstinate fidelity to him.[1]

The history of the world for Egypt was therefore only the history of the struggle between the adherents of Osiris and the followers of Sît ; an interminable warfare

[1] This incident in the wars of Horus and Sît is drawn by Faucher-Gudin from a bas-relief of the temple of Edfû. On the right, Har-Hûdîti, standing up in the solar bark, pierces with his lance the head of a crocodile, a partisan of Sît, lying in the water below; Harmâkhis, standing behind him, is present at the execution. Facing this divine pair, is the young Horus, who kills a man, another partisan of Sît, while Isis and Har-Hûdîti hold his chains ; behind Horus, Isis and Thot are leading four other captives bound and ready to be sacrificed before Harmâkhis.

in which sometimes one and sometimes the other of the rival parties obtained a passing advantage, without ever gaining a decisive victory till the end of time. The divine kings of the second and third Ennead devoted most of the years of their earthly reign to this end; they were portrayed under the form of the great warrior Pharaohs, who, from the eighteenth to the twelfth century before our era, extended their rule from the plains of the Euphrates to the marshes of Ethiopia. A few peaceful sovereigns are met with here and there in this line of conquerors—a few sages or legislators, of whom the most famous was styled Thot, the doubly great, ruler of Hermopolis and of the Hermopolitan Ennead. A legend of recent origin made him the prime minister of Horus, son of Isis; a still more ancient tradition would identify him with the second king of the second dynasty, the immediate successor of the divine Horuses, and attributes to him a reign of 3226 years. He brought to the throne that inventive spirit and that creative power which had characterized him from the time when he was only a feudal deity. Astronomy, divination, magic, medicine, writing, drawing—in fine, all the arts and sciences emanated from him as from their first source. He had taught mankind the methodical observation of the heavens and of the changes that took place in them, the slow revolutions of the sun, the rapid phases of the moon, the intersecting movements of the five planets, and the shapes and limits of the constellations which each night were lit up in the sky. Most of the latter either remained, or appeared to remain immovable, and seemed never to pass out of the regions accessible to the human eye. Those which were situate on the extreme margin of the firmament accomplished movements there analogous to those of the planets. Every year at fixed times they were seen to sink one after another below the horizon, to disappear, and rising again after an eclipse of greater or less duration, to regain insensibly their original positions. The constellations were reckoned to be thirty-six in number, the thirty-six *decani* to whom were attributed mysterious powers, and of whom Sothis was queen — Sothis transformed into the star of Isis, when Orion (Sâhû, became the star of Osiris. The nights are so clear and the atmosphere so transparent in Egypt, that the eye can readily penetrate the depths of space, and distinctly see points of light which would be invisible in our foggy climate. The Egyptians did not therefore need special instruments to ascertain the existence of a

ONE OF THE ASTRONOMICAL TABLES OF THE TOMB OF RAMSES IV.[1]

[1] Drawn by Faucher-Gudin, from a copy by LEPSIUS, *Denkm.*, iii. 227, 3.

considerable number of stars which we could not see without the help of our telescopes; they could perceive with the naked eye stars of the fifth magnitude, and note them upon their catalogues.[1] It entailed, it is true, a long training and uninterrupted practice to bring their sight up to its maximum keenness; but from very early times it was a function of the priestly colleges to found and maintain schools of astronomy. The first observatories established on the banks of the Nile seem to have belonged to the temples of the sun; the high priests of Râ—who, to judge from their title, were alone worthy to behold the sun face to face—were actively employed from the earliest times in studying the configuration and preparing maps of the heavens. The priests of other gods were quick to follow their example: at the opening of the historic period, there was not a single temple, from one end of the valley to the other, that did not possess its official astronomers, or, as they were called, "watchers of the night."[2] In the evening they went up on to the high terraces above the shrine, or on to the narrow platforms which terminated the pylons, and fixing their

[1] Biot, however, states that stars of the third and fourth magnitude "are the smallest which can be seen with the naked eye." I believe I am right in affirming that several of the fellahin and Bedawin attached to the "service des Antiquités" can see stars which are usually classed with those of the fifth magnitude.

[2] *Urshu*: this word is also used for the soldiers on watch during the day upon the walls of a fortress. Birch believed he had discovered in the British Museum a catalogue of observations made at Thebes by several astronomers upon a constellation which answered to the Hyades or the Pleiades; it was merely a question in this text of the quantity of water supplied regularly to the astronomers of a Theban temple for their domestic purposes.

eyes continuously on the celestial vault above them, followed the movements of the constellations and carefully noted down the slightest phenomena which they observed. A portion of the chart of the heavens, as known to Theban Egypt between the eighteenth and twelfth centuries before our era, has survived to the present time; parts of it were carved by the decorators on the ceilings of temples, and especially on royal tombs. The deceased Pharaohs were identified with Osiris in a more intimate fashion than their subjects. They represented the god even in the most trivial details; on earth —where, after having played the part of the beneficent Onnophris of primitive ages, they underwent the most complete and elaborate embalming, like Osiris of the lower world; in Hades—where they embarked side by side with the Sun-Osiris to cross the night and to be born again at daybreak; in heaven—where they shone with Orion-Sâhu under the guardianship of Sothis, and, year by year, led the procession of the stars. The maps of the firmament recalled to them, or if necessary taught them, this part of their duties: they there saw the planets and the *decani* sail past in their boats, and the constellations follow one another in continuous succession. The lists annexed to the charts indicated the positions occupied each month by the principal heavenly bodies—their risings, their culminations, and their settings. Unfortunately, the workmen employed to execute these pictures either did not understand much about the subject in hand, or did not trouble themselves to copy the originals exactly: they omitted many passages, transposed others, and made endless mistakes, which made it impossible for us to transfer accurately to a modern map the information possessed by the ancients.

In directing their eyes to the celestial sphere, Thot had at the same time revealed to men the art of measuring time, and the knowledge of the future. As he was the moon-god *par excellence*, he watched with jealous care over the divine eye which had been entrusted to him by Horus, and the thirty days during which he was engaged in conducting it through all the phases of its nocturnal life, were reckoned as a month. Twelve of these months formed the year, a year of three hundred and sixty days, during which the earth witnessed the gradual beginning and ending of the circle of the seasons. The Nile rose, spread over the fields, sank again into its channel; to the vicissitudes of the inundation succeeded the work of cultivation; the harvest followed the seedtime : these formed three distinct divisions of the year, each of nearly equal duration. Thot made of them the three seasons,—that of the waters, Shaît; that of vegetation, Pirûît; that of the harvest, Shômû—each comprising four months, numbered one to four; the 1st, 2nd, 3rd, and 4th months of Shait; the 1st, 2nd, 3rd, and 4th months of Pirûît; the 1st, 2nd, 3rd, and 4th months of Shômû. The twelve months completed, a new year began, whose birth was heralded by the rising of Sothis in the early days of August. The first month of the Egyptian year thus coincided with the eighth of ours. Thot became its patron, and gave it his name, relegating each of the others to a special protecting divinity; in this manner the third month of Shait fell to Hathor, and was called after her; the fourth of Pirûît belonged to Ranûît or Ramûît, the lady of harvests, and derived from her its appellation of Pharmûti. Official documents always designated the months by the ordinal number attached to them in each season, but the people gave them by preference the names of their tutelary deities, and these names, transcribed into Greek, and then into Arabic, are still used by the Christian inhabitants of Egypt, side by side with the Mussulman appellations. One patron for each month was, however, not deemed sufficient: each month was subdivided into three decades, over which presided as many *decani*, and the days themselves were assigned to genii appointed to protect them. A number of festivals were set apart at irregular intervals during the course of the year: festivals for the new year, festivals for the beginning of the seasons, months and decades, festivals for the dead, for the supreme gods, and for local divinities. Every act of civil life was so closely allied to the religious life, that it could not be performed without a sacrifice or a festival. A festival celebrated the cutting of the dykes, another the opening of the canals, a third the reaping of the first sheaf, or the carrying of the grain; a crop gathered or stored without a festival to implore the blessing of the gods, would have been an act of sacrilege and fraught with disaster. The first year of three hundred and sixty days, regulated by the revolutions of the moon, did not long meet the needs of the Egyptian people; it did not correspond with the length of the solar year, for it fell short of it by five and a quarter days, and this deficit, accumulating from twelvemonth to twelvemonth, caused such a serious difference between the

calendar reckoning and the natural seasons, that it soon
had to be corrected. They intercalated, therefore, after
the twelfth month of each year and before the first day of
the ensuing year, five epagomenal days, which they termed
the " five days over and above the year." [1] The legend of
Osiris relates that Thot created them in order to permit
Nûit to give birth to all her children. These days constituted, at the end of the " great year," a " little month,"
which considerably lessened the difference between the
solar and lunar computation, but did not entirely do away
with it, and the six hours and a few minutes of which the
Egyptians had not taken count gradually became the source
of fresh perplexities. They at length amounted to a whole
day, which needed to be added every four years to the
regular three hundred and sixty days, a fact which was
unfortunately overlooked. The difficulty, at first only
slight, which this caused in public life, increased with
time, and ended by disturbing the harmony between the
order of the calendar and that of natural phenomena :
at the end of a hundred and twenty years, the legal year
had gained a whole month on the actual year, and the 1st
of Thot anticipated the heliacal rising of Sothis by thirty

[1] There appears to be a tendency among Egyptologists now to doubt the
existence, under the Ancient Empire, of the five epagomenal days, and as a
fact they are nowhere to be found expressly mentioned ; but we know that
the five gods of the Osirian cycle were born during the epagomenal day (cf.
p. 247 of this History), and the allusions to the Osirian legend which are
met with in the Pyramid texts, prove that the days were added long before
the time when those inscriptions were cut. As the wording of the texts
often comes down from prehistoric times, it is most likely that the invention
of the epagomenal days is anterior to the first Thinite and Memphite
dynasties.

days, instead of coinciding with it as it ought. The astronomers of the Græco-Roman period, after a retro-spective examination of all the past history of their country, discovered a very ingenious theory for obviating this unfortunate discrepancy. If the omission of six hours annually entailed the loss of one day every four years, the time would come, after three hundred and sixty-five times four years, when the deficit would amount to an entire year, and when, in consequence, fourteen hundred and sixty whole years would exactly equal fourteen hundred and sixty-one incomplete years. The agreement of the two years, which had been disturbed by the force of circumstances, was re-established of itself after rather more than fourteen and a half centuries : the opening of the civil year became identical with the beginning of the astronomical year, and this again coincided with the heliacal rising of Sirius, and therefore with the official date of the inundation. To the Egyptians of Pharaonic times, this simple and eminently practical method was unknown : by means of it hundreds of generations, who suffered endless troubles from the recurring difference between an uncertain and a fixed year, might have consoled themselves with the satisfaction of knowing that a day would come when one of their descendants would, for once in his life, see both years coincide with mathe-matical accuracy, and the seasons appear at their normal times. The Egyptian year might be compared to a watch which loses a definite number of minutes daily. The owner does not take the trouble to calculate a cycle in which the total of minutes lost will bring the watch round to the correct time : he bears with the irregularity as long as his affairs do not suffer by it; but when it causes him inconvenience, he alters the hands to the right · hour, and repeats this operation each time he finds it necessary, without being guided by a fixed rule. In like manner the Egyptian year fell into hopeless confusion with regard to the seasons, the discrepancy continually increasing, until the difference became so great, that the king or the priests had to adjust the two by a process similar to that employed in the case of the watch.

The days, moreover, had each their special virtues, which it was necessary for man to know if he wished to profit by the advantages, or to escape the perils which they possessed for him. There was not one among them that did not recall some incident of the divine wars, and had not witnessed a battle between the partisans of Sît and those of Osiris or Râ; the victories or the disasters which they had chronicled had as it were stamped them with good or bad luck, and for that reason they remained for ever auspicious or the reverse. It was on the 17th of Athyr that Typhon had enticed his brother to come to him, and had murdered him in the middle of a banquet. Every year, on this day, the tragedy that had taken place in the earthly abode of the god seemed to be repeated afresh in the heights of heaven. Just as at the moment of the death of Osiris, the powers of good were at their weakest, and the sovereignty of evil everywhere prevailed, so the whole of Nature, abandoned to the powers of darkness, became inimical to man. Whatever he undertook on that day issued in failure. If he went out to walk by the river-side, a crocodile would attack him, as the crocodile sent by Sit had attacked Osiris.   If he set out on a journey, it was a last farewell which he bade to his family and friends: death would meet him by the way.   To escape this fatality, he must shut himself up at home, and wait in inaction until the hours of danger had passed and the sun of the ensuing day had put the evil one to flight.[1]   It was to his interest to know these adverse influences; and who would have known them all, had not Thot pointed them out and marked them in his calendars?   One of these, long fragments of which have come down to us, indicated briefly the character of each day, the gods who presided over it, the perils which accompanied their patronage, or the good fortune which might be expected of them.   The details of it are not always intelligible to us, as we are still ignorant of many of the episodes in the life of Osiris.   The Egyptians were acquainted with the matter from childhood, and were guided with sufficient exactitude by these indications.   The hours of the night were all inauspicious; those of the day were divided into three "seasons" of four hours each, of which some were lucky, while others were invariably of ill omen.   "THE 4TH OF TYBI: *good, good, good.*   Whatsoever thou seest on this day will be fortunate.   Whosoever is

---

[1] On the 20th of Thot no work was to be done, no oxen killed, no stranger received.   On the 22nd no fish might be eaten, no oil lamp was to be lighted.   On the 23rd "put no incense on the fire, nor kill big cattle, nor goats, nor ducks ; eat of no goose, nor of that which has lived."   On the 26th "do absolutely nothing on this day," and the same advice is found on the 7th of Paophi, on the 18th, on the 26th, on the 27th, and more than thirty times in the remainder of the Sallier Calendar.   On the 30th of Mechir it is forbidden to speak aloud to any one.

born on this day, will die more advanced in years than any of his family; he will attain to a greater age than his father. THE 5TH OF TYBI: *inimical, inimical, inimical.* This is the day on which the goddess Sokhît, mistress of the double white Palace, burnt the chiefs when they raised an insurrection, came forth, and manifested themselves. Offerings of bread to Shû, Phtah, Thot: burn incense to Râ, and to the gods who are his followers, to Phtah, Thot, Hû-Sû, on this day. Whatsoever thou seest on this day will be fortunate. THE 6TH OF TYBI: *good, good, good.* Whatsoever thou seest on this day will be fortunate. THE 7TH OF TYBI: *inimical, inimical, inimical.* Do not join thyself to a woman in the presence of the Eye of Horus. Beware of letting the fire go out which is in thy house. THE 8TH OF TYBI: *good, good, good.* Whatsoever thou seest with thine eye this day, the Ennead of the gods will grant to thee: the sick will recover. THE 9TH OF TYBI: *good, good, good.* The gods cry out for joy at noon this day. Bring offerings of festal cakes and of fresh bread, which rejoice the heart of the gods and of the manes. THE 10TH OF TYBI: *inimical, inimical, inimical.* Do not set fire to weeds on this day: it is the day on which the god Sap-hôû set fire to the land of Bûto. THE 11TH OF TYBI: *inimical, inimical, inimical.* Do not draw nigh to any flame on this day, for Râ entered the flames to strike all his enemies, and whosoever draws nigh to them on this day, it shall not be well with him during his whole life. THE 12TH OF TYBI: *inimical, inimical, inimical.* See that thou beholdest not a rat on this day, nor approachest any rat within thy house: it is the day wherein Sokhît gave forth the decrees." In these cases a little watchfulness or exercise of memory sufficed to put a man on his guard against evil omens; but in many circumstances all the vigilance in the world would not protect him, and the fatality of the day would overtake him, without his being able to do ought to avert it. No man can at will place the day of his birth at a favourable time; he must accept it as it occurs, and yet it exercises a decisive influence on the manner of his death. According as he enters the world on the 4th, 5th, or 6th of Paophi, he either dies of marsh fever, of love, or of drunkenness. The child of the 23rd perishes by the jaws of a crocodile: that of the 27th is bitten and dies by a serpent. On the other hand, the fortunate man whose birthday falls on the 9th or the 29th lives to an extreme old age, and passes away peacefully, respected by all.

Thot, having pointed out the evil to men, gave to them at the same time the remedy. The magical arts of which he was the repository, made him virtual master of the other gods. He knew their mystic names, their secret weaknesses, the kind of peril they most feared, the ceremonies which subdued them to his will, the prayers which they could not refuse to grant under pain of misfortune or death. His wisdom, transmitted to his worshippers, assured to them the same authority which he exercised upon those in heaven, on earth, or in the nether world. The magicians instructed in his school had, like the god, control of the words and sounds which, emitted at the favourable moment with the "correct voice," would evoke the most formidable deities from beyond the confines of the universe: they could bind and loose at will Osiris, Sit, Anubis, even Thot himself; they could send them forth, and recall them, or constrain them to work and fight for them. The extent of their power exposed the magicians to terrible temptations; they were often led to use it to the detriment of others, to satisfy their spite, or to gratify their grosser appetites. Many, moreover, made a gain of their knowledge, putting it at the service of the ignorant who would pay for it. When they were asked to plague or get rid of an enemy, they had a hundred different ways of suddenly surrounding him

THE GODS FIGHTING FOR THE MAGICIAN WHO HAS INVOKED THEM.[1]

without his suspecting it: they tormented him with deceptive or terrifying dreams; they harassed him with apparitions and mysterious voices; they gave him as a, prey to sicknesses, to wandering spectres, who entered into him and slowly consumed him. They constrained, even at a distance, the wills of men; they caused women to be the victims of infatuations, to forsake those they had loved, and to love those they had previously detested. In order to compose an irresistible charm, they merely required a little blood from a person,

[1] Drawn by Faucher-Gudin, from the tracing by GOLÉNISCHEFF, *Die Metternich-Stele*, pl. iii. 14.

a few nail-parings, some hair, or a scrap of linen which he had worn, and which, from contact with his skin, had become impregnated with his personality. Portions of these were incorporated with the wax of a doll which they modelled, and clothed to resemble their victim; thenceforward all the inflictions to which the image was subjected were experienced by the original; he was consumed with fever when his effigy was exposed to the fire, he was wounded when the figure was pierced by a knife. The Pharaohs themselves had no immunity from these spells.[1] These machinations were wont to be met by others of the same kind, and magic, if invoked at the right moment, was often able to annul the ills which magic had begun. It was not indeed all-powerful against fate: the man born on the 27th of Paophi would die of a snake-bite, whatever charm he might use to protect himself. But if the day of his death were foreordained, at all events the year in which it would occur was uncertain, and it was easy for the magician to arrange that it should not take place prematurely. A formula recited opportunely, a sentence of prayer traced on a papyrus, a little statuette worn about the person, the smallest amulet blessed and consecrated, put to flight the serpents who were the instruments of fate. Those curious stelæ on which we see Horus half naked, standing on two crocodiles and brandishing in his fists creatures which had reputed powers of fascination, were so many

---

[1] Spells were employed against Ramses III., and the evidence in the criminal charge brought against the magicians explicitly mentions the wax figures and the philters used on this occasion.

protecting talismans; set up at the entrance to a room or a house, they kept off the animals represented and

THE CHILD HORUS ON THE CROCODILES.[1]

[1] Drawn by Faucher-Gudin, from an Alexandrian stele in the Gizeh Museum. The reason for the appearance of so many different animals in this stele and in others of the same nature, has been given by MASPERO,

brought the evil fate to nought. Sooner or later destiny would doubtless prevail, and the moment would come when the fated serpent, eluding all precautions, would succeed in carrying out the sentence of death. At all events the man would have lived, perhaps to the verge of old age, perhaps to the years of a hundred and ten, to which the wisest of the Egyptians hoped to attain, and which period no man born of mortal mother might exceed. If the arts of magic could thus suspend the law of destiny, how much more efficacious were they when combating the influences of secondary deities, the evil eye, and the spells of man? Thot, who was the patron of sortilege, presided also over exorcisms, and the criminal acts which some committed in his name could have reparation made for them by others in his name. To malicious genii, genii still stronger were opposed; to harmful amulets, those which were protective; to destructive measures, vitalizing remedies; and this was not even the most troublesome part of the magicians' task. Nobody, in fact, among those delivered by their intervention escaped unhurt from the trials to which he had been subjected. The possessing spirits when they quitted their victim generally left behind them traces of their occupation, in the brain, heart, lungs, intestines—in fact, in the whole body. The illnesses to which the human race is prone, were not indeed all brought about by enchanters relentlessly

Études de Mythologie et d'Archéologie Égyptiennes, vol. ii. pp. 417–419 ; they were all supposed to possess the evil eye and to be able to fascinate their victim before striking him.

persecuting their enemies, but they were all attributed to the presence of an invisible being, whether spectre or demon, who by some supernatural means had been made to enter the patient, or who, unbidden, had by malice or necessity taken up his abode within him. It was needful, after expelling the intruder, to re-establish the health of the sufferer by means of fresh remedies. The study of simples and other *materiæ medicæ* would furnish these; Thot had revealed himself to man as the first magician, he became in like manner for them the first physician and the first surgeon.

Egypt is naturally a very salubrious country, and the Egyptians boasted that they were "the healthiest of all mortals;" but they did not neglect any precautions to maintain their health. "Every month, for three successive days, they purged the system by means of emetics or clysters. The study of medicine with them was divided between specialists; each physician attending to one kind of illness only. Every place possessed several doctors; some for diseases of the eyes, others for the head, or the teeth, or the stomach, or for internal diseases." But the subdivision was not carried to the extent that Herodotus would make us believe. It was the custom to make a distinction only between the physician trained in the priestly schools, and further instructed by daily practice and the study of books,— the bone-setter attached to the worship of Sokhît who treated fractures by the intercession of the goddess,— and the exorcist who professed to cure by the sole virtue of amulets and magic phrases. The professional doctor treated all kinds of maladies, but, as with us, there were specialists for certain affections, who were consulted in preference to general practitioners. If the number of these specialists was so considerable as to attract the attention of strangers, it was because the climatic character of the country necessitated it. Where ophthalmia and affections of the intestines raged violently, we necessarily find many oculists[1] as well as doctors for internal maladies. The best instructed, however, knew but little of anatomy. As with the Christian physicians of the Middle Ages, religious scruples prevented the Egyptians from cutting open or dissecting, in the cause of pure science, the dead body which was identified with that of Osiris. The processes of embalming, which would have instructed them in anatomy, were not intrusted to doctors; the horror was so great with which any one was regarded who mutilated the human form, that the "paraschite," on whom devolved the duty of making the necessary incisions in the dead, became the object of universal execration: as soon as he had finished his task, the assistants assaulted him, throwing stones at him with such violence that he had to take to his heels to escape with his life.[2] The knowledge of what went on within the body was therefore but vague. Life seemed to be a little air, a breath which was conveyed by the veins from member to member. "The head contains twenty-two vessels, which draw the spirits into it and send them thence to all parts of the body.

---

[1] Affections of the eyes occupy one-fourth of the *Ebers Papyrus*.
[2] DIODORUS SICULUS, i. 91.

There are two vessels for the breasts, which communicate heat to the lower parts. There are two vessels for the thighs, two for the neck, two for the arms, two for the back of the head, two for the forehead, two for the eyes, two for the eyelids, two for the right ear by which enter the breaths of life, and two for the left ear which in like manner admit the breaths of death."

A DEAD MAN RECEIVING THE BREATH OF LIFE.[1]

The "breaths" entering by the right ear, are "the good airs, the delicious airs of the north ;" the sea-breeze which tempers the burning of summer and renews the strength of man, continually weakened by the heat and threatened with exhaustion. These vital spirits, entering the veins and arteries by the ear or nose, mingled with the blood, which carried them to all parts of the body ; they sustained the animal, and were, so to speak, the cause of its movement. The heart, the perpetual mover—*hâiti*—collected them and redistributed them throughout the body : it was regarded as "the beginning of all the members," and whatever part

[1] Drawn by Faucher-Gudin, from a sketch by NAVILLE, in the *Ægyptische Todtenbuch*, vol. i. pl. lxix. The deceased carries in this hand a sail inflated by the wind, symbolizing the air, and holds it to his nostrils that he may inhale the breaths which will fill anew his arteries, and bring life to his limbs.

of the living body the physician touched, "whether the head, the nape of the neck, the hands, the breast, the arms, the legs, his hand lit upon the heart," and he felt it beating under his fingers. Under the influence of the good breaths, the vessels were inflated and worked regularly; under that of the evil, they became inflamed, were obstructed, were hardened, or gave way, and the physician had to remove the obstruction, allay the inflammation, and re-establish their vigour and elasticity. At the moment of death, the vital spirits "withdrew with the soul; the blood," deprived of air, "became coagulated, the veins and arteries emptied themselves, and the creature perished" for want of breaths.

The majority of the diseases from which the ancient Egyptians suffered, are those which still attack their successors; ophthalmia, affections of the stomach, abdomen, and bladder, intestinal worms, varicose veins, ulcers in the leg, the Nile pimple, and finally the "divine mortal malady," the *divinus morbus* of the Latins, epilepsy. Anæmia, from which at least one-fourth of the present population suffers, was not less prevalent than at present, if we may judge from the number of remedies which were used against hæmaturia, the principal cause of it. The fertility of the women entailed a number of infirmities or local affections which the doctors attempted to relieve, not always with success.[1] The science of those days treated

---

[1] With regard to the diseases of women, cf. *Ebers Papyrus*, pls. xciii., xcviii., etc. Several of the recipes are devoted to the solution of a problem which appears to have greatly exercised the mind of the ancients, viz. the determination of the sex of a child before its birth.

externals only, and occupied itself merely with symptoms easily determined by sight or touch; it never suspected that troubles which showed themselves in two widely remote parts of the body might only be different effects of the same illness, and they classed as distinct maladies those indications which we now know to be the symptoms of one disease. They were able, however, to determine fairly well the specific characteristics of ordinary affections, and sometimes described them in a precise and graphic fashion. " The abdomen is heavy, the pit of the stomach painful, the heart burns and palpitates violently. The clothing oppresses the sick man and he can barely support it. Nocturnal thirsts. His heart is sick, as that of a man who has eaten of the sycamore gum. The flesh loses its sensitiveness as that of a man seized with illness. If he seek to satisfy a want of nature he finds no relief. Say to this, ' There is an accumulation of humours in the abdomen, which makes the heart sick. I will act.'" This is the beginning of gastric fever so common in Egypt, and a modern physician could not better diagnose such a case; the phraseology would be less flowery, but the analysis of the symptoms would not differ from that given us by the ancient practitioner. The medicaments recommended comprise nearly everything which can in some way or other be swallowed, whether in solid, mucilaginous, or liquid form. Vegetable remedies are reckoned by the score, from the most modest herb to the largest tree, such as the sycamore, palm, acacia, and cedar, of which the sawdust and shavings were supposed to possess both antiseptic and emollient properties. Among the mineral substances are to be noted sea-salt, alum, nitre, sulphate of copper, and a score of different kinds of stones—among the latter the "memphite stone" was distinguished for its virtues; if applied to parts of the body which were lacerated or unhealthy, it acted as an anæsthetic and facilitated the success of surgical operations. Flesh taken from the living subject, the heart, the liver, the gall, the blood—either dried or liquid—of animals, the hair and horn of stags, were all customarily used in many cases where the motive determining their preference above other *materiæ medicæ* is unknown to us. Many recipes puzzle us by their originality and by the barbaric character of the ingredients recommended: "the milk of a woman who has given birth to a boy," the dung of a lion, a tortoise's brains, an old book boiled in oil.[1] The medicaments compounded of these incongruous substances were often very complicated. It was thought that the healing power was increased by multiplying the curative elements; each ingredient acted upon a specific region of the body, and after absorption, separated itself from the rest to bring its influence to bear upon that region. The physician made use of all the means which we employ to-day to introduce remedies into the human system, whether pills or potions,

---

[1] *Ebers Papyrus*, pl. lxxviii. l. 22—lxxix. l. 1: "To relieve a child who is constipated.—An old book. Boil it in oil, and apply half to the stomach, to provoke evacuation." It must not be forgotten that, the writings being on papyrus, the old book in question, once boiled, would have an effect analogous to that of our linseed-meal poultices. If the physician recommended taking an old one, it was for economical reasons merely; the Egyptians of the middle classes would always have in their possession a number of letters, copy-books, and other worthless waste papers, of which they would gladly rid themselves in such a profitable manner.

poultices, or ointments, draughts or clysters. Not only did he give the prescriptions, but he made them up, thus combining the art of the physician with that of the dispenser. He prescribed the ingredients, pounded them either separately or together, he macerated them in the proper way, boiled them, reduced them by heating, and filtered them through linen. Fat served him as the ordinary vehicle for ointments, and pure water for potions; but he did not despise other liquids, such as wine, beer (fermented or un-fermented), vinegar, milk, olive oil, "ben" oil either crude or refined, even the urine of men and animals: the whole, sweetened with honey, was taken hot, night and morning. The use of more than one of these remedies became world-wide; the Greeks borrowed them from the Egyytians; we have piously accepted them from the Greeks; and our contemporaries still swallow with resignation many of the abominable mixtures invented on the banks of the Nile, long before the building of the Pyramids.

It was Thot who had taught men arithmetic; Thot had revealed to them the mysteries of geometry and mensuration; Thot had constructed instruments and promulgated the laws of music; Thot had instituted the art of drawing, and had codified its unchanging rules. He had been the inventor or patron of all that was useful or beautiful in the Nile valley, and the climax of his beneficence was reached by his invention of the principles of writing, without which humanity would have been liable to forget his teaching, and to lose the advantage of his discoveries. It has been sometimes questioned whether writing, instead of having been a benefit to the Egyptians, did not rather

injure them. An old legend relates that when the god
unfolded his discovery to King Thamos, whose minister
he was, the monarch immediately raised an objection to it.
Children and young people, who had hitherto been forced
to apply themselves diligently
to learn and retain whatever
was taught them, now that
they possessed a means of
storing up knowledge without
trouble, would cease to apply
themselves, and would neglect
to exercise their memories.
Whether Thamos was right or
not, the criticism came too
late : " the ingenious art of
painting words and of speaking
to the eyes " had once for
all been acquired by the
Egyptians, and through them
by the greater part of mankind. It was a very complex
system, in which were united
most of the methods fitted for
giving expression to thought,

THOT RECORDS THE YEARS OF THE LIFE
OF RAMSES II.[1]

namely : those which were limited to the presentment of

---

[1] Bas-relief of the temple of Seti I. at Abydos, drawn by Boudier, from a
photograph by Beato. The god is marking with his reed-pen upon the
notches of a long frond of palm, the duration in millions of years of the
reign of Pharaoh upon this earth, in accordance with the decree of the
gods.

the idea, and those which were intended to .suggest sounds. At the outset the use was confined to signs intended to awaken the idea of the object in the mind of the reader by the more or less faithful picture of the object itself; for example, they depicted the sun by a centred disc ☉, the moon by a crescent ☽, a lion by a lion in the act of walk-ing 𓃯, a man by a small figure in a squatting attitude 𓀀. As by this method it was possible to convey only a very restricted number of entirely materialistic concepts, it became necessary to have recourse to various artifices in order to make up for the shortcomings of the ideograms properly so-called. The part was put for the whole, the pupil ⦿ in place of the whole eye 𓁹, the head of the ox 𓃾 instead of the complete ox 𓃂. The Egyptians sub-stituted cause for effect and effect for cause, the instrument for the work accomplished, and the disc of the sun ☉ signi-fied the day; a smoking brazier 𓊶 the fire: the brush, inkpot, and palette of the scribe 𓏞 denoted writing or written documents. They conceived the idea of employing some object which presented an actual or supposed re-semblance to the notion to be conveyed; thus, the foreparts of a lion 𓄂 denoted priority, supremacy, command; .the wasp symbolized royalty 𓆤, and a tadpole 𓆐 stood for hundreds of thousands. They ventured finally to use con-ventionalisms, as for instance when they drew the axe 𓌹 for a god, or the ostrich-feather 𓆄 for justice; the sign in these cases had only a conventional connection with the concept assigned to it. At times two or three of these symbols were associated in order to express conjointly an idea which would have been inadequately rendered by one

of them alone : a five-pointed star placed under an inverted
crescent moon ⌣ denoted a month, a calf running before
the sign for water ⤚≣ indicated thirst.   All these artifices combined furnished, however, but a very incomplete
means of seizing and transmitting thought.   When the
writer had written out twenty or thirty of these signs and
the ideas which they were supposed to embody, he had
before him only the skeleton of a sentence, from which the
flesh and sinews had disappeared ; the tone and rhythm of
the words were wanting, as were also the indications of
gender, number, person, and inflection, which distinguish
the different parts of speech and determine the varying
relations between them.   Besides this, in order to understand for himself and to guess the meaning of the author,
the reader was obliged to translate the symbols which he
deciphered, by means of words which represented in the
spoken language the pronunciation of each symbol.   Whenever he looked at them, they suggested to him both the
idea and the word for the idea, and consequently a sound
or group of sounds ; when each of them had thus acquired
three or four invariable associations of sound, he forgot
their purely ideographic value and accustomed himself to
consider them merely as notations of sound.

The first experiment in phonetics was a species of rebus,
where each of the signs, divorced from its original sense,
served to represent several words, similar in sound, but
differing in meaning in the spoken language.   The same
group of articulations, *Naûfir, Nofir,* conveyed in Egyptian
the concrete idea of a lute and the abstract idea of beauty ;
the sign 𝍦 expressed at once the lute and beauty.

The beetle was called *Khopirrû*, and the verb "to be" was pronounced *khopirû*: the figure of the beetle 🪲 consequently signified both the insect and the verb, and by further combining with it other signs, the articulation of each corresponding syllable was given in detail. The sieve ⊙ *khaû*, the mat ▪ *pû*, *pi*, the mouth ⌒ *ra*, *rû*, gave the formula *khaû-pi-rû*, which was equivalent to the sound of *khopirû*, the verb "to be:" grouped together 🪲, they denoted in writing the concept of "to be" by means of a triple rebus. In this system, each syllable of a word could be represented by one of several signs, all sounding alike. One-half of these "syllabics" stood for open, the other half for closed syllables, and the use of the former soon brought about the formation of a true alphabet. The final vowel in them became detached, and left only the remaining consonant—for example, *r* in *rû*, *h* in *ha*, *n* in *ni*, *b* in *bû*—so that ⌒ *rû*, ⊓ *ha*, ⚊ *ni*, ⌐ *bû*, eventually stood for *r*, *h*, *n*, and *b* only. This process in the course of time having been applied to a certain number of syllables, furnished a fairly large alphabet, in which several letters represented each of the twenty-two chief articulations, which the scribes considered sufficient for their purposes. The signs corresponding to one and the same letter were homophones or "equivalents in sound"—⬟, ⌐, ↑, are homophones, just as ⚊ and 🦉, because each of them, in the group to which it belongs, may be indifferently used to translate to the eye the articulations *m* or *n*. One would have thought that when the Egyptians had arrived thus far, they would have been led, as a matter of course, to reject the various characters which they had used each in its turn, in order to retain an alphabet only. But the true spirit of invention, of which they had given proof, abandoned them here as elsewhere : if the merit of a discovery was often their due, they were rarely able to bring their invention to perfection. They kept the ideographic and syllabic signs which they had used at the outset, and, with the residue of their successive notations, made for themselves a most complicated system, in which syllables and ideograms were mingled with letters properly so called. There is a little of everything in an Egyptian phrase, sometimes even in a word; as, for instance, in 𓏶𓏺𓏼 *maszirû*, the ear, or 𓄿𓏺𓏺𓏺 *kherôu*, the voice; there are the syllabics 𓏶 *mas*, 𓏺 *zir*, 𓏺 *rû*, 𓏺 *kher*, the ordinary letters 𓏺 *s*, 𓏺 *û*, 𓏺 *r*, which complete the phonetic pronunciation, and finally the ideograms, namely, 𓏺, which gives the picture of the ear by the side of the written word for it, and 𓏺 which proves that the letters represent a term designating an action of the mouth. This medley had its advantages ; it enabled the Egyptians to make clear, by the picture of the object, the sense of words which letters alone might sometimes insufficiently explain. The system demanded a serious effort of memory and long years of study; indeed, many people never completely mastered it. The picturesque appearance of the sentences, in which we see representations of men, animals, furniture, weapons, and tools grouped together in successive little pictures, rendered hieroglyphic writing specially suitable for the decoration of the temples of the gods or the palaces of kings. Mingled with scenes of worship, sacrifice, battle, or private life, the inscriptions frame or separate groups of personages, and occupy the vacant spaces which the sculptor or painter was at a loss to fill; hieroglyphic writing is pre-eminently a monumental script. For the ordinary purposes of life it was traced in black or red ink on fragments of limestone or pottery, or on wooden tablets covered with stucco, and specially on the fibres of papyrus. The exigencies of haste and the unskilfulness of scribes soon changed both its appearance and its elements; the characters when contracted, superimposed and united to one another with connecting strokes, preserved only the most distant resemblance to the persons or things which they had originally represented. This cursive writing, which was somewhat incorrectly termed hieratic, was used only for public or private documents, for administrative correspondence, or for the propagation of literary, scientific, and religious works.

It was thus that tradition was pleased to ascribe to the gods, and among them to Thot—the doubly great— the invention of all the arts and sciences which gave to Egypt its glory and prosperity. It was clear, not only to the vulgar, but to the wisest of the nation, that, had their ancestors been left merely to their own resources, they would never have succeeded in raising themselves much above the level of the brutes. The idea that a discovery of importance to the country could have risen in a human brain, and, once made known, could have been spread and developed by the efforts of successive generations, appeared to them impossible to accept. They believed that every art, every trade, had remained unaltered from the outset, and if some novelty in its aspect tended to show them their error, they preferred to imagine a divine intervention, rather than be undeceived. The mystic writing, inserted as chapter sixty-four in the *Book of the Dead*, and which subsequently was supposed to be of decisive moment to the future life of man, was, as they knew, posterior in date to the other formulas of which this book was composed; they did not, however, regard it any the less as being of divine origin. It had been found one day, without any one knowing whence it came, traced in blue characters on a plaque of alabaster, at the foot of the statue of Thot, in the sanctuary of Hermopolis. A prince, Hardidûf, had discovered it in his travels, and regarding it as a miraculous object, had brought it to his sovereign. This king, according to some, was Hûsaphaîti of the first dynasty, but by others was believed to be the pious Mykerinos. In the same way, the book on medicine, dealing with the diseases of women, was held not to be the work of a practitioner; it had revealed itself to a priest watching at night before the Holy of Holies in the temple of Isis at Coptos. "Although the earth was plunged into darkness, the moon shone upon it and enveloped it with light. It was sent as a great wonder to the holiness of King Kheops, the just of speech." The gods had thus exercised a direct influence upon men until they became entirely civilized, and this work of culture was apportioned among the three divine dynasties according to the strength of each. The first, which comprised the most vigorous divinities, had accomplished the more difficult task of establishing the world on a solid basis; the second had carried on the education of the Egyptians; and the third had regulated, in all its minutiæ, the religious constitution of the country. When there was nothing more demanding supernatural strength or intelligence to establish it, the gods returned to heaven, and were succeeded on the throne by mortal men. One tradition maintained dogmatically that the first human king whose memory it preserved, followed immediately after the last of the gods, who, in quitting the palace, had made over the crown to man as his heir, and that the change of nature had not entailed any interruption in the line of sovereigns. Another tradition would not allow that the contact between the human and divine series had been so close. Between the Ennead and Menes, it intercalated one or more lines of Theban or Thinite kings ; but these were of so formless, shadowy, and undefined an aspect, that they were called Manes, and there was attributed to them at most only a passive existence, as of persons who had always been in the condition of the dead, and had never been subjected to the trouble of passing through life. Menes was the first in order of those who were actually living. From his time, the Egyptians claimed to possess an uninterrupted list of the Pharaohs who had ruled over the Nile valley. As far back as the XVIIIth dynasty this list was written upon papyrus, and furnished the number of years that each prince occupied the throne, or the length of his life.[1] Extracts from it were inscribed in the temples,

---

[1] The only one of these lists which we possess, the "Turin Royal Papyrus," was bought, nearly intact, at Thebes, by Drovetti, about 1818, but was accidentally injured by him in bringing home. The fragments of it were acquired, together with the rest of the collection, by the Piedmontese Government in 1820, and placed in the Turin Museum, where Champóllion

or even in the tombs of private persons; and three of
these abridged catalogues are still extant, two coming
from the temples of Seti I. and Ramses II. at Abydos,[1]
while the other was discovered in the tomb of a person
of rank named Tunari, at Saqqâra.[2] They divided this
interminable succession of often problematical personages
into dynasties, following in this division, rules of which
we are ignorant, and which varied in the course of ages.
In the time of the Ramessides, names in the list which
subsequently under the Lagides formed five groups were
made to constitute one single dynasty.[3] Manetho of

saw and drew attention to them in 1824. Seyffarth carefully collected and
arranged them in the order in which they now are; subsequently Lepsius
gave a facsimile of them in 1840, in his *Auswahl der wichtigsten Urkunden*,
pls. i.–vi., but this did not include the verso; Champollion-Figeac edited in
1847, in the *Revue Archéologique*, 1st series, vol. vi., the tracings taken by
the younger Champollion before Seyffarth's arrangement; lastly, Wilkinson
published the whole in detail in 1851. Since then, the document has been
the subject of continuous investigation : E. de Rougé has reconstructed, in
an almost conclusive manner, the pages containing the first six dynasties,
and Lauth, with less certainty, those which deal with the eight following
dynasties.

[1] The first table of Abydos, unfortunately incomplete, was discovered in
the temple of Ramses II. by Banks, in 1818; the copy published by Caillaud
and by Salt served as a foundation for Champollion's first investigations on
the history of Egypt. The original, brought to France by Mimaut, was
acquired by England, and is now in the British Museum. The second
table, which is complete, all but a few signs, was brought to light by
Mariette in 1864, in the excavations at Abydos, and was immediately
noticed and published by DUMICHEN. The text of it is to be found in
MARIETTE, *La Nouvelle Table d'Abydos* (*Revue Archéologique*, 2nd series, vol.
xiii.), and *Abydos*, vol. i. pl. 43.

[2] The table of Saqqâra, discovered in 1863, has been published by
MARIETTE, *La Table de Saqqâra* (*Revue Archéologique*, 2nd series, vol. x. p.
169, et seq.), and reproduced in the *Monuments Divers*, pl. 58.

[3] The Royal Canon of Turin, which dates from the Ramesside period,

Sebennytos, who wrote a history of Europe for the use of Alexandrine Greeks, had adopted, on some unknown authority, a division of thirty-one dynasties from Menes to the Macedonian Conquest, and his system has prevailed—not, indeed, on account of its excellence, but because it is the only complete one which has come down to us.[1] All the families inscribed in his lists ruled in succession.[2] The country was no doubt frequently broken up into a dozen or more independent states, each possessing its own kings during several generations; but the annalists had from the outset discarded these collateral lines, and recognized only one legitimate dynasty, of which the rest were but vassals. Their theory of legitimacy does not always agree with actual history, and the particular line of princes which they rejected as

gives, indeed, the names of these early kings without a break, until the list reaches Unas; at this point it sums up the number of Pharaohs and the aggregate years of their reigns, thus indicating the end of a dynasty. In the intervals between the dynasties rubrics are placed, pointing out the changes which took place in the order of direct succession. The division of the same group of sovereigns into five dynasties has been preserved to us by Manetho.

[1] The best restoration of the system of Manetho is that by LEPSIUS, *Das Königsbuch der Alten Ægypter*, which should be completed and corrected from the memoirs of Lauth, Lieblein, Krall, and Unger. A common fault attaches to all these memoirs, so remarkable in many respects. They regard the work of Manetho, not as representing a more or less ingenious system applied to Egyptian history, but as furnishing an authentic scheme of this history, in which it is necessary to enclose all the royal names which the monuments have revealed, and are still daily revealing to us.

[2] E. de Rougé triumphantly demonstrated, in opposition to Bunsen, now nearly fifty years ago, that all Manetho's dynasties are successive, and the monuments discovered from year to year in Egypt have confirmed his demonstration in every detail.

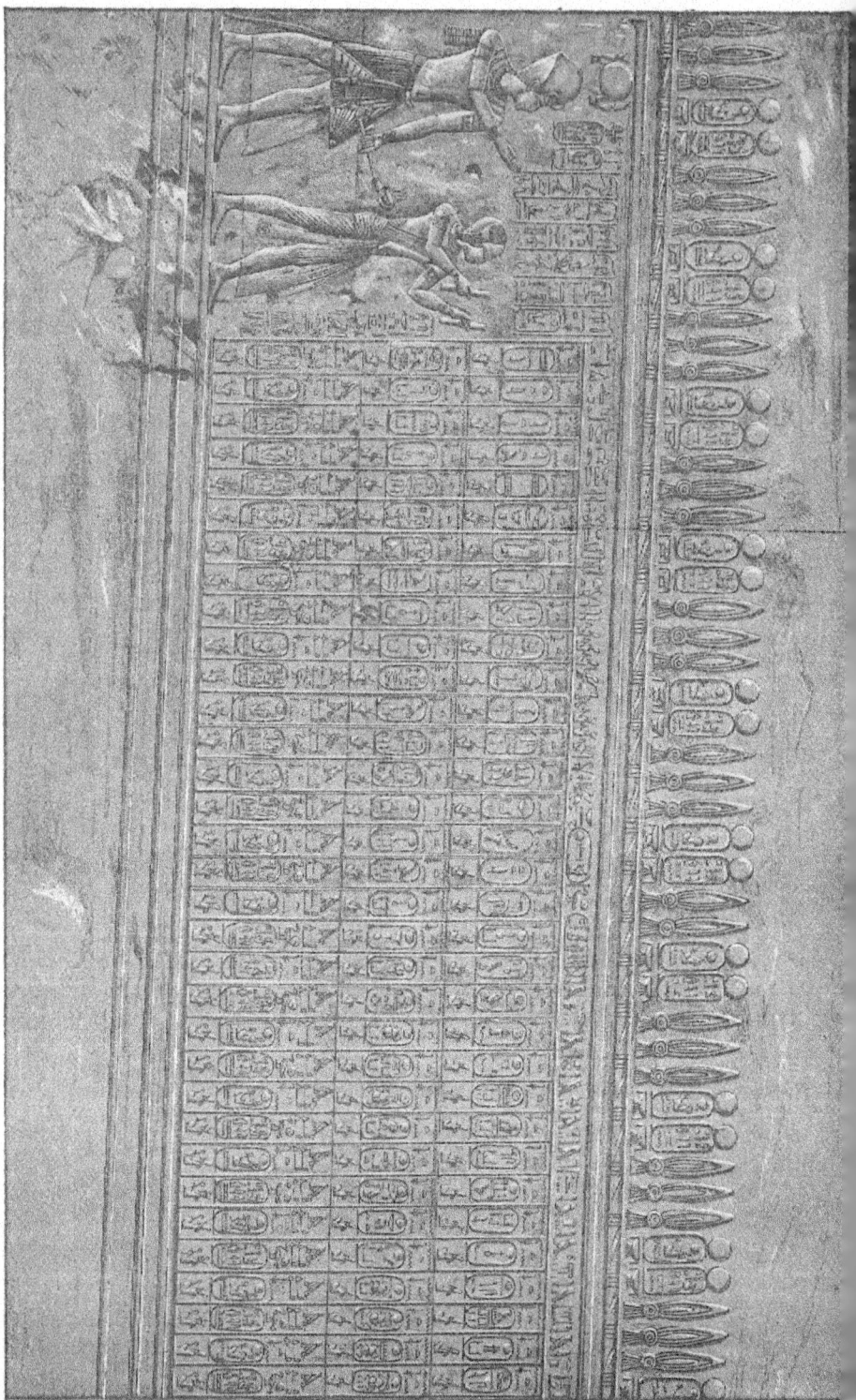

THE TABLE OF THE KINGS IN THE TEMPLE OF SETI I. AT ABYDOS.

From a photograph.

usurpers represented at times the only family possessing true rights to the crown.[1] In Egypt, as elsewhere, the official chroniclers were often obliged to accommodate the past to the exigencies of the present, and to manipulate the annals to suit the reigning party; while obeying their orders the chroniclers deceived posterity, and it is only by a rare chance that we can succeed in detecting them in the act of falsification, and can re-establish the truth.

The system of Manetho, in the state in which it has been handed down to us by epitomizers, has rendered, and continues to render, service to science; if it is not the actual history of Egypt, it is a sufficiently faithful substitute to warrant our not neglecting it when we wish to understand and reconstruct the sequence of events. His dynasties furnish the necessary framework for most of the events and revolutions, of which the monuments have preserved us a record. At the outset, the centre to which the affairs of the country gravitated was in the extreme north of the valley. The principality which extended from the entrance of the Fayûm to the

---

[1] It is enough to give two striking examples of this. The royal lists of the time of the Ramessides suppress, at the end of the XVIIIth dynasty, Amenôthes IV. and several of his successors, and give the following sequence —Amenôthes III., Harmhabît, Ramses I., without any apparent hiatus; Manetho, on the contrary, replaces the kings who were omitted, and keeps approximately to the real order between Horos (Amenôthes III.) and Armaïs (Harmhabît). Again, the official tradition of the XXth dynasty gives, between Ramses II. and Ramses III., the sequence—Mînephtah, Seti II., Nakht-Seti; Manetho, on the other hand, gives Amenemes followed by Thûôris, who appear to correspond to the Amenmeses and Siphtah of contemporary monuments, but, after Mînephtah, he omits Seti II. and Nakhîtou-Seti, the father of Ramses III.

apex of the Delta, and subsequently the town of Memphis itself, imposed their sovereigns upon the remaining nomes, served as an emporium for commerce and national industries, and received homage and tribute from neighbouring peoples. About the time of the VIth dynasty this centre of gravity was displaced, and tended towards the interior ; it was arrested for a short time at Heracleopolis (IXth and Xth dynasties), and ended by fixing itself at Thebes (XIth dynasty). From henceforth Thebes became the capital, and furnished Egypt with her rulers. With the exception of the XIVth Xoïte dynasty, all the families occupying the throne from the XIth to the XXth dynasty were Theban. When the barbarian shepherds invaded Africa from Asia, the Thebaïd became the last refuge and bulwark of Egyptian nationality; its chiefs struggled for many centuries against the conquerors before they were able to deliver the rest of the valley. It was a Theban dynasty, the XVIIIth, which inaugurated the era of foreign conquest; but after the XIXth, a movement, the reverse of that which had taken place towards the end of the first period, brought back the centre of gravity, little by little, towards the north of the country. From the time of the XXIst dynasty, Thebes ceased to hold the position of capital : Tanis, Bubastis, Mendes, Sebennytos, and above all, Sais, disputed the supremacy with each other, and political life was concentrated in the maritime provinces. Those of the interior, ruined by Ethiopian and Assyrian invasions, lost their influence and gradually dwindled away. Thebes became impoverished and depopulated; it fell into ruins, and soon was nothing more than a resort for devotees or travellers. The history of Egypt is, therefore, divided into three periods, each corresponding to the suzerainty of a town or a principality:—

I.—MEMPHITE PERIOD, usually called the "Ancient Empire," from the Ist to the Xth dynasty: kings of Memphite origin ruled over the whole of Egypt during the greater part of this epoch.

II.—THEBAN PERIOD, from the XIth to the XXth dynasty. It is divided into two parts by the invasion of the Shepherds (XVIth dynasty):

    a. The first Theban Empire (Middle Empire), from the XIth to the XIVth dynasty.

    b. The new Theban Empire, from the XVIIth to the XXth dynasty.

III.—SAITE PERIOD, from the XXIst to the XXXth dynasty, divided into two unequal parts by the Persian Conquest:

    a. The first Saïte period, from the XXIst to the XXVIth dynasty.

    b. The second Saïte period, from the XXVIIIth to the XXXth dynasty.

The Memphites had created the monarchy. The Thebans extended the rule of Egypt far and wide, and made of her a conquering state: for nearly six centuries she ruled over the Upper Nile and over Western Asia. Under the Saïtes she retired gradually within her natural frontiers, and from having been aggressive became assailed, and suffered herself to be crushed in turn by all the nations she had once oppressed.[1] The monuments have as yet yielded no account of the events which tended to unite the country under the rule of one man; we can only surmise that the feudal principalities had gradually been drawn together into two groups, each of which formed a separate kingdom. Heliopolis became the chief focus in the north, from which civilization radiated over the rich plains and the marshes of the Delta. Its colleges of priests had collected, condensed, and arranged the principal myths of the local religions; the Ennead to which it gave conception would never have obtained the popularity which we must acknowledge it had, if its princes had not exercised, for at least some period, an actual suzerainty over the neighbouring plains. It was around Heliopolis that the kingdom of Lower Egypt was organized; everything there bore traces of Heliopolitan theories—the protocol of the kings, their supposed descent from Râ, and the enthusiastic worship which they offered to the sun. The Delta, owing to its compact and restricted area, was aptly suited for government from one centre; the Nile valley proper, narrow, tortuous, and stretching like a thin strip on either bank of the river, did not lend itself to so complete a unity. It, too, represented a

---

[1] The division into Ancient, Middle, and New Empire, proposed by Lepsius, has the disadvantage of not taking into account the influence which the removal of the seat of the dynasties exercised on the history of the country. The arrangement which I have here adopted was first put forward in the *Revue critique*, 1873, vol. i. pp. 82, 83.

single kingdom, having the reed ⌡ and the lotus ⚱
for its emblems; but its component parts were more
loosely united, its religion was less systematized, and
it lacked a well-placed city to serve as a political and
sacerdotal centre. Hermopolis contained schools of
theologians who certainly played an important part in
the development of myths and dogmas; but the influence
of its rulers was never widely felt. In the south, Siût
disputed their supremacy, and Heracleopolis stopped
their road to the north. These three cities thwarted
and neutralized one another, and not one of them ever
succeeded in obtaining a lasting authority over Upper
Egypt. Each of the two kingdoms had its own natural
advantages and its system of government, which gave
to it a particular character, and stamped it, as it were,
with a distinct personality down to its latest days. The
kingdom of Upper Egypt was more powerful, richer,
better populated, and was governed apparently by more
active and enterprising rulers. It is to one of the latter,
Mîni or Menes of Thinis, that tradition ascribes the
honour of having fused the two Egypts into a single
empire, and of having inaugurated the reign of the
human dynasties. Thinis figured in the historic period
as one of the least of Egyptian cities. It barely maintained an existence on the left bank of the Nile, if not
on the exact spot now occupied by Girgeh, at least only
a short distance from it.[1] The principality of the Osirian

---

[1] The site of Thinis is not yet satisfactorily identified. It is neither at
Kom-es-Sultân, as Mariette thought, nor, according to the hypothesis of A.
Schmidt, at El-Kherbeh. Brugsch has proposed to fix the site at the village

Reliquary, of which it was the metropolis, occupied the valley from one mountain range to the other, and gradually extended across the desert as far as the Great Theban Oasis. Its inhabitants worshipped a sky-god, Anhûri, or rather two twin gods, Anhûri-Shû, who were speedily

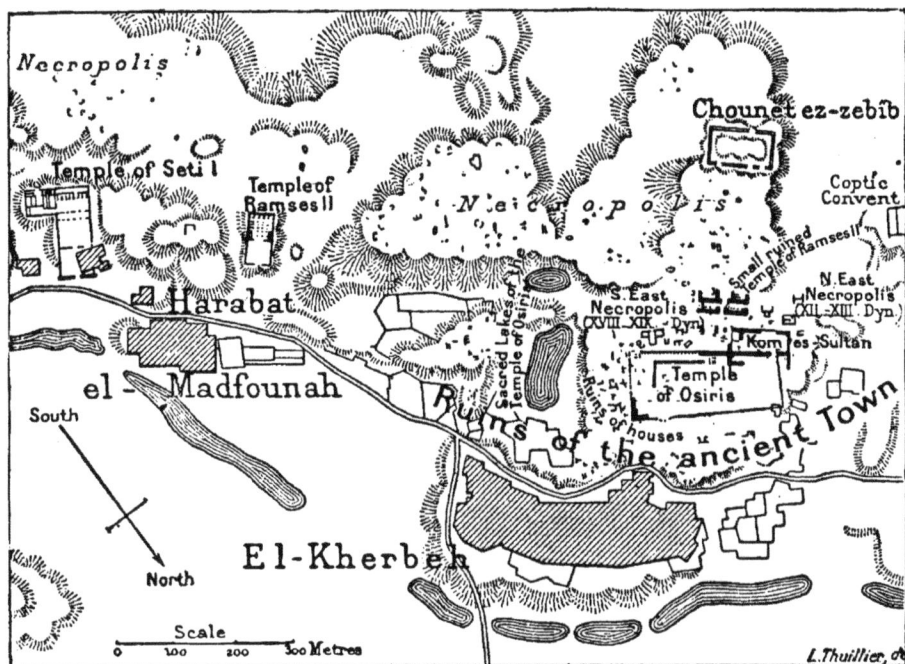

PLAN OF THE RUINS OF ABYDOS, MADE BY MARIETTE IN 1865 AND 1875.

amalgamated with the solar deities and became a war-like personification of Râ. Anhûri-Shû, like all the other

of Tineh, near Berdis, and is followed in this by Dümichen. The present tendency is to identify it either with Girgeh itself, or with one of the small neighbouring towns—for example, Birbeh—where there are some ancient ruins; this was also the opinion of Champollion and of Nester L'hôte. I may mention that, in a frequently quoted passage of Hellanicos, Zoëga corrects the reading Τίνδιον ὄνομα into Θῖν δὲ οἱ ὄνομα, which would once more give us the name of Thinis: the mention of this town as being ἐπιποταμίη, "situated on the river," would be a fresh reason for its identification with Girgeh.

solar manifestations, came to be associated with a goddess having the form or head of a lioness—a Sokhît, who took for the occasion the epithet of Mîhît, the northern one. Some of the dead from this city are buried on the other side of the Nile, near the modern village of Mesheikh, at the foot of the Arabian chain, whose steep cliffs here approach somewhat near the river : the principal necropolis was at some distance to the east, near the sacred town of Abydos. It would appear that, at the outset, Abydos was the capital of the country, for the entire nome bore the same name as the city, and had adopted for its symbol the representation of the reliquary in which the god reposed. In very early times Abydos fell into decay, and resigned its political rank to Thinis, but its religious importance remained unimpaired. The city occupied a long and narrow strip of land between the canal and the first slopes of the Libyan mountains. A brick fortress defended it from the incursions of the Bedouin, and beside it the temple of the god of the dead reared its naked walls. Here, Anhûri, having passed from life to death, was worshipped under the name of Khontamentît, the chief of that western region whither souls repair on quitting this earth. It is impossible to say by what blending of doctrines or by what political combinations this Sun of the Night came to be identified with Osiris of Mendes, since the fusion dates back to a very remote antiquity; it had become an established fact long before the most ancient sacred books were compiled. Osiris Khontamentît grew rapidly in popular favour, and his temple attracted annually an increasing number of pilgrims. The Great Oasis had been considered at first as a sort of mysterious paradise, whither the dead went in search of peace and happiness. It was called Uît, the Sepulchre; this name clung to it after it had become an actual Egyptian province, and the remembrance of its ancient purpose survived in the minds of the people, so that the " cleft," or gorge in the mountain through which the doubles journeyed towards it, never ceased to be regarded as one of the gates of the other world. At the time of the New Year festivals, spirits flocked thither from all parts of the valley; they there awaited the coming of the dying sun, in order to embark with him and enter safely the dominions of Khontamentît. Abydos, even before the historic period, was the only town, and its god the only god, whose worship, practised by all Egyptians, inspired them all with an equal devotion.

The excavations of the last few years have brought to light some, at all events, of the oldest Pharaohs known to the Egyptian annalists, namely, those whom they placed in their first human dynasties; and the locality where the monuments of these princes were discovered, shows us that these writers were correct in representing Thinis as playing an important part in the history of the early ages of their country. If the tomb of Menes— that sovereign whom we are inclined to look upon as the first king of the official lists—lies near the village of Nagadeh, not far from Thebes,[1] those of his immediate successors are close to Thinis, in the cemeteries of

---

[1] The objects found during these excavations are now in the Gizeh Museum.

Abydos.¹ They stand at the very foot of the Libyan
hills, near the entrance to the ravine—the " Cleft "—
through which the mysterious oasis was reached, and
thither the souls flocked in order that they might enter
by a safe way the land beyond the grave.² The mass
of pottery, whole and broken, which has accumulated
on this site from the offerings of centuries has obtained
for it among the Fellahin the name of Omm-el-Gaâb—
" the mother of pots." The tombs there lie in serried
ranks. They present for the most part a rough model
of the pyramids of the Memphite period—rectangular
structures of bricks without mortar rising slightly above
the level of the plain. The funeral chamber occupies
the centre of each, and is partly hollowed out of the
soil, like a shallow well, the sides being bricked. It
had a flat timber roof, covered by a layer of about three
feet of sand; the floor also was of wood, and in several
cases the remains of the beams of both ceiling and pavement have been brought to light. The body of the
royal inmate was laid in the middle of the chamber,
surrounded by its funeral furniture and by a part of the
offerings. The remainder was placed in the little rooms
which opened out of the principal vault, sometimes on

¹ The credit of having discovered this important necropolis, and of having
brought to light the earliest known monuments of the first dynasties, is
entirely due to Amélineau. He carried on important work there during
four years, from 1895 to 1899 : unfortunately its success was impaired by
the theories which he elaborated with regard to the new monuments, and
by the delay in publishing an account of the objects which remained in his
possession.

² For the " Cleft," cf. *supra*, pp. 281, 282, 334.

the same level, sometimes on one higher than itself; after their contents had been laid within them, the entrance to these rooms was generally walled up. Human bodies have been found inside them, probably those of slaves killed at the funeral that they might wait upon the dead in his life beyond the grave.[1] The objects placed in these chambers were mostly offerings, but besides these were coarse stelæ bearing the name of a person, and dictated to " the double of his luminary."[2] Some of them mention a dwarf[3] or a favourite dog of the sovereign, who accompanied his master into the tomb. Tablets of ivory or bone skilfully incised furnish us with scenes representing some of the ceremonies of the deification of the king in his lifetime and the sacrifices offered at the time of his burial;[4] in rarer instances they record his exploits. The offerings themselves were such as we meet with in burials of a subsequent age— bread, cakes, meat, and poultry of various sorts—indeed, everything we find mentioned in the lists inscribed in the tombs of the later dynasties, particularly the jars of wine and liquors, on the clay bungs of which are still legible the impression of the signet bearing the name of

[1] FL. PETRIE, The Royal Tombs of the First Dynasty, part i. p. 14.

[2] The " luminous double " or the " double of his luminary " is doubtless that luminous spectre which haunted the tombs and even the houses of the living during the night, and which I have mentioned, supra, p. 160.

[3] Petrie found the skeletons of two dwarfs, probably the very two to whom the two stelæ (Nos. 36, 37) in the tomb of Semempses were raised. Was one of these dwarfs one of the Danga of Puanît who were sought after by the Pharaohs of the Memphite dynasties?

[4] This was the ceremony called by the Egyptians " The Festival of the Foundation."—habu sudu.

the sovereign for whose use they were sealed. Besides stuffs and mats, the furniture comprised chairs, beds, stools, an enormous number of vases, some in coarse pottery for common use, others in choice stone such as diorite, granite, or rock crystal very finely worked, on the fragments of all of which may be read cut in outline the names and preamble of the Pharaoh to whom the object belonged. The ceremonial of the funerary offering and its significance was already fully developed at this early period; this can be gathered by the very nature of the objects buried with the deceased, by their number, quantity, and by the manner in which they were arranged. Like their successors in the Egypt of later times, these ancient kings expected to continue their material existence within the tomb, and they took precautions that life there should be as comfortable as circumstances should permit. Access to the tomb was sometimes gained by a sloping passage or staircase; this made it possible to see if everything within was in a satisfactory condition. After the dead had been enclosed in his chamber, and five or six feet of sand had been spread over the beams which formed its roof, the position of the tomb was shown merely by a scarcely perceptible rise in the soil of the necropolis, and its site would soon have been forgotten, if its easternmost limits had not been marked by two large stelæ on which were carefully engraved one of the appellations of the king—that of his double, or his Horus name.[1] It was on this spot, upon an altar placed between the two

---

[1] For the Horus name of the Pharaohs, see vol. ii., pp. 23–25.

stelæ, that the commemorative ceremonies were celebrated, and the provisions renewed on certain days fixed
by the religious law. Groups of private tombs were
scattered around,—the resting-places of the chief officers
of the sovereign, the departed Pharaoh being thus surrounded in death by the same courtiers as those who
had attended him during his earthly existence.

The princes, whose names and titles have been revealed
to us by the inscriptions on these tombs, have not by any
means been all classified as yet, the prevailing custom at
that period having been to designate them by their Horus
names, but rarely by their proper names, which latter is
the only one which figures in the official lists which we
possess of the Egyptian kings. A few texts, more explicit
than the rest, enable us to identify three of them with
the Usaphais, the Miebis, and the Semempses of Manetho
—the fifth, sixth, and seventh kings of the I[st] dynasty.[1]
The fact that they are buried in the necropolis of Abydos
apparently justifies the opinion of the Egyptian chroniclers
that they were natives of Thinis. Is the Menes who
usually figures at their head[2] also a Thinite prince?

---

[1] The credit is due to SETHE of having attributed their ordinary names
to several of the kings of the I[st] dynasty with Horus names only which were
found by Amélineau, and these identifications have been accepted by all
Egyptologists. Petrie discovered quite recently on some fragments of vases
the Horus names of these same princes, together with their ordinary names.
The Usaphais, the Miebis, and the Semempses of Manetho are now satisfactorily identified with three of the Pharaohs discovered by Amélineau and
by Petrie. ——

[2] In the time of Seti I. and Ramses II. he heads the list of the Table of
Abydos. Under Ramses II. his statue was carried in procession, preceding
all the other royal statues. Finally, the "Royal Papyrus" of Turin,

Several scholars believe that his ordinary name, Mînî, is to be read on an ivory tablet engraved for a sovereign whose Horus name—Ahauîti, the warlike—is known to us from several documents, and whose tomb also has been discovered, but at Nagadeh. It is a great rectangular structure of bricks 165 feet long and 84 broad, the external walls of which were originally ornamented by deep polygonal grooves, resembling those which score the façade of Chaldæan buildings, but the Nagadeh tomb has a second brick wall which fills up all the hollows left in the first one, and thus hides the primitive decoration of the monument. The building contains twenty-one chambers, five of which in the centre apparently constituted the dwelling of the deceased, while the others, grouped around these, serve as storehouses from whence he could draw his provisions at will. Did the king buried within indeed bear the name of Menes,[1] and if such was the case, how are we to reconcile the tradition of his Thinite origin with the existence of his far-off tomb in the neighbourhood of Thebes? Objects bearing his Horus name have been found at Omm-el-Gaâb, and it is evident that he belonged to the same age as the sovereigns interred in this necropolis. If, indeed, Menes was really his personal name, there is no reason against his being the Menes of tradition, he whom the Pharaohs

written in the time of Ramses I., begins the entire series of the human Pharaohs with his name.

[1] The sign *Manu*, which appears on the ivory tablet found in this tomb, has been interpreted as a king's name, and consequently inferred to be Menes. This reading has been disputed on various sides, and the point remains, therefore, a contested one until further discovery.

of the glorious Theban dynasties regarded as the earliest of their purely human ancestors. Whether he was really the first king who reigned over the whole of Egypt, or whether he had been preceded by other sovereigns whose monuments we may find in some site still unexplored, is a matter for conjecture. That princes had exercised authority in various parts of the country is still uncertain, but that the Egyptian historians did not know them, seems to prove that they had left no written records of their names. At any rate, a Menes lived who reigned at the outset of history, and doubtless before long the Nile valley, when more carefully explored, will yield us monuments recording his actions and determining his date. The civilization of the Egypt of his time was ruder than that with which we have hitherto been familiar on its soil, but even at that early period it was almost as complete. It had its industries and its arts, of which the cemeteries furnish us daily with the most varied examples : weaving, modelling in clay, wood-carving, the incising of ivory, gold, and the hardest stone were all carried on; the ground was cultivated with hoe and plough; tombs were built showing us the model of what the houses and palaces must have been; the country had its army, its administrators, its priests, its nobles, its writing, and its system of epigraphy differs so little from that to which we are accustomed in later ages, that we can decipher it with no great difficulty. Frankly speaking, all that we know at present of the first of the Pharaohs beyond the mere fact of his existence is practically *nil*, and the stories related of him by the writers of classical times are mere legends arranged to suit the fancy of the compiler.. "This Menes, according to the priests, surrounded Memphis with dykes. For the river formerly followed the sandhills for some distance on the Libyan side. Menes, having dammed up the reach about a hundred stadia to the south of Memphis, caused the old bed to dry up, and conveyed the river through an artificial channel dug midway between the two mountain ranges. Then Menes, the first who was king, having enclosed a firm space of ground with dykes, there founded that town which is still called Memphis; he then made a lake round it, to the north and west, fed by the river, the city being bounded on the east by the Nile." [1] The history of Memphis, such as it can be gathered from the monuments, differs considerably from the tradition current in Egypt at the time of Herodotus. It appears, indeed, that at the outset, the site on which it subsequently arose was occupied by a small fortress, Ânbû-hazû—the white wall—which was dependent on Heliopolis, and in which Phtah possessed a sanctuary. After the "white wall" was separated from the Heliopolitan principality to form a nome by itself, it assumed a certain importance, and furnished, so it was said, the dynasties which succeeded the Thinite. Its prosperity dates only, however, from the time when the sovereigns of the Vth and VIth dynasties fixed on it for their residence; one of them, Papi I., there founded for himself and for his "double" after

---

[1] The dyke supposed to have been made by Menes is evidently that of Qosheîsh, which now protects the province of Gizeh, and regulates the inundation in its neighbourhood.

him, a new town, which he called Minnofîrû, from his
tomb. Minnofîrû, which is the correct pronunciation and
the origin of Memphis, probably signified "the good
refuge," the haven of the good, the burying-place where
the blessed dead came to rest beside Osiris. The people
soon forgot the true interpretation, or probably it did not
fall in with their taste for romantic tales. They were
rather disposed, as a rule, to discover in the beginnings
of history individuals from whom the countries or cities
with which they were familiar took their names: if no
tradition supplied them with this, they did not experience
any scruple in inventing one. The Egyptians of the time
of the Ptolemies, who were guided in their philological
speculations by the pronunciation in vogue around them,
attributed the patronship of their city to a Princess
Memphis, a daughter of its founder, the fabulous
Uchoreus; those of preceding ages before the name
had become altered, thought to find in Minnofîrû a " Mini
Nofir," or "Menes the Good," the reputed founder of
the capital of the Delta. Menes the Good, divested of
his epithet, is none other than Menes, the first king,
and he owes this episode in his life to a popular attempt at
etymology. The legend which identifies the establishment of the kingdom with the construction of the city,
must have originated at the time when Memphis was
still the residence of the kings and the seat of government, at latest about the end of the Memphite period.
It must have been an old tradition in the time of the
Theban dynasties, since they admitted unhesitatingly the
authenticity of the statements which ascribed to the

northern city so marked a superiority over their own country.

When once this half-mythical Menes was firmly established in his position, there was little difficulty in inventing a story which would portray him as an ideal sovereign. He was represented as architect, warrior, and statesman; he had begun the temple of Phtah, written laws and regulated the worship of the gods, particularly that of Hâpis, and he had conducted expeditions against

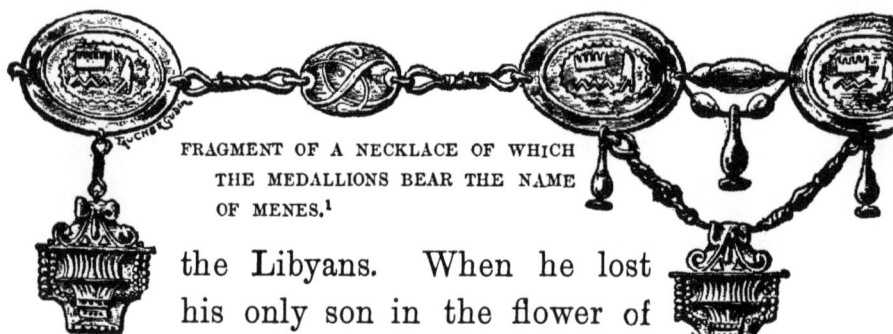

FRAGMENT OF A NECKLACE OF WHICH THE MEDALLIONS BEAR THE NAME OF MENES.[1]

the Libyans. When he lost his only son in the flower of his age, the people improvised a hymn of mourning to console him—the "Maneros"—both the words and the tune of which were handed down from generation to generation. He did not, moreover, disdain the luxuries of the table, for he invented the art of serving a dinner, and the mode of eating it in a reclining posture. One day, while hunting, his dogs, excited by something or other, fell upon him to devour him. He escaped with difficulty, and, pursued by them, fled to the shore of Lake Mœris, and was there brought to bay; he was on

[1] Drawn by Faucher-Gudin after PRISSE D'AVENNES. The gold medallions engraved with the name of Menes are ancient, and perhaps go back to the XXth dynasty; the setting is entirely modern, with the exception of the three oblong pendants of cornelian.

the point of succumbing to them, when a crocodile took him on his back and carried him across to the other side.[1] In gratitude he built a new town, which he called Crocodilopolis, and assigned to it for its god the crocodile which had saved him; he then erected close to it the famous labyrinth and a pyramid for his tomb. Other traditions show him in a less favourable light. They accuse him of having, by horrible crimes, excited against him the anger of the gods, and allege that after a reign of sixty to sixty-two years, he was killed by a hippopotamus which came forth from the Nile.[2] They also related that the Saïte Tafnakhti, returning from an expedition against the Arabs, during which he had been obliged to renounce the pomp and luxuries of royal life, had solemnly cursed him, and had caused his imprecations to be inscribed upon a stele set up in the temple of Amon at Thebes. Nevertheless, in the memory that Egypt preserved of its first Pharaoh, the good outweighed the evil. He was worshipped in Memphis side by side with Phtah and

---

[1] This is an episode from the legend of Osiris: at Philæ, in the little building of the Antonines, may be seen a representation of a crocodile crossing the Nile, carrying on his back the mummy of the god. The same episode is also found in the tale of Onûs el-Ujûd and of Uard f'il-Ikmâm, where the crocodile leads the hero to his beautiful prisoner in the Island of Philæ. EBERS, l'Égypte, French trans., vol. ii. pp. 415, 416, has shown how this episode in the Arab story must have been inspired by the bas-relief at Philæ and by the scene which it portrays: the temple is still called " Kasr," and the island " Geziret Onûs el-Ujûd."

[2] In popular romances, this was the usual end of criminals of every kind; we shall see that another king, Akhthoes the founder of the IXth dynasty, after committing horrible misdeeds, was killed, in the same way as Menes, by a hippopotamus.

Ramses II.; his name figured at the head of the royal lists, and his cult continued till the time of the Ptolemies.

His immediate successors had an actual existence, and their tombs are there in proof of it. We know where Usaphais, Miebis, and Semempses[1] were laid to rest, besides more than a dozen other princes whose real names and whose position in the official lists are still uncertain. The order of their succession was often a matter of doubt to the Egyptians themselves, but perhaps the discoveries of the next few years will enable us to clear up and settle definitely matters which were shrouded in mystery in the time of the Theban Pharaohs. As a fact, the forms of such of their names as have been handed down to us by later tradition, are curt and rugged, indicative of an early state of society, and harmonizing with the more primitive civilization to which they belong: Ati the Wrestler, Teti the Runner, Qenqoni the Crusher, are suitable rulers for a people, the first duty of whose chief was to lead his followers into battle, and to strike harder than any other man in the thickest of the fight.[2] Some of the monuments they have left us, seem to show that their reigns were as much devoted to war as those of the later Pharaohs. The

---

[1] FLINDERS PETRIE, *The Royal Tombs of the First Dynasty*, vol. i. p. 56.

[2] The Egyptians were accustomed to explain the meaning of the names of their kings to strangers, and the Canon of Eratosthenes has preserved several of their derivations, of which a certain number, as, for instance, that of Menes from αἰώνιος, the "lasting," are tolerably correct. M. Krall is, to my knowledge, the only Egyptologist who has attempted to glean from the meaning of these names indications of the methods by which the national historians of Egypt endeavoured to make up the lists of the earliest dynasties.

king whose Horus name was Nârumîr, is seen on a contemporary object which has come down to us, standing
before a heap of beheaded foes; the bodies are all stretched
out on the ground, each with his head placed neatly
between his legs: the king had overcome, apparently in
some important engagement, several thousands of his
enemies, and was inspecting the execution of their leaders.
That the foes with whom these early kings contended were
in most cases Egyptian princes of the nomes, is proved by
the list of city names which are inscribed on the fragments
of another document of the same nature, and we gather
from them that Dobu (Edfu), Hasutonu (Cynopolis),
Habonu (Hipponon), Hakau (Memphis) and others were
successively taken and dismantled.[1] On this fragment
King Den is represented standing over a prostrate chief of
the Bedouin, striking him with his mace. Sondi, who is
classed in the IInd dynasty, received a continuous worship
towards the end of the IIIrd dynasty. But did all those
whose names preceded or followed his on the lists, really
exist as he did? and if they existed, to what extent do the

[1] Palette resembling the preceding one, and with it deposited in the
Gizeh Museum; reproduced by STEINDORFF, and by J. DE MORGAN. The
names of the towns were enclosed within the embattled line which was used
later on to designate foreign countries. The animals which surmount them
represent the gods of Egypt, the king's protectors; and the king himself,
identified with these gods, is making a breach in the wall with a pick-axe.
The names of the towns have not been satisfactorily identified: Hat-kau,
for instance, may not be Memphis, but it appears that there is no doubt
with regard to Habonu. Cf. SAYCE, *The Beginnings of the Egyptian Monarchy*
in the *Proceedings of the Biblical Archæological Society*, 1898, vol. xx. pp.
99–101.
[3] The ivory plaque, which doubtless came from the king's tomb at Abydos,
is in the collection of Mr. McGregor.—ED.

order and the relation assigned to them agree with the actual truth? The different lists do not contain the same names in the same positions; certain Pharaohs are added or suppressed without appreciable reason. Where Manetho inscribes Kenkenes and Ouenephes, the tables of the time of Seti I. gave us Ati and Ata; Manetho reckons nine kings to the IInd dynasty, while they register only five.[1] The monuments, indeed, show us that Egypt in the past obeyed princes whom her annalists were unable to classify: for instance, they associate with Sondi a Pirsenû, who is not mentioned in the annals. We must, therefore, take the record of all this opening period of history for what it is—namely, a system invented at a much later date, by means of various artifices and combinations—to be partially accepted in default of a better, but without according to it that excessive confidence which it has hitherto received. The two Thinite dynasties, in direct descent from the first human king Menes, furnish, like this hero himself, only a tissue of romantic tales and miraculous legends in the place of history. A double-headed stork, which had appeared in the first year of Teti, son of Menes, had foreshadowed to Egypt a long prosperity, but a famine under Ouenephes, and a terrible plague under Semempses, had depopulated the country: the laws had been relaxed, great crimes had been committed, and revolts had broken

---

[1] The impossibility of reconciling the names of ↓he Greek with those of the Pharaonic lists has been admitted by most of the savants who have discussed the matter, viz. Mariette, E. de Rougé, Lieblein, Wiedemann; most of them explain the differences by the supposition that, in many cases, one of the lists gives the cartouche name, and the other the cartouche prenomen of the same king.

out. During the reign of Boêthos, a gulf had opened near Bubastis, and swallowed up many people, then the Nile had flowed with honey for fifteen days in the time of Nephercheres, and Sesochris was supposed to have been a giant in stature. A few details about royal edifices were mixed up with these prodigies. Teti had laid the foundation of the great palace of Memphis, Ouenephes had built the pyramids of Ko-komè near Saqqâra. Several of the ancient Pharaohs had published books on theology, or had written treatises on anatomy and medicine; several had made laws which lasted down to the beginning of the Christian era. One of them was called Kakôû, the male of males, or the bull of bulls. They explained his name by the statement that he had concerned himself about the sacred animals; he had proclaimed as gods, Hâpis of Memphis, Mnevis of Heliopolis, and the goat of Mendes. After him, Binôthris had conferred the right of succession upon all the women of the blood-royal. The accession of the IIIrd dynasty, a Memphite one according to Manetho, did not at first change the miraculous character of this history. The Libyans had revolted against Necherophes, and the two armies were encamped before each other, when one night the disk of the moon became immeasurably enlarged, to the great alarm of the rebels, who recognized in this phenomenon a sign of the anger of heaven, and yielded without fighting. Tosorthros, the successor of Necherophes, brought the hieroglyphs and the art of stone-cutting to perfection. He composed, as Teti did, books of medicine, a fact which caused him to be identified with the healing god Imhotpû. The priests related these things

seriously, and the Greek writers took them down from their
lips with the respect which they offered to everything
emanating from the wise men of Egypt.

What they related of the human kings was not more
detailed, as we see, than their accounts of the gods.
Whether the legends dealt with deities or kings, all
that we know took its origin, not in popular imagination, but in sacerdotal dogma : they were invented
long · after the times they dealt with, in the recesses
of the temples, with an intention and a method of
which we are enabled to detect flagrant instances on the
monuments. Towards the middle of the third century
before our era, the Greek troops stationed on the southern
frontier, in the forts at the first cataract, developed a
particular veneration for Isis of Philæ. Their devotion
spread to the superior officers who came to inspect them,
then to the whole population of the Thebäid, and finally
reached the court of the Macedonian kings. The latter,
carried away by force of example, gave every encouragement
to a movement which attracted worshippers to a common
sanctuary, and united in one cult the two races over which
they ruled. They pulled down the meagre building of the
Saïte period which had hitherto sufficed for the worship
of Isis, constructed at great cost the temple which still
remains almost intact, and assigned to it considerable
possessions in Nubia, which, in addition to gifts from
private individuals, made the goddess the richest land-
owner in Southern Egypt. Khnûmû and his two
wives, Anûkit and Satît, who, before Isis, had been the
undisputed suzerains of the cataract, perceived with

jealousy their neighbour's prosperity: the civil wars and
invasions of the centuries immediately preceding had

SATÎT PRESENTS THE PHARAOH AMENÔTHES III. TO KHNÛMÛ.[1]

ruined their temples, and their poverty contrasted pain-
fully with the riches of the new-comer.   The priests

[1] Drawn by Faucher-Gudin, from one of the bas-reliefs of the temple of
Khnûmû, at Elephantinê.   This bas-relief is now destroyed.

resolved to lay this sad state of affairs before King Ptolemy, to represent to him the services which they had rendered and still continued to render to Egypt, and above all to remind him of the generosity of the ancient Pharaohs, whose example, owing to the poverty of the times, the recent Pharaohs had been unable to follow. Doubtless authentic documents were wanting in their archives to support their pretensions: they therefore inscribed upon a rock, in the island of Sehel, a long inscription which they attributed to Zosiri of the IIIrd dynasty. This sovereign had left behind him a vague reputation for greatness. As early as the XIIth dynasty Usirtasen III. had claimed him as "his father"—his ancestor—and had erected a statue to him; the priests knew that, by invoking him, they had a chance of obtaining a hearing. The inscription which they fabricated, set forth that in the eighteenth year of Zosiri's reign he had sent to Madîr, lord of Elephantinê, a message couched in

ANÛKIT.

these terms: " I am overcome with sorrow for the throne, and for those who reside in the palace, and my heart is afflicted and suffers greatly because the Nile has not risen in my time, for the space of eight years. Corn is scarce, there is a lack of herbage, and nothing is left to eat: when any one calls upon his neighbours for help, they take pains not to go. The child weeps, the young man is uneasy, the hearts of the old men are in despair, their limbs are bent,

they crouch on the earth, they fold their hands; the courtiers have no further resources; the shops formerly furnished with rich wares are now filled only with air, all that was in them has disappeared. My spirit also, mindful of the beginning of things, seeks to call upon the Saviour who was here where I am, during the centuries of the gods, upon Thot-Ibis, that great wise one, upon Imhotpû, son of Phtah of Memphis. Where is the place in which the Nile is born? Who is the god or goddess concealed there? What is his likeness?" The lord of Elephantinê brought his reply in person. He described to the king, who was evidently ignorant of it, the situation of the island and the rocks of the cataract, the phenomena of the inundation, the gods who presided over it, and who alone could relieve Egypt from her disastrous plight. Zosiri repaired to the temple of the principality and offered the prescribed sacrifices; the god arose, opened his eyes, panted and cried aloud, "I am Khnûmû who created thee!" and promised him a speedy return of a high Nile and the cessation of the famine. Pharaoh was touched by the benevolence which his divine father had shown him; he forthwith made a decree by which he ceded to the temple all his rights of suzerainty over the neighbouring nomes within a radius of twenty miles. Henceforward the entire population, tillers and vinedressers, fishermen and hunters, had to yield the tithe of their incomes to the priests; the quarries could not be worked without the consent of Khnûmû, and the payment of a suitable indemnity into his coffers, and finally, all metals and precious woods shipped thence for Egypt had to submit to a toll on behalf of the temple. Did the

THE STEP-PYRAMID OF SAQQÂRA.[1]

Ptolemies admit the claims which the local priests attempted to deduce from this romantic tale? and did the god regain possession of the domains and dues which they declared had been his right? The stele shows us with what ease the scribes could forge official documents, when the exigencies of daily life forced the necessity upon them; it teaches us at the same time how that fabulous chronicle was elaborated, whose remains have been preserved for us by classical writers. Every prodigy, every fact related by Manetho, was taken from some document analogous to the supposed inscription of Zosiri.[2]

[1] Drawn by Boudier, from a photograph by Dévèria (1864); in the foreground, the tomb of Ti.

[2] The legend of the yawning gulf at Bubastis must be connected with the gifts supposed to have been offered by King Boêthos to the temple of

The real history of the early centuries, therefore, eludes
our researches, and no contemporary record traces for us
those vicissitudes which Egypt passed through before being
consolidated into a single kingdom, under the rule of one
man. Many names, apparently of powerful and illustrious
princes, had survived in the memory of the people; these
were collected, classified, and grouped in a regular manner
into dynasties, but the people were ignorant of any exact
facts connected with the names, and the historians, on
their own account, were reduced to collect apocryphal
traditions for their sacred archives. The monuments of
these remote ages, however, cannot have entirely disappeared: they exist in places where we have not as yet
thought of applying the pick, and chance excavations will
some day most certainly bring them to light. The few
which we do possess barely go back beyond the IIIrd
dynasty: namely, the hypogeum of Shiri, priest of Sondi
and Pirsenû; possibly the tomb of Khûîthotpû at Saqqâra;
the Great Sphinx of Gîzeh; a short inscription on the
rocks of the Wady Maghâra, which represents Zosiri (the
same king of whom the priests of Khnûmû in the Greek
period made a precedent) working the turquoise or copper
mines of Sinai; and finally the Step-Pyramid where this

that town, to repair the losses sustained by the goddess on that occasion;
the legend of the pestilence and famine is traceable to some relief given by
a local god, and for which Semempses and Ûenephes might have shown
their gratitude in the same way as Zosiri. The tradition of the successive
restorations of Denderah accounts for the constructions attributed to Teti I.
and to Tosorthros; finally, the pretended discoveries of sacred books, dealt
with elsewhere, show how Manetho was enabled to attribute to his Pharaohs
the authorship of works on medicine or theology.

same Pharaoh rests.[1] It forms a rectangular mass, in-correctly orientated, with a variation from the true north of 4° 35′, 393 ft. 8 in. long from east to west, and 352 ft. deep, with a height of 159 ft. 9 in. It is composed of six cubes, with sloping sides, each being about 13 ft. less in width than the one below it; that nearest to the ground measures 37 ft. 8 in. in height, and the uppermost one 29 ft. 9 in. It was entirely constructed of limestone from the neighbouring mountains. The blocks are small, and badly cut, the stone courses being concave to offer a better resistance to downward thrust and to shocks of earthquake. When breaches in the masonry are examined, it can be seen that the external surface of the steps has, as it were, a double stone facing, each facing being carefully dressed. The body of the pyramid is solid, the chambers being cut in the rock beneath. These chambers have been often enlarged, restored, and reworked in the course of centuries, and the passages which connect them form a perfect laby-rinth into which it is dangerous to venture without a guide. The columned porch, the galleries and halls, all lead to a sort of enormous shaft, at the bottom of which the architect had contrived a hiding-place, destined, no doubt, to contain the more precious objects of the funerary furniture. Until the beginning of this century, the vault had preserved its

---

[1] The stele of Sehêl has enabled us to verify the fact that the preamble [a string of titles] to the inscription of the king, buried in the Step-Pyramid, is identical with that of King Zosiri: it was, therefore, Zosiri who con-structed, or arranged for the construction of this monument as his tomb. The Step-Pyramid of Saqqâra was opened in 1819, at the expense of the Prussian General Minutoli, who was the first to give a brief description of the interior, illustrated by plans and drawings.

original lining of glazed pottery. Three quarters of the wall surface were covered with green tiles, oblong and slightly convex on the outer side, but flat on the inner: a

ONE OF THE CHAMBERS OF THE STEP-PYRAMID, WITH ITS WALL-COVERING OF GLAZED TILES.[1]

square projection pierced with a hole, served to fix them at the back in a horizontal line by means of flexible wooden

[1] Drawn by Faucher-Gudin, from the coloured sketch by Segato. M. Stern attributes the decoration of glazed pottery to 'the XXVIth dynasty, which opinion is shared by BORCHARDT. The yellow and green glazed tiles bearing the cartouche of Papi I., show that the Egyptians of the Memphite dynasties used glazed facings at that early date; we may, therefore, believe, if the tiles of the vault of Zosiri are really of the Saite period, that they replaced a decoration of the same kind, which belonged to the time of its construction, and of which some fragments still exist among the tiles of more recent date.

rods. The three bands which frame one of the doors are
inscribed with the titles of the Pharaoh: the hieroglyphs
are raised in either blue, red, green, or yellow, on a fawn-
coloured ground. Other kings had built temples, palaces,
and towns,—as, for instance, King Khâsakhimu, of whose
constructions some traces exist at Hieracônpolis, opposite
to El-Kab, or King Khâsakhmui, who preceded by a few
years the Pharaohs of the IVth dynasty—but the monuments
which they raised to be witnesses of their power or piety to
future generations, have, in the course of ages, disappeared
under the tramplings and before the triumphal blasts of
many invading hosts: the pyramid alone has survived, and
the most ancient of the historic monuments of Egypt is
a tomb.

END OF VOL. I.

INDEX

INDEX

Denderah, 102, 129
" Destruction of Men," The, 149
Didû of Osiris, The, 183
Domestic implements, 67
Domestic life of Egyptians, 64
Dom-palm (Egyptian *Mama*), 41
" Double Truth," The, 271
Dynasties of Egypt, The, 321, 322, *et seq.*

E

Edfû (Apollinopolis Magna), (Tbû), 102, 130, 286
Egyptian language, The, 58
Egyptians,
    Costumes of ancient, 68, 72
    Customs of ancient, 63
    Early civilization, 66
    Origin of the, 56, 57
    Types and characteristics of, 58–63
    Weapons of ancient, 73–76
Ekhmîm. *See* Akhmîm
Embalming, Process of, 153, 309
Enneads, The, 203, *et seq.*, 213, 215, 226, 272, 273
Epagomenal days, The five, 298
Eratosthenes, Canon of, 345
Erment, 135
Esneh (Latopolis), 130

F

Fauna of Egypt, 41, 42
Fennec, The, 139
Festivals, Ancient Egyptian, 297, 300
Feudal gods of Egypt, 140, 151, 183, 203
Fish of the Nile, 44, 45
" Five, House of the," 210
Flora of Egypt, 35, 36, 39, 40
Food-plants, 83
Funeral rites, Ancient, 160, 257
Funerary gods, The, 204

G

Gebel Abûfêda, 12
Gebel el-Ahmar, 12
Gebel et-Têr, 12
Gebel Mokattam, 11
Gebelên, 13
Girgeh. *See* Cerkasoros
Gizeh, 354
Gods of Egypt, 107, 132, 146, 162
Gods, Endowment of, 177
Granites of Egypt, 15, 16

H

Hades, The Egyptian, 280, 282, 295
Hahû-Hehît, 213

Hâikûphtah (Hakûphtah), 54
Hâpi, 47, 48, 51, 54, 205, 260
Hâpi, Hymn to, 51
Hâpis (Apis), 343, 348
Hardidûf, 321
Hare, Nome of the, 95
Harhûdîti (Hor-hud), 133, 204, 291
Harkhobi, 135
Harmâkhis, 286
Harmakhûîti, 134, 196, 198
Harmerati, 133
Harnûbi, 134, 142
Haroêris (Horus), 114, 117, 123, 124, 130, 133, 134, 137, 142–145, 152, 166, 202–205, 216, 217, 225, 227, 252, 253, 265, 286, 292
Harpoon, Nome of the, 98, 100
Har-Sapdi (Hor-Sopd), 133
Harshâfîtû (Her-shafui), 132, 140, 168
Harsiesis, 203
Harsiîsît, 186
Hartimâ, 134
Hâthor, 112, 115, 117, 119, 133, 137, 141, 144, 163, 172, 206, 215, 235, 253, 263, 266, 268, 296
Haunch constellation, The, 125–127
Haunch, Nome of the, 97
Hâûrit, 132
Heliopolis (*see also* Aûnû of the North), 163, 166, 190, 191, 274, 330, 341
Hermopolis Magna. *See* Khmûnû
Hibonû (Minieh), 287, 288
Hierodules, 178
Hieroglyphs, The, 315–319
Hininsû, 95
Hor-hud. *See* Harhûdîti
Horse, The, 41
Hor-Sopd. *See* Har-Sapdi
Horus (Haroêris), 114, 117, 123, 124, 130, 133, 134, 137, 142–145, 152, 202–206, 215, 216, 225, 227, 252, 253, 265, 286, 288, 292, 305
Hunting, Ancient methods of, 76–82
Hûsaphaîti, 321
Hû-Sû, 302

I

Ialû. *See* " Reeds, Field of "
Iâûhû, 128
Ibis, The, 44
Ibrâhimîyeh, 8
Ichneumon, The, 42
Imhotep. *See* Imhotpû
Imhotpû, 143, 146, 348, 352
Incantations, etc., 303, 304
Irrigation. *See* Agriculture in Egypt
Isis, 28, 119, 132, 143, 145, 183, 186, 187, 200, 206, 215, 221, 231, 232, 246, 249, 252, 255, 260, 269, 349

INDEX

"Islands of the Blest," 266, 277–283
Iûsasît, 141, 216

K

Kabhsonûf (Kabhsnuf), 205
Kahiri (planet Saturn), 128
Kakôû, 348
Kakû-Kakît, 213
Kasr-es-Sayad, 12
Kenkenes, 347
Kerkesoura. *See* Cerkasoros
Kha, Lake of, 266
Khait-nûtrît, 287
Khamsîn, The, 30
Khartum, 21
Kheops, 321
Kheper. *See* Khopri
Khmûnû (Hermopolis Magna), 95, 102, 137, 181, 207, 211, 214, 331
Khnûmû (god of Elephantinê), 52, 132, 140, 152, 168, 181, 217, 222, 349, 352
Khomninû, 213
Khonsû, 151
Khontamentît (Khent-Amenti), 163, 164, 258, 280, 281, 333
Khopri (Kheper), 163, 197, 198, 233, 265
Khû (Khûû), 160
Khûfûi (*see also* Kheops)
Khûihotep. *See* Khûithotpû
Khûithotpû, 354
Kings, Tables of, 322, *et seq*
Ko-komè, Pyramids of, 348

L

"Land of Shades," 25
Letopolis (Sokhem), 144
Life, Ancient Egyptian theory of, 309
Lotus, The, 36, 47, 84, 85, 193, 195

M

Madîr, 351
Magicians, 303
Magicians, The king's, 311
Mâît, 208, 268
"Maneros," The, 343
Manes, 322
Manû, 23, 56, 120
Marriage amongst Egyptians, 63, 64
Mars-Doshiri, 128
Maskhaît, 126
Maskhonît, 108
Mathematical calculations, Early, 314
Mâzît, 120
"Meadow of Reeds." *See* "Reeds, Field of"
"Meadow of Rest." *See* "Rest, Field of"
Medamôt Taûd, 135

Medicine, Early practice of, 308, 311, 312
"Melayahs," 95
Meloukhia, The, 84
Memphis (Minnofirû), 328, 341, 342
Memphite period, The, 328, 329
Mendes, 163, 168, 200
Menes, 5, 90, 322, 333–343, 347
Menkaûri. *See* Mykerinos
Mihît, 333
Mîn (God of Koptos). *See* Minû
Minnofirû. *See* Memphis
Minû, 133, 168, 205
Miriri Papi I. *See* Papi I.
Mirit Mihit, 48
Mirit Qimâit, 48
Mnevis, 193, 348
Mœris, King, 90
Mœris, Lake (Birket-Kerun), 343
Monad, The, 214
Monâit, 123, 142
Montu (Mentu), god of Hermonthis, 135, 168, 215, 228
Moon, Ancient traditions of the, 123
Music, Invention of, 314
Mykerinos (Menkaûri), 321

N

Nahmâûît, 141, 142
Napri, 51, 54
Naprît, 108
Nebthôtpît, 141, 216
Nekhabît (Eileithyapolis, El-Kab), 56, 96, 102
Nekhabit, the vulture goddess, 137
Nephercheres, 348
Nephthys, 189, 200, 201, 215, 247, 249, 252, 260, 269
Ngagu oirû, 115
"Night of the Drop," 28, 30
Nile,
 Blue, 29
 Festivals of the, 50
 Green, 29
 Inundations of the, 29, 50, 53, 89
 Mouths of the, 6
 Red, 30
 Rise of the, 30, 50, 53, 89
 Source of the, 25, 26
 Valley of the, 6
 White, 34
Nile-gods, The (Hâpi and his two goddesses, Mirit Qimâit and Mirit Mihit; also Khnûmû, Osiris, Harshâfiû), 46–48, 132, 140, 168, 181
Ninû-Ninît, 213
Nit, 53, 133, 137, 141, 163, 166, 180, 206, 263, 268
Nofir-horû, 141

INDEX

Nofir-tumu, 144
Nome-gods, 132, 163, 183, 184, 205
Nomes of Egypt, The, 92–103
Nû, or Nûn, 180, 209, 227, 234–239
Nûbit, Ombos, 286
Nûit (Nut), 115, 120, 123, 172, 181, 182, 188, 199, 200, 210, 215, 228, 238–242, 247, 263
Nû-Nûit, 213
Nut. See Nûit

O

Oasis, The Great (Uit, Uhat), (Oasis of El-Khargeh), 334
Œdipus Egyptiacus (Kircher), Map from, 27
Ogdoad, The, 212, 217
Oirû maû (Ur-ma), 177, 230
Oleander (Narû), Nome of, 95, 100
Ombos (Nûbit), 137
Omens and auspicious days, 301, 302
On. See Aûnû of the North
Onkhit (Ankht), 23
Onnophris (Osiris), 184, 259, 270, 273, 279, 280, 295
Onouris, 135
"Opening of the Mouth," 257
Oracles, Egyptian, 168, 169
Orion-Sâhû. See Sâhû
Osiris, 90, 132, 140, 141–145, 152, 163, 164, 168, 181–191, 200, 215, 245–262, 268, 273–291, 295, 300–304, 309, 333
Osiris Khontamentit, 280, 281
Ouenephes, 347, 348
Oxyrrhynchos (Pi-mâzit, Bahnasa), 286, 287
Oxyrrhynchus (*mormyrus* fish), 137, 252

P

Panopolis (Apû). See Akhmîm
Paophi, 303
Papi I., 341
Papyrus, The, 47, 85
Paradise, The Egyptian idea of, 284. *See also* Hades
Pasht. See Bastit
Paûiti, 203
Pelusiac branch of Nile, 6
Pepi. See Papi
Pharaoh, 352
Pharmûti, 297
Phœnix, The, 193
Phtah, 51, 132, 143, 152, 163, 168, 206, 222, 228, 302, 341, 344, 352
Phtah-Sokar-Osiris, 280
Piarit, 244, 245
Pi-râ. See Heliopolis
Pirûit, 296, 297

Priesthood, The Egyptian, 173–177
Princes and nobility, 92, 93
Ptolemy, King, 351
Pûanit, 112
Punt. See Pûanit
Pyramid, The Step-, 354

Q

Qabhsonûf, 260
Qasr-es-Sayad, 12
Qenqoni, 345
Qimit, 55
Qosheish, 89, 90
Qûbti, 96

R

Ra, 51, 114–128, 133, 139, 152, 166, 168, 194–199, 222–247, 255, 265, 281, 285 294, 300, 330
Râ-Harmakhis, 242
Râ-Harmakhûiti, 197
Raiân, 8
Ramses II., 323, 340, 345
Raninit, 109
Ranûit (Ramûit), 297
Ra-qririt, 163
"Reeds, Field of," 241, 258, 262, 280
Religious rites and ceremonies, 174
Remedies, Egyptian. See Medicine
Rert. See Ririt
"Respondents," 276
"Rest, Field of," 241, 258
Ririt (Rert), 126
Romitû (Rotû), 55

S

"Sa," The, 151
Safir, 110
Sâhû, 128, 129, 293, 295
Sahu-Orion, 295
Said (Arabic name of Upper Egypt), 45, 96
Sais, 102
Saïte period, The, 329
Sâkieh, The, 19
Saktit, The, 120
Samiû Sit, 252
Sapdi, 181
Sap-hôû, 302
Saqqâra, 323, 348, 354
Satit (Sati), 141, 349
"Satni, Tale of," 208
Saza, 110
Seb. See Sibû
Sebek. See Sovkû (or Sobkhû)
Sebennytic branch of Nile, 6
Sehel, 15
Sehêl stele, The, 355
Selkit, 216
Semempses, 347

www.ingramcontent.com/pod-product-compliance
Lightning Source LLC
Chambersburg PA
CBHW040425110426
42814CB00021B/321